The Campus History Series

BURKE HIGH SCHOOL 1894–2006

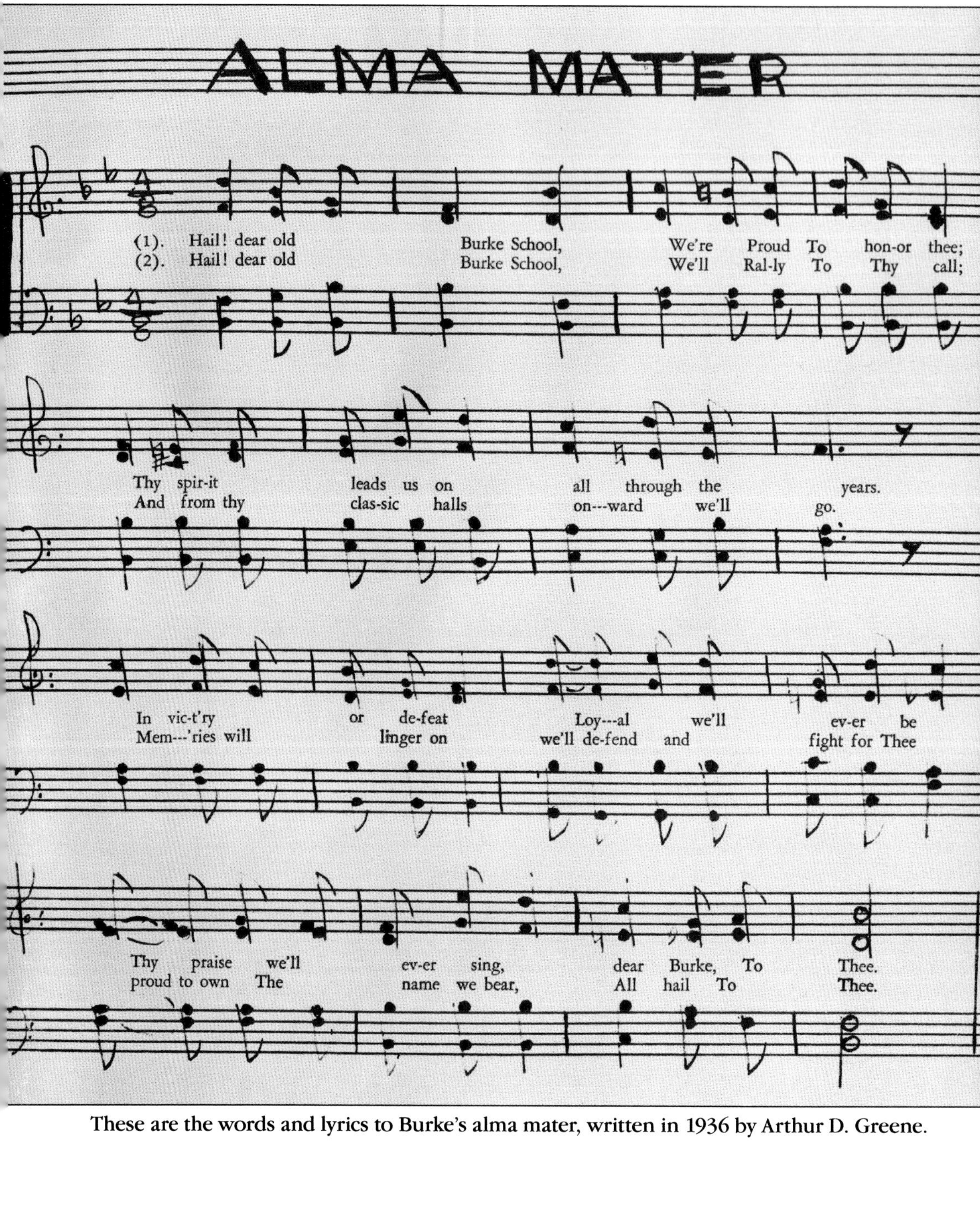

These are the words and lyrics to Burke's alma mater, written in 1936 by Arthur D. Greene.

ON THE COVER: The senior graduating class *c.* 1942 poses on the front steps of the administration building. The image in the background depicts a woodwork course *c.* 1920. (Courtesy of the Avery Research Center.)

The Campus History Series

BURKE HIGH SCHOOL 1894–2006

SHERMAN E. PYATT

ARCADIA PUBLISHING

ISBN 978-0-7385-4412-0

Published by Arcadia Publishing
Charleston, South Carolina

Printed in the United States of America

Library of Congress Catalog Card Number: 2006937177

For all general information contact Arcadia Publishing at:
Telephone 843-853-2070
Fax 843-853-0044
E-mail sales@arcadiapublishing.com
For customer service and orders:
Toll-Free 1-888-313-2665

Visit us on the Internet at www.arcadiapublishing.com

This book is dedicated to all of the students, teachers, family members, friends, and community people who care about Burke High School.

CONTENTS

ACKNOWLEDGMENTS

The author would like to acknowledge the assistance and support of several individuals: Phalarma L. (Washington) Freeman, Alice A. Pyatt, Edelle P. Gaillard, Virginia F. Howard, Gwendolyn Brown, Rodney E. Jenkins, Rudolph A. Pyatt Jr., Richard Brewer Jr., Stephen Graham III, Debra Manigault, Myrtice Brown, Cheryl Williams, Linard McCloud, Deborah Wright, Marguerite Middleton, Evelyn Brown, and Gwendolyn Brown. I would like to thank the Avery Research Center at the College of Charleston and the Burke High Media Center for the use of their materials. I would like to recognize the contributions of Lois Simms, Marilyn Pyatt, and Sean Pyatt, who have given so generously of their time and talent in support of this project. Finally, I would like to thank Maggie Bullwinkel and all the other staff members of Arcadia Publishing for their interest in this project.

INTRODUCTION

The history of Burke High School could best be described as a school constantly struggling for its survival. During the mid- to late 1800s, a majority of state and local governments throughout the South, particularly South Carolina, opposed compulsory public education for African Americans. In the early 1890s, Rev. John L. Dart sought to rectify this problem by establishing a school for African American boys and girls in downtown Charleston.

In 1894, he opened what was known as the Charleston Industrial Institute, located on the corner of Bogard and Kracke Streets. The school was an overwhelming success, and it was funded by private donations. As early as 1901, Dart and a group of African American citizens appealed to the Charleston City School Board to assume responsibility for governing his school. Several years would elapse before the board would reluctantly agree to assume responsibility of the private school.

It is safe to say that Reverend Dart was one of many educators responsible for advancing and improving the educational needs of African American boys and girls in Charleston during the late 19th and early 20th centuries. If it were not for his vision and dedication, there would not have been an established Burke High School as early as 1910.

The doors to Burke High School, then called the Charleston Colored Industrial School, opened in 1911 with 375 African American boys and girls. Ironically, the faculty consisted of one principal and five teachers, all whom were white. According to the city school board financial records, the school was built at a cost of $18,741. Furthermore, $10,000 of that amount was contributed by parties outside of the state (Year Book, 1880). A. W. Hoursey, a 1916 graduate and former acting principal of Burke, indicated that when the school was being built, workers unearthed skeletons. Undoubtedly, the school was built on a burial site. In 1919, 16 African American teachers and an African American principal by the name of David Hill replaced the all-white faculty. After the death of city board member James E. Burke in 1921, the name of the school was changed to Burke Industrial School.

Initially, the school opened as an industrial and elementary school. By 1925, it became a combination industrial, elementary, and high school. Despite inadequate funding and the incredulous attitude of the district superintendent, A. B. Rhett, the school made great strides over the next two decades. During the 1930s, principal Joseph Berry organized an athletic program and departmentalized the high school from eighth grade up. The normal class, the senior class of the high school, and the senior class of the grammar school held graduation exercises in the school auditorium.

During the mid-1940s, an education subcommittee of Charleston County reported the following: in 1944–1945, there were 13 high schools for white pupils and two for African Americans in the county. There was no bus service available for students from the Sea Islands attending Burke Industrial School, but buses were operated for white children at an estimated monthly cost of $10,000 (Charleston, 1945).

Moreover, it was not until after a group of concerned parents and citizens such as Robert Morrison, John Bennett, William Bluford, and R. E. Brogdon began to press the school board that Burke was finally accredited by the state school board in 1949 (Charleston, 1950). Still, by the early 1940s, there were major changes taking place in the school. Principal William Henry Grayson hired Eugene Hunt as an English teacher and also to teach choral singing. He established a 250-voice choir at the school. Also, Grayson hired Holland W. Daniels to teach mathematics and organize a school band (Drago, 1990). Finally, in 1949, a report published by the George Peabody College for Teachers indicated that Burke had an enrollment of 1,827 students and a student capacity for 1,500 pupils. The rooms in the old Burke building, along with the tailor shop and home economics laboratory, were in need of renovations. There were approximately 300 nonresident students attending Burke, which contributed to overcrowding.

In 1951, a group of parents and community leaders addressed their concerns to the Charleston County School Board regarding the inequalities that existed between white and African American students. Specifically, they pointed out the stark differences in the vocational programs that were offered at Burke and those offered at predominately white Murray Vocational School. There were 20 different trade courses offered at Murray. Conversely, there were only 10 courses offered at Burke. These courses included both evening and day programs. The amount of federal aid for teachers provided to Murray teachers was $11,473, and at Burke, the amount was $4,300. Surprisingly, there were five times as many students enrolled in trades at Burke as at Murray. Lastly, the school enrollment on September 12, 1951, revealed that there were 290 students attending Murray Vocational and 1,737 students attending Burke (Charleston, 1952).

By 1954, the enrollment at Burke neared the 2,000 mark. This increase was a result of the merging of students from Avery Normal Institute with those at Burke. Subsequently, Burke became the only public high school for African Americans in the city of Charleston until 1962, when Charles A. Brown High School opened. According to the enrollment figures of that year, Burke became the largest of all the schools in Charleston County (*Parvenue*, 1965).

The increase in enrollment brought additional changes to the physical structure of the campus. Several buildings were added to accommodate the ever-growing student body. Not surprising, the Charleston County School Board minutes in 1956 indicated that the school still did not have a functioning auditorium or gymnasium. Furthermore, the school's administration reported that a portion of the annex building and north wing were in need of repairs. As late as 1955, African American community leaders such as Robert Morrison were voicing their concerns regarding the delay of building a new gymnasium. Through it all, the faculty continued teaching and the students continued learning (Charleston, 1956).

The opening of Charles A. Brown High School in the city gave way to a decline in the enrollment at Burke. The enrollment for the 1962–1963 school years at Burke was approximately 1,450 (*Parvenue*, 1963). In 1961, the supervisor of the Schoolhouse Planning Committee recommended the construction of an industrial arts shop and enlargement of the present gymnasium (Charleston, 1962). It took nearly seven years from the date of these recommendations before the school acquired a new gymnasium.

Several students and faculty members were participants in the civil rights movement in Charleston during the 1960s. It was reported that two members of the faculty, Eugene Hunt and J. Michael Graves, challenged the students to become active in the civil rights struggle. As a result, approximately 24 students were arrested for attempting to desegregate downtown lunch counters such as Woolworth, W. T. Grant, and S. H. Kress (Drago, 1990).

Coincidentally, three of the 24 students arrested would later affect the desegregation of academic institutions on a broader stage. In 1963, Harvey Gantt became the first African American to integrate Clemson University. During that same year, Delano Meriwether became the first of his race to enter Duke University School of Medicine. Both of these men were graduates of the class of 1960. Lastly, Bernard Deas (class of 1961) became the first African American to graduate from the Medical University School of Medicine in 1971.

On March 13, 1972, Joseph Jenkins, president of the Student Council, led approximately 1,500 of the school's 1,700 students on a massive walkout. The students were seeking to address the lack of cafeteria space, additional library shelving, more classroom space, and alleviation of overcrowding. Through their determination and unwavering commitment, the students were able to convince the administration and the school board to address their concerns (*Parvenue*, 1972).

During the late 1970s and early 1980s, Charles A. Brown, Rivers, and Charleston High Schools were closed due to a decline in enrollment. Subsequently, these students were merged with the students at Burke. Again the school board failed to provide adequate funding for facilities to accommodate the additional students on the campus. This was evident during a District 20 Constituent Board meeting in 1984, when a parent indicated that it was poor planning to design a new cafeteria with seating for 250 students with a student body of 1,700 students. (Charleston, 1984).

In 1988, the school board moved the Charleston County magnet school to the Burke campus. For the next eight years, there were two high schools, two principals, two student bodies and two different curriculums on one campus. The Burke student body witnessed another historic event in 1995. Jeannetta Scott was named principal, making her the first female to hold that position. By 1996, the academic magnet school had moved from the campus.

There were several things occurring in Charleston County that would impact the school both directly and indirectly. During the 1990s, the school would witness a decline in enrollment brought on by the opening of magnet and charter schools in Charleston County. Secondly, there was a slow migration of African Americans moving out of the city. Finally, there was the untimely resignation of Jeannetta Scott in 1998.

Over the next three years, the school would be without a permanent principal, resulting in frustration from the parents and the Burke community. Supporters of Burke no longer felt that the Charleston County School Board was willing to provide adequate resources that would produce a positive learning environment for the students. The supporters pushed for a new school, and by 2002, groundbreaking ceremonies were held for the new school. The new school was designed by a Burke graduate, Harvey Gantt (Pyatt, 2005).

Burke graduates and supporters have always demonstrated an overwhelming sense of pride and loyalty towards the school. Conversely, there were those who had always felt that the school board never gave its full support to the school. As late as 2006, Burke was threatened with infractions that could have resulted in the State Board of Education taking control of the school. Also, the principal hired in 2005 abruptly resigned in 2006. A new principal was hired, and the school was given a reprieve by the board of education.

There are countless numbers of Burke graduates throughout Charleston and the country. Many of them would probably agree that part of their success and accomplishments in life were the result of the nurturing that they received from the dedicated faculty and strong parental involvement. The struggle for Burke High School will continue as long as the school exists. Yet those who have supported the school in the past can take solace by remembering these words from the alma mater:

Hail, dear old Burke school!
We'll rally to thy call
And from thy classic halls,
Onward we'll go.
Mem'ries will linger on.
We'll defend and fight for thee.
Proud to own the name we bear,
All hail to thee!"

One

BUILDINGS

In fact, when the first building was built, workmen dug up skeletons.

—A. W. Hoursey (Class of 1916)

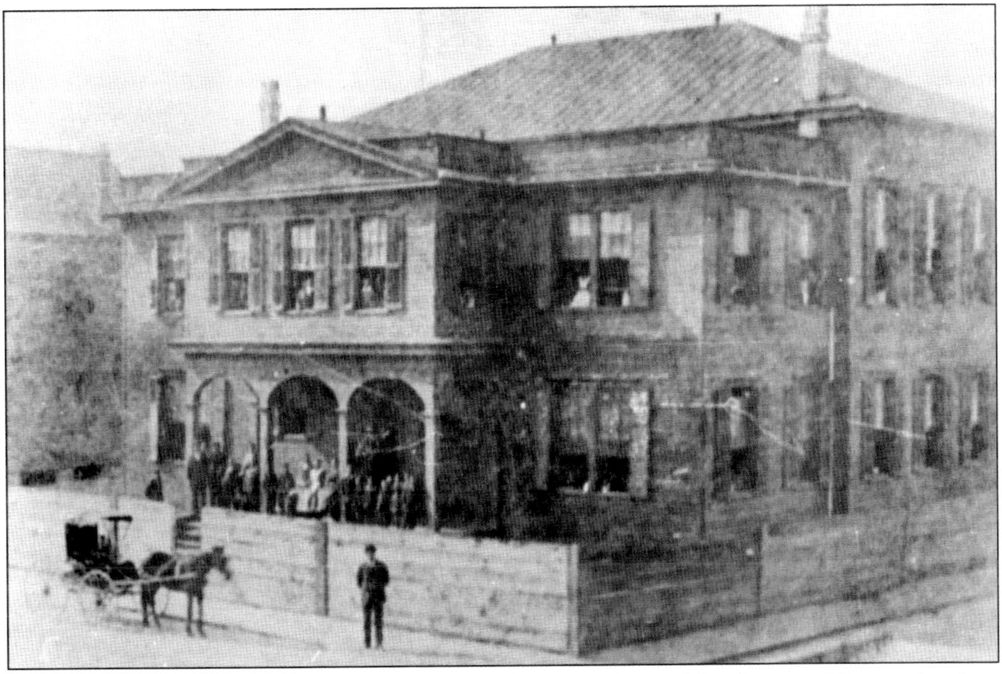

In 1894, Rev. John L. Dart established the Charleston Industrial Institute on his own land on Kracke Street. This six-room building, known as Dart Hall, accommodated approximately 150 children. A few years later, Dart purchased the adjoining lots and upon them built what was considered a large and beautiful building at the corner of Bogard and Kracke Streets, seen *c.* 1897. Dart Hall would eventually serve as the first public library for African Americans in the city of Charleston. (Courtesy of the Avery Research Center.)

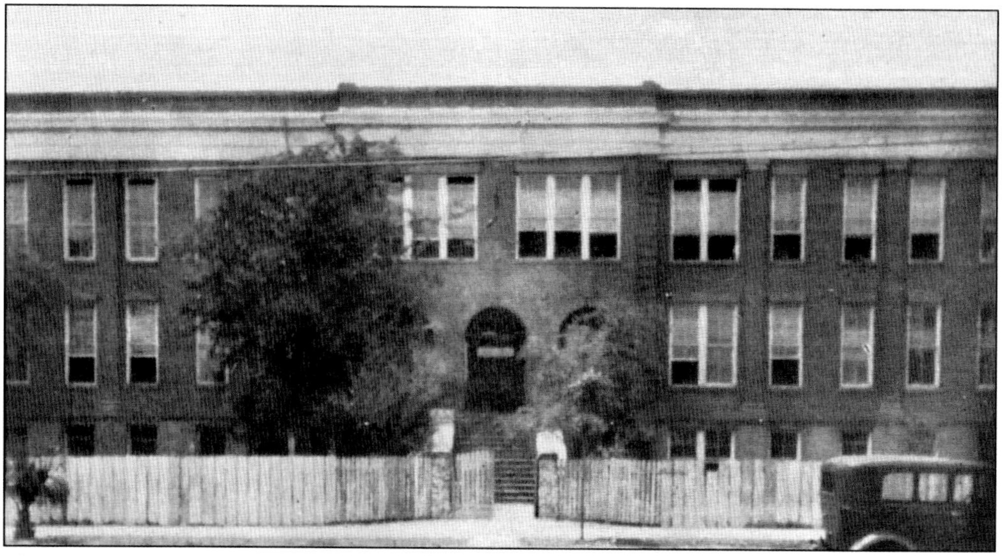

This was the first building erected for the Charleston Colored Industrial School in 1910 on the corner of Fishburne and President Streets. It opened in January 1911 and housed students and eight teachers. (Courtesy of the Avery Research Center.)

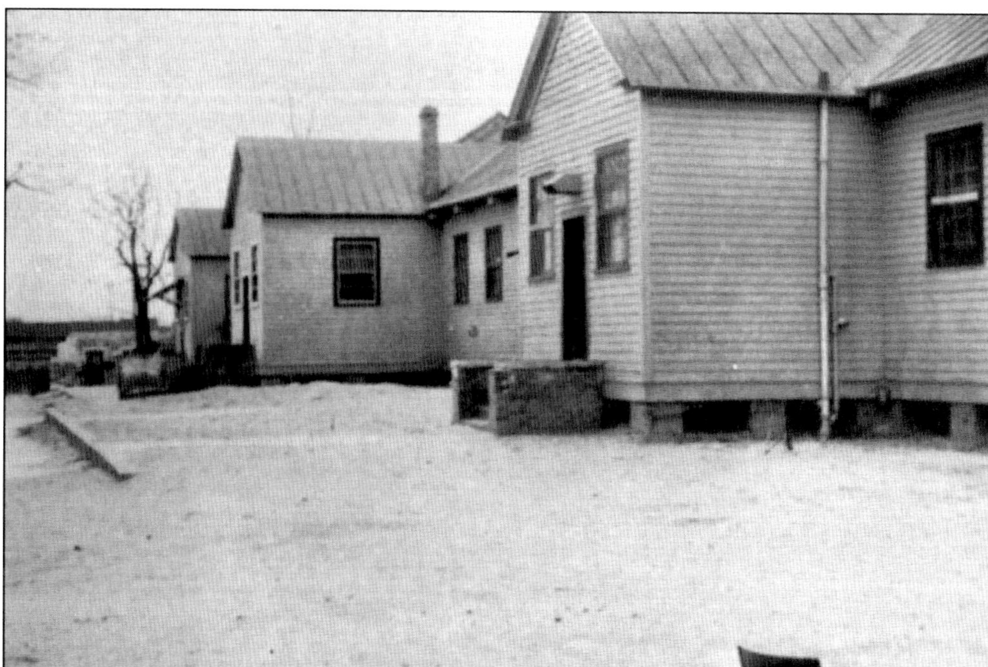

Prior to the erection of the Fields-Sims-Wright Center, trade classes were held in wood-frame structures. The structures, *c.* 1958, were in extremely poor condition. (Courtesy of the Avery Research Center.)

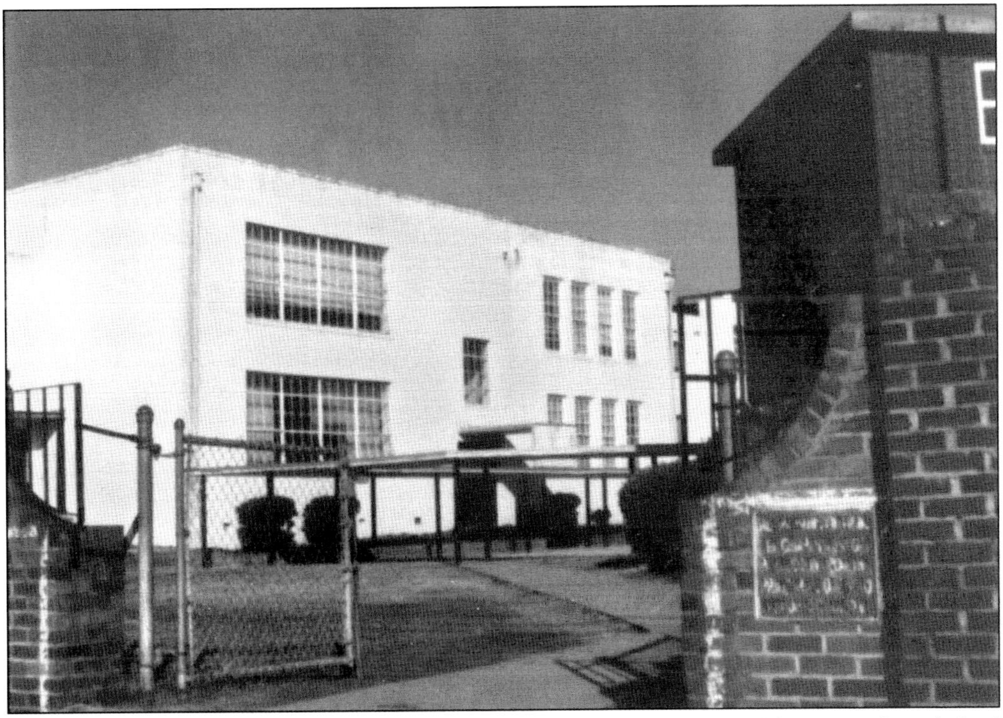

The structure to the left was known as the annex building. The building was demolished during the late 1970s. This was the main entrance when one entered the campus. (Courtesy of the Avery Research Center.)

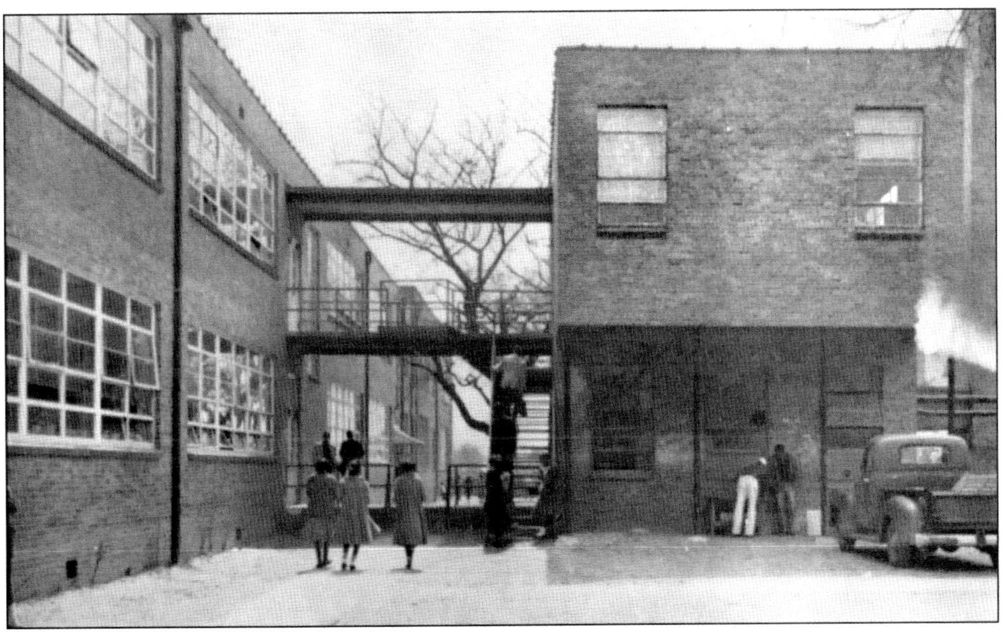

During the late 1950s and 1960s, the building to the right served as the band room. By 1968, a new facility was built which housed the band and choir. The old band room was demolished a year later. (Courtesy of Burke High School.)

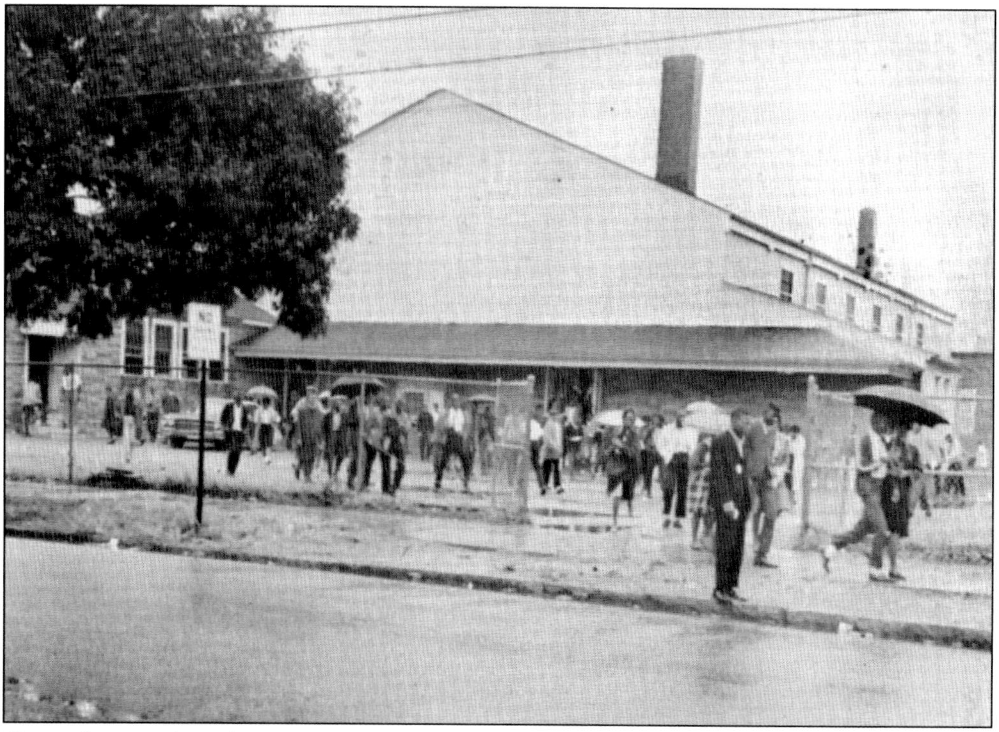

Pictured are students leaving assembly on a rainy day in 1963. The building was the gymnasium that was remodeled in 1960. It was located on the corner of President and Fishburne Streets. This was the site of the remodeled structure of the old USO building. The new ROTC building is now located at this site. (Courtesy of the Avery Research Center.)

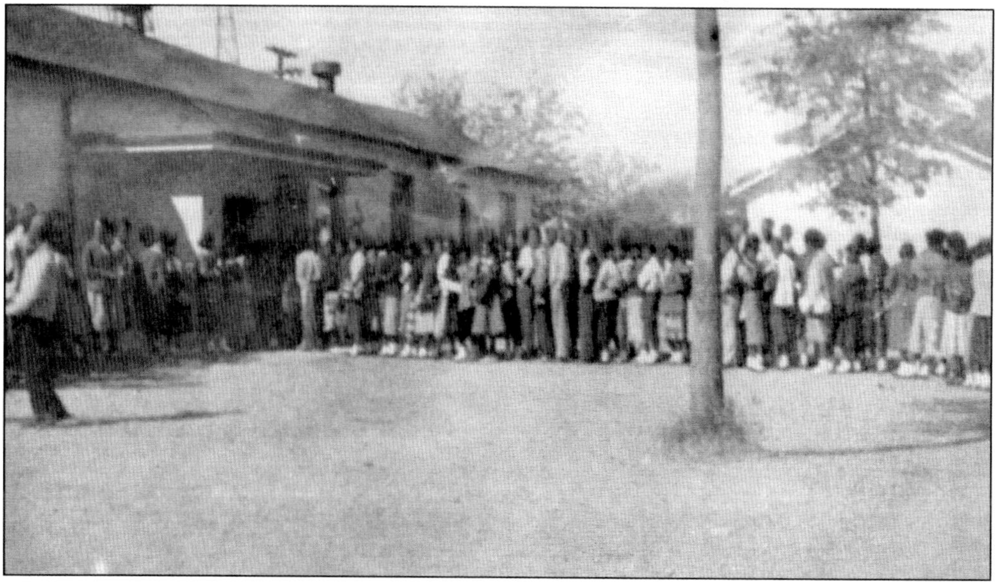

Here is a scene in 1954 of the exterior of the cafeteria during a normal lunch period. There was never enough seating to accommodate the student body. Yet this was still a far cry from the old portable trailer that was used until this structure was built in 1950. (Courtesy of the Avery Research Center.)

This building project began in 1953. The building above was demolished to make way for the buildings below, which were completed in the fall of 1954. The building project was initiated to accommodate the students who were coming from Avery to Burke after Avery closed in 1954. (Courtesy of the Avery Research Center.)

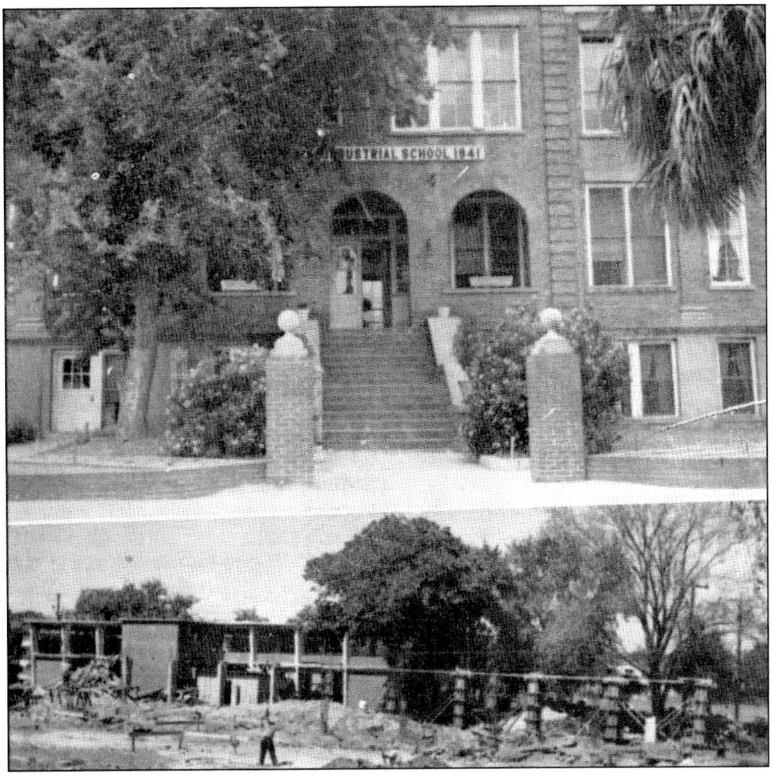

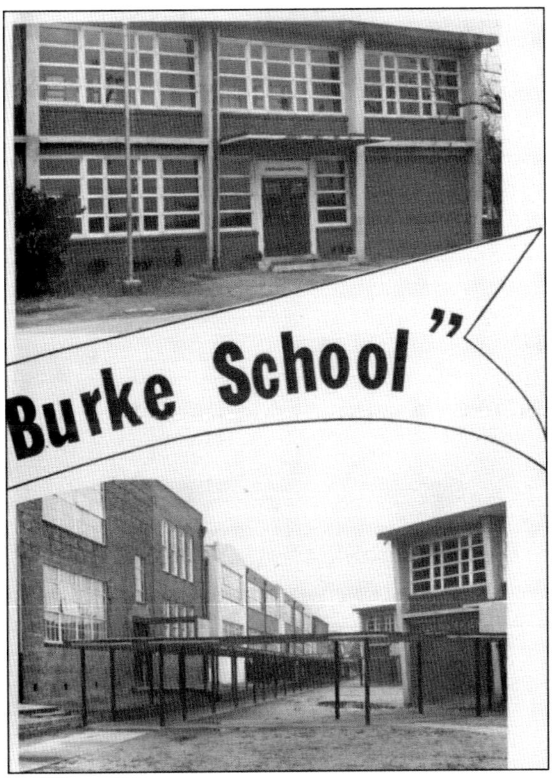

The buildings were part of the campus until the late 1980s. They consisted of the library, administration, science, and home economics facilities. The buildings to the left were classrooms. They were built during the 1930s and 1940s. As late as 1988, the buildings to the right housed science, mathematics, special education, business occupation, and home economics classes. (Courtesy of the Avery Research Center.)

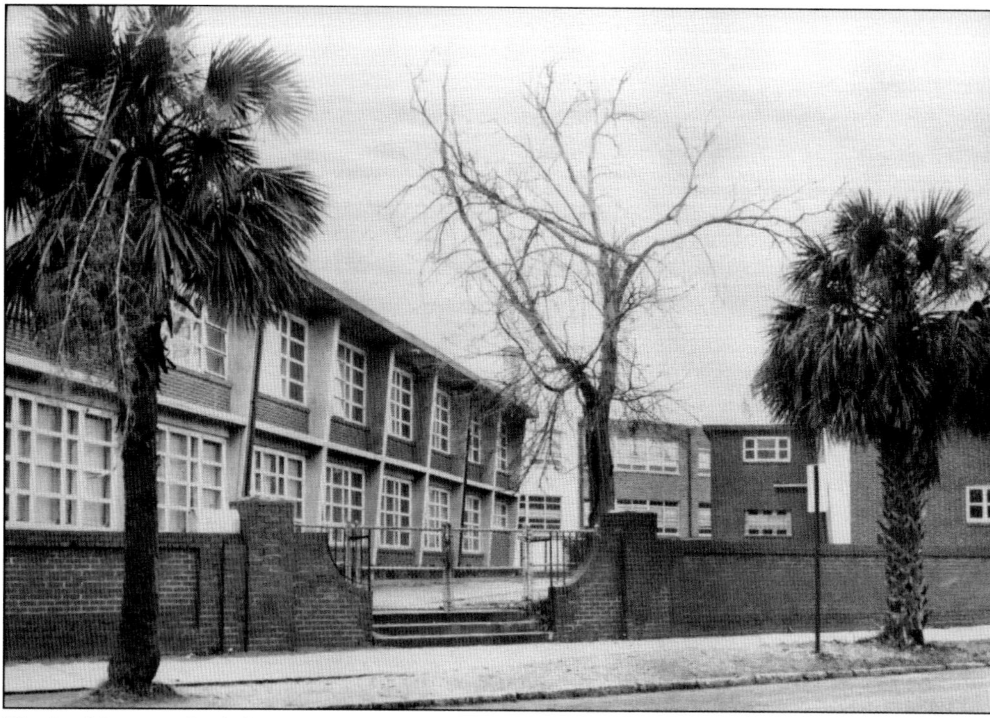

The building to the left was erected in 1954 and housed the main offices on the first floor. The second level was used for classroom instruction. (Courtesy of Burke High School.)

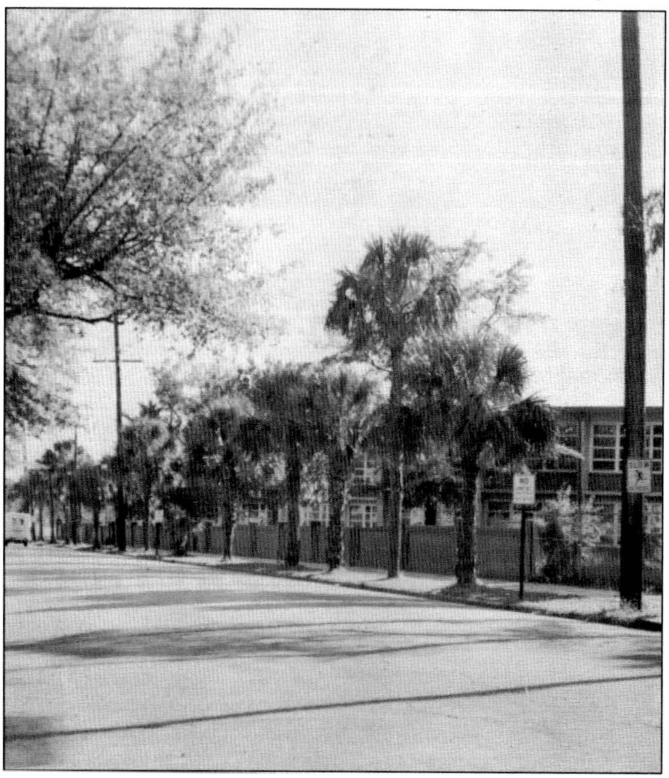

These four structures lined President Street from 1954 until the late 1990s, when they were demolished to make way for the new Burke High School. (Courtesy of Burke High School.)

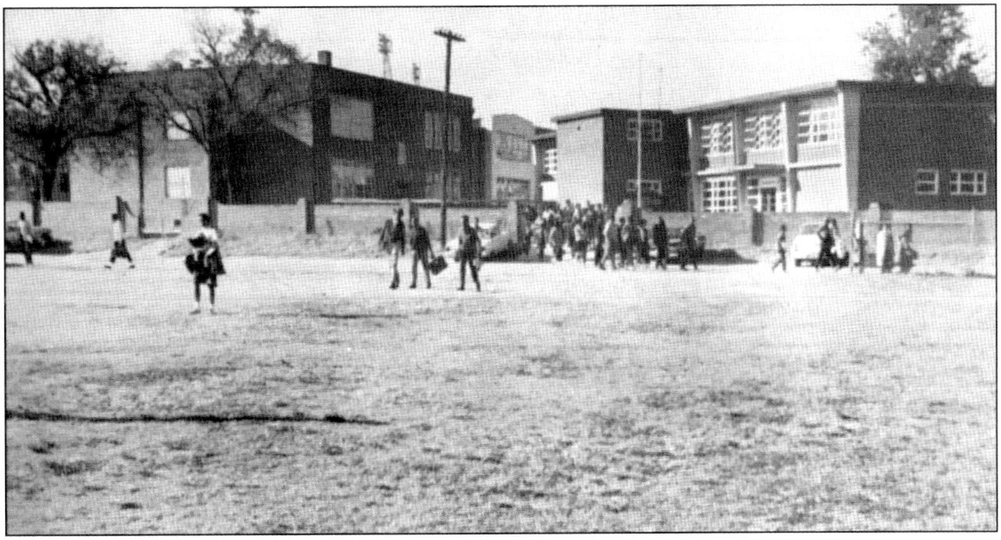

This view of the campus during the 1980s shows students departing for home. The open area is known as Harmon Field. The buildings no longer exist, but the field is used as a practice area for the marching band and the football team. (Courtesy of Burke High School.)

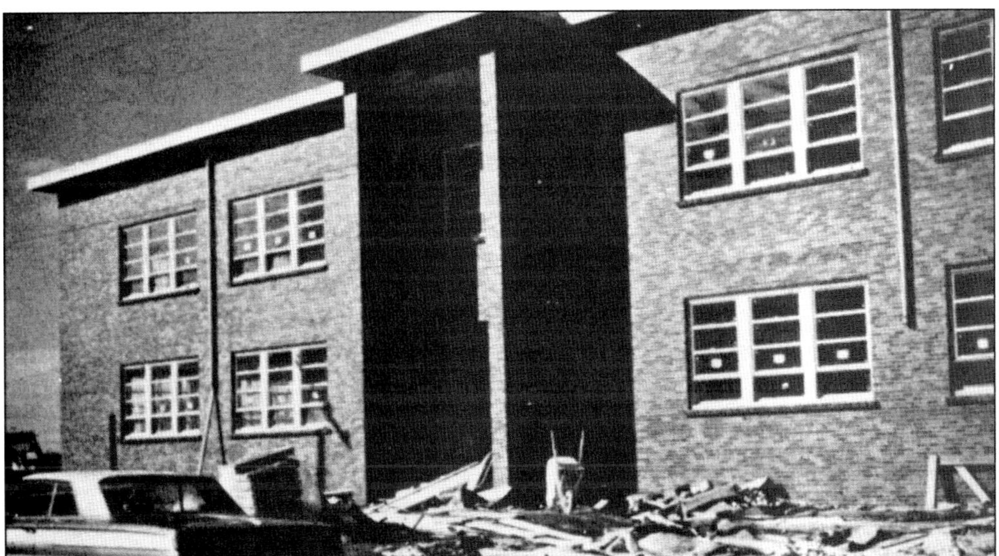

Completed in 1968, the new gymnasium was approximately 13,500 square feet. It contained physical education classrooms, showers for boys and girls, and sections for the band and choir. The auditorium had bleachers seating a least 1,700 people. The building was located on Fishburne Street across from Harmon Field. By 1983, the band and choir facilities were moved to the Fine Arts Center on the Rhett campus. (Courtesy of the Avery Research Center.)

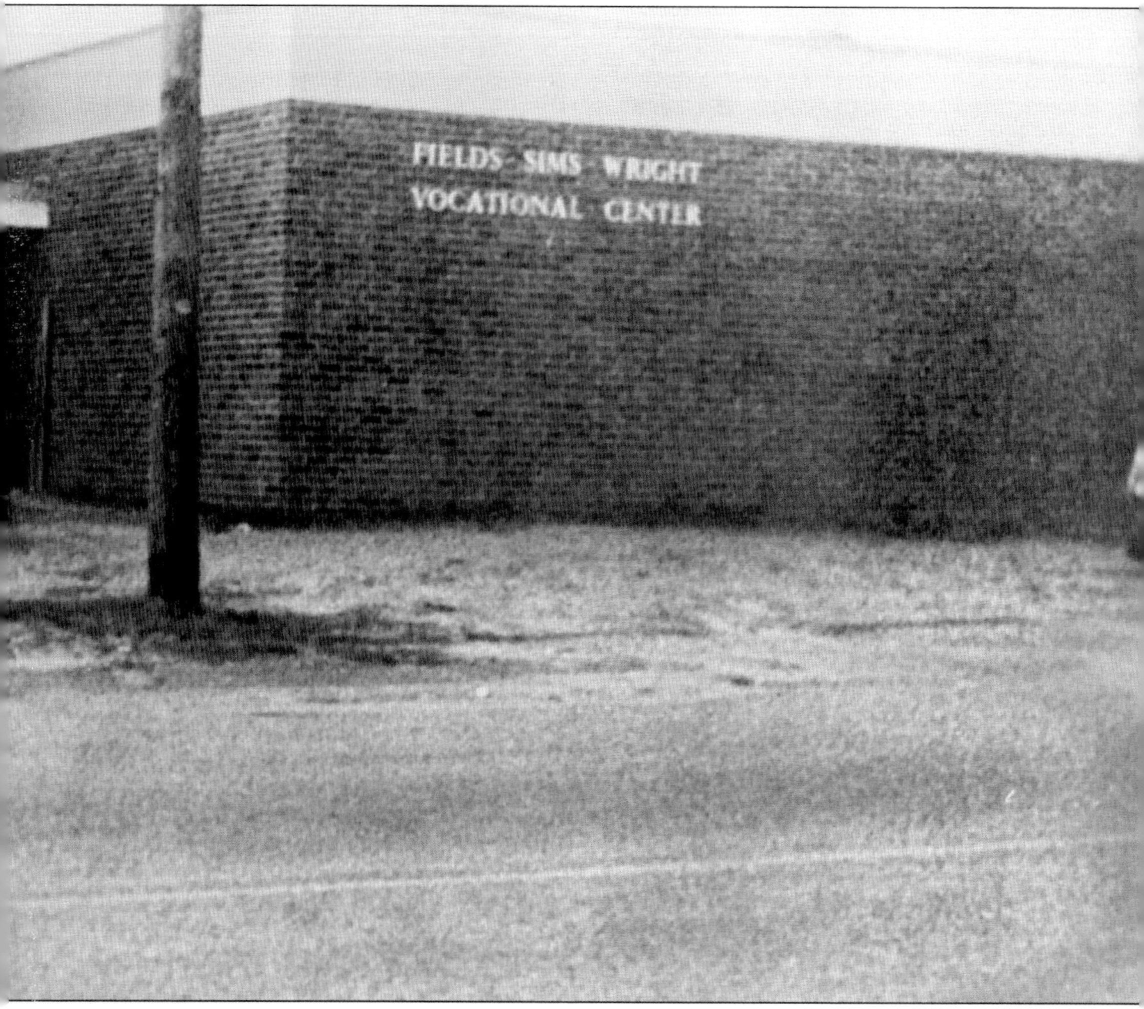

The Fields-Sims-Wright Vocational Center was dedicated in 1980. The renovation and construction began in 1977 and was completed a year later. Plumbing, masonry, electronics, auto body repair, and carpentry were just a few of the trade classes taught in this building. (Courtesy of the Avery Research Center.)

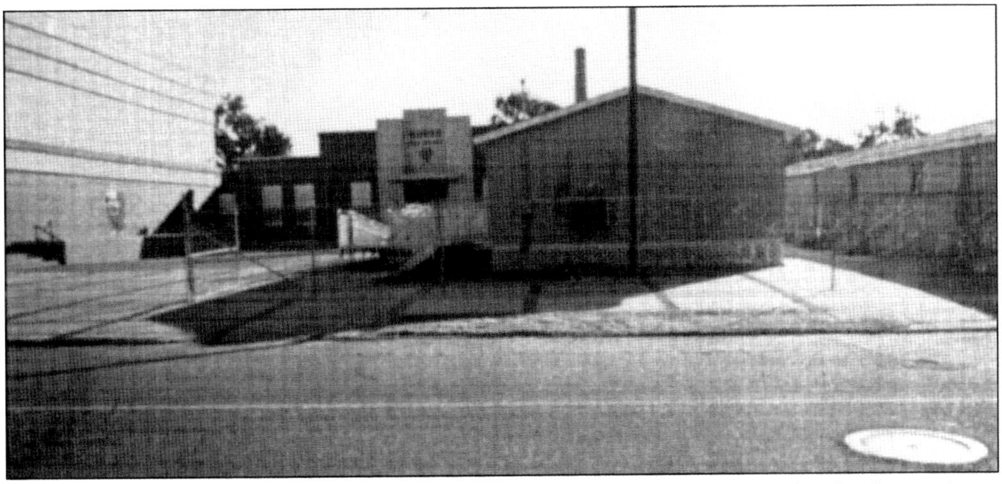

By 2002, construction had begun on the campus for the new Burke School. The students were restricted to one side of the campus. The building in the foreground housed the main offices, guidance department, library, and the cafeteria. The facility to the left is still the Fine Arts Center. (Courtesy of Sherman Pyatt.)

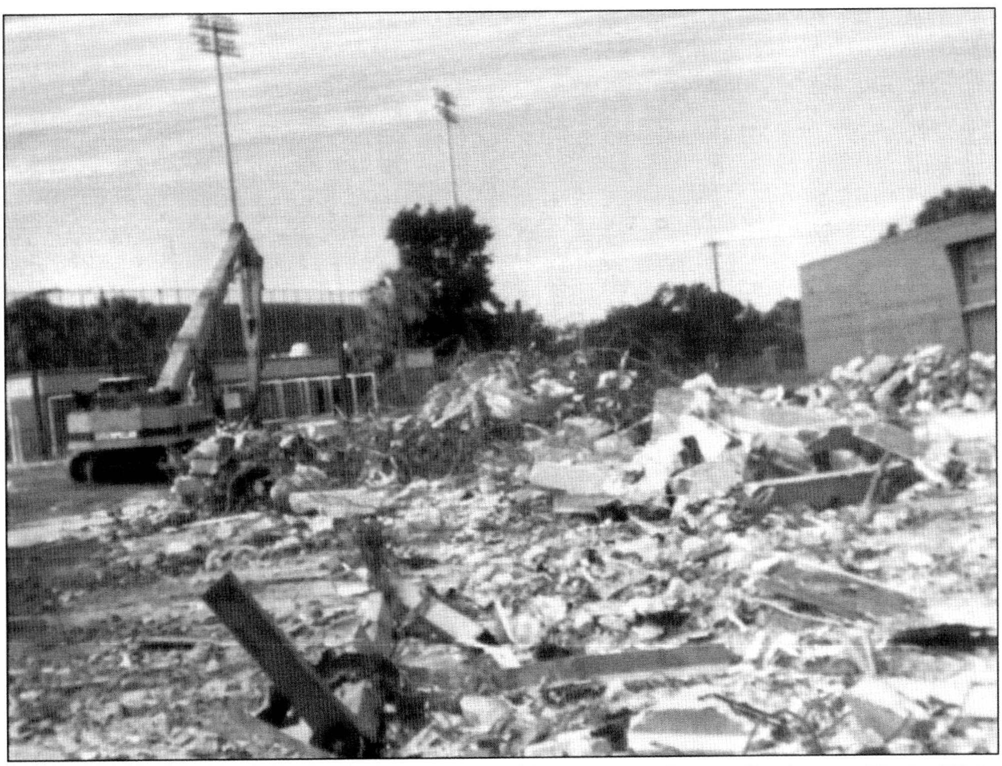

By 2003, the demolition of the old buildings had begun to make way for the new Burke High, which was designed by Harvey Gantt, a Burke graduate. (Courtesy of Sherman Pyatt.)

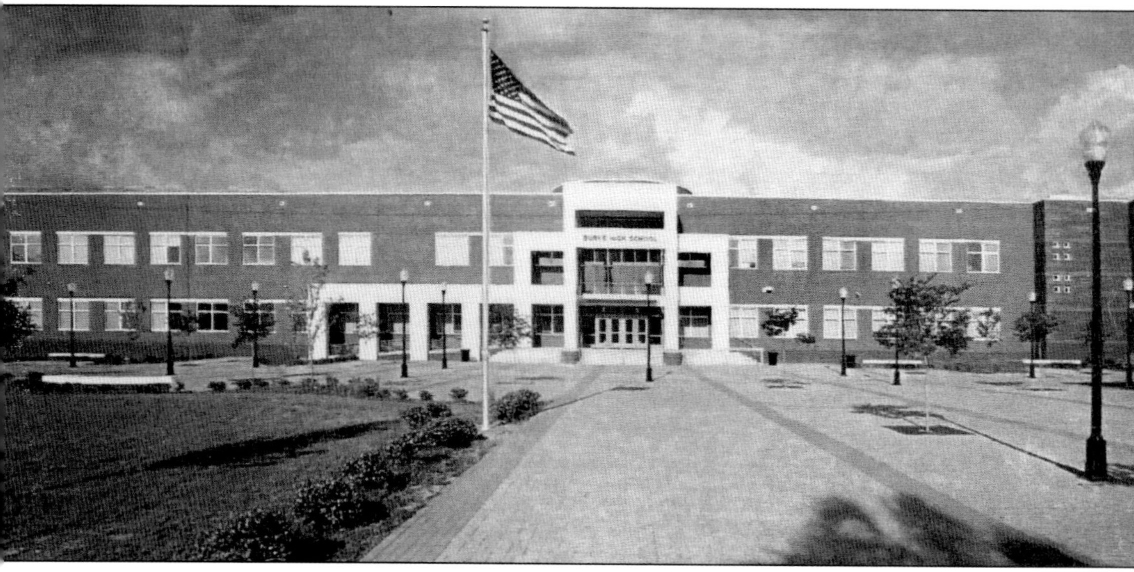

Pictured is a front view of the newly renovated Burke High School. The facility provides a state-of-the-art educational environment for 1,200 students. It includes academic, art, and vocational classrooms, a media center, and the physical education department with a 1,500-seat gymnasium, 700-seat auditorium, a cafeteria, and dining for approximately 400 students. The school was dedicated in December 2005. (Courtesy of Sherman Pyatt.)

Two

PRINCIPALS AND FACULTY

The faculty was bold, unafraid of challenges, very competent, talented and competitive.

—Marguerite S. Middleton, English teacher (1971, 1979–1980)

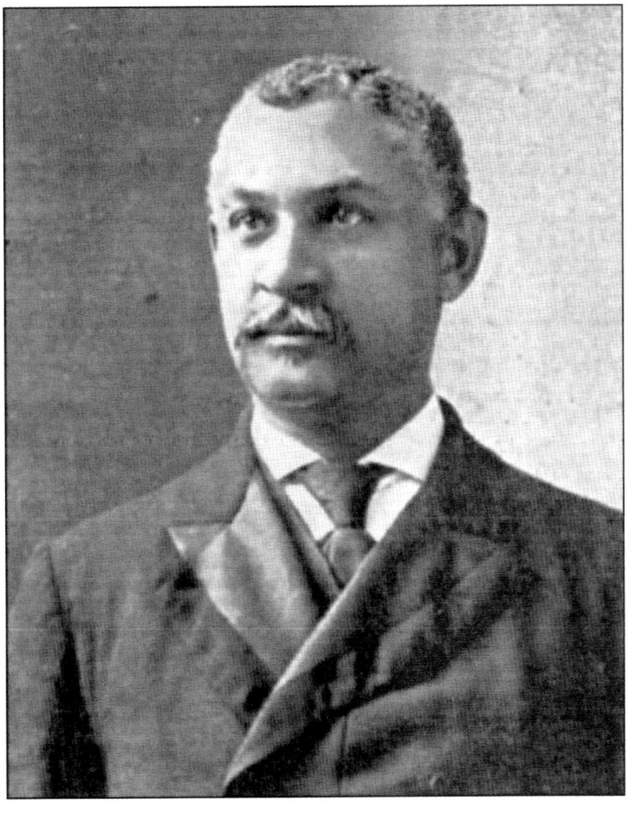

Rev. John L. Dart was born a free person of color in Charleston in 1854. He graduated from Avery Normal Institute in 1872. Dart attended Atlanta University and Newton Theological Seminary in Newton, Massachusetts, where he was ordained as a Baptist minister. He returned to Charleston in 1886 and became pastor of Morris Street Baptist Church. In 1894, he opened the Charleston Normal and Industrial Institute to educate African American children in the city of Charleston. He died in 1915. (Courtesy of Sherman Pyatt.)

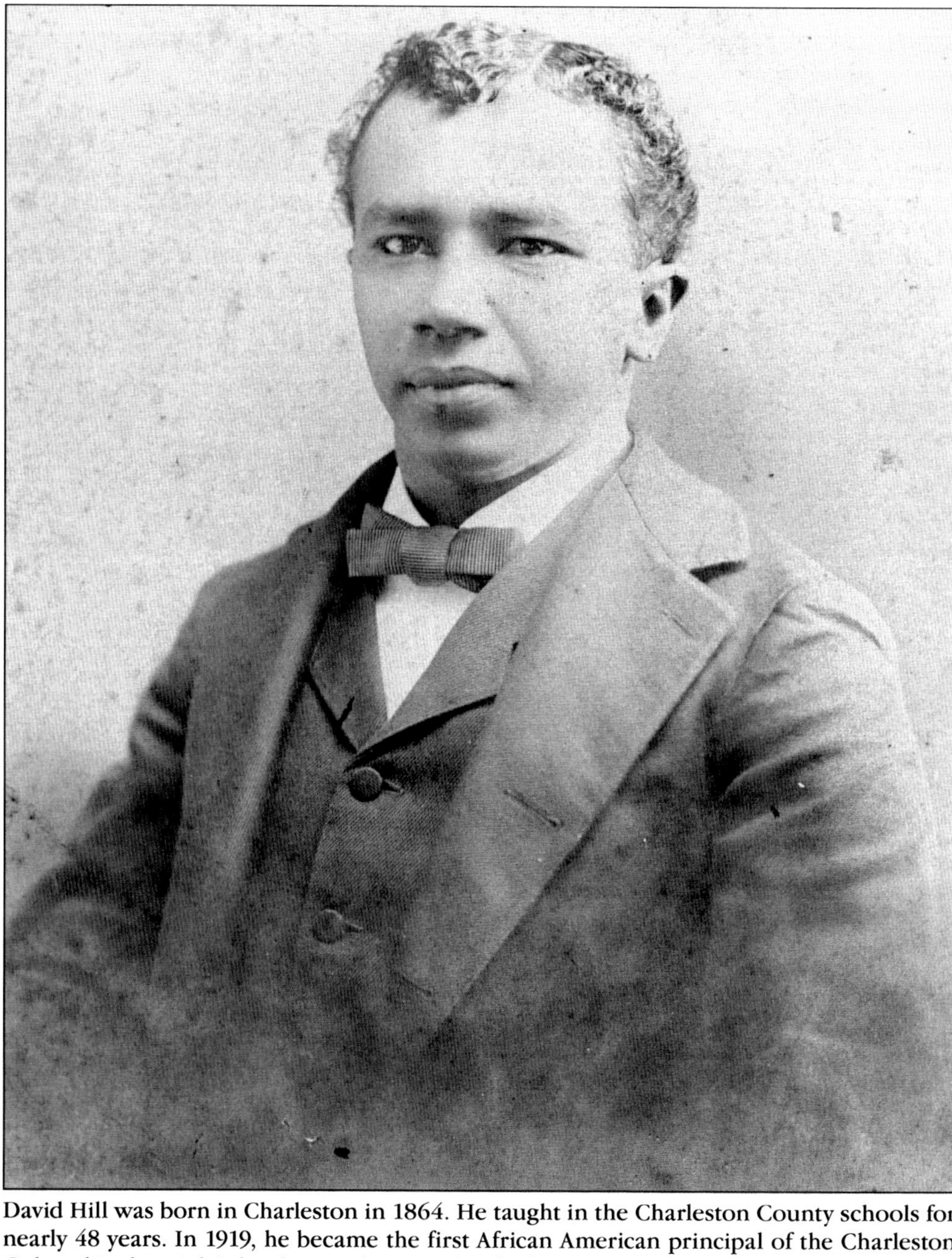

David Hill was born in Charleston in 1864. He taught in the Charleston County schools for nearly 48 years. In 1919, he became the first African American principal of the Charleston Colored Industrial School. He, along with 16 African American teachers, replaced the formerly all-white faculty. In 1925, he became the first principal of Buist Elementary School in downtown Charleston. (Courtesy of the Avery Research Center.)

In 1936, Arthur D. Greene wrote the Burke school alma mater. Even though he was hired to teach science, Greene volunteered to become the school's athletic coach and music director. He was also credited with organizing Burke's baccalaureate service and formal graduation. In 1937, Greene was appointed vice principal at Burke, and a year later the football team won its first championship. (Courtesy of Burke High School.)

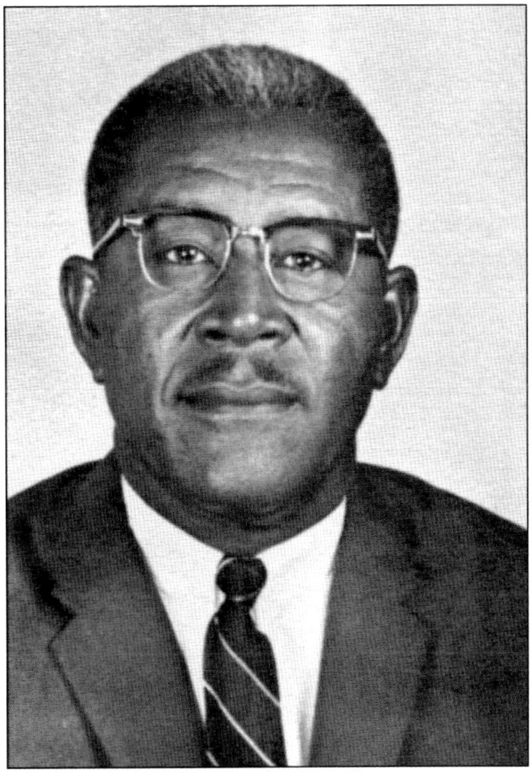

The Alma Mater

HAIL! DEAR OLD BURKE SCHOOL,
WE'LL BOW TO HONOR THEE,
THY SPIRIT LEADS US ON
THRU ALL THE YEARS

IN VICTORY OR DEFEAT,
LOYAL WE'LL EVER BE,
THY PRAISE WE'LL EVER SING,
DEAR BURKE TO THEE.

HAIL DEAR OLD BURKE SCHOOL,
WE'LL RALLY TO THY CALL,
AND FROM THE CLASSIC HALLS,
ONWARD WE'LL GO.

MEMORIES WILL LINGER ON,
WE'LL DEFEND AND FIGHT FOR THEE,
PROUD TO OWN THE NAME WE BEAR,
ALL HAIL TO THEE.

Composed by Mr. A. D. Greene

Arthur D. Greene wrote the alma mater in 1936 so that the student body would have a spirited song to sing during the annual Thanksgiving Day football game played against Avery Normal Institute. (Courtesy of Burke High School.)

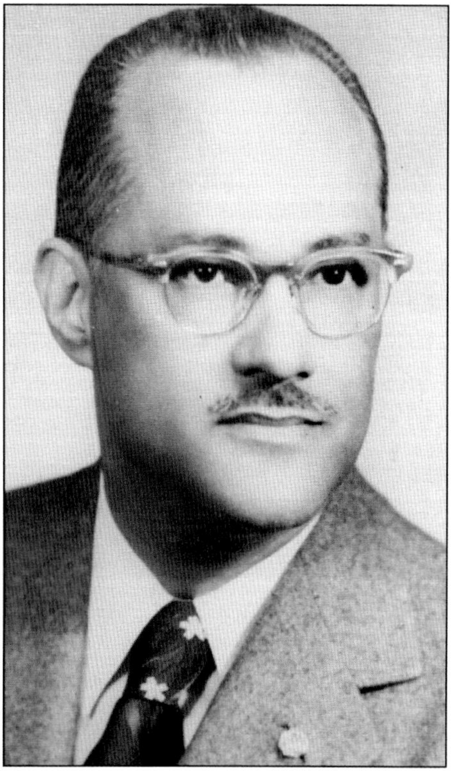

A native Charlestonian, William Henry Grayson graduated from Fisk University and received a master's degree in business administration from the University of Michigan. Grayson was principal of Burke School from 1939 to 1945. Under his administration, Burke became a full, four-year high school, the curriculum was broadened, and the faculty was upgraded. Several new trades were added, such as tailoring, printing, cosmetology, and welding. Moreover, the music program was expanded. After serving as principal, Grayson became supervisor of elementary schools for the City of Charleston. (Courtesy of the Avery Research Center.)

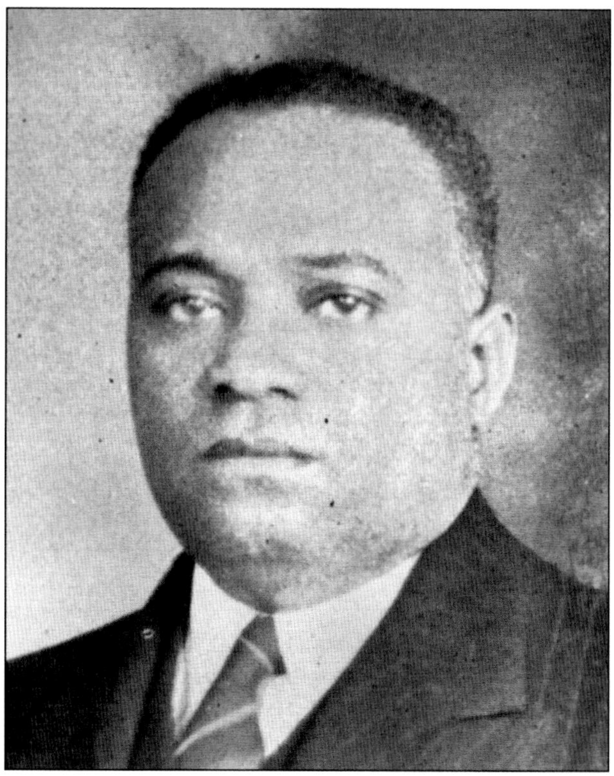

In 1935, Samuel Higgins assumed the responsibilities as Burke's principal. Under his watch, all departments were enlarged, and extracurricular activities were broadened. The first school newspaper was published, and the student government was formed. Higgins resigned in 1939 to assume the duties of president of Allen University in Columbia, South Carolina. (Courtesy of the Avery Research Center.)

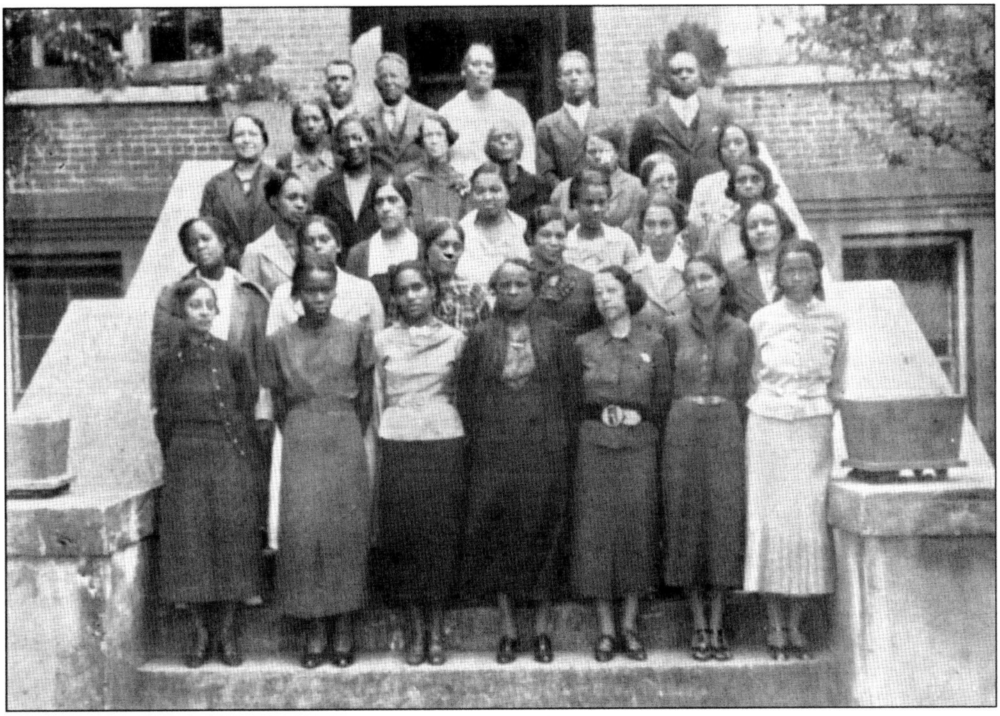

This 1937 photograph reveals that the majority of the faculty were female. Excluding principal Higgins to the far right, there were only three male teachers. (Courtesy of the Avery Research Center.)

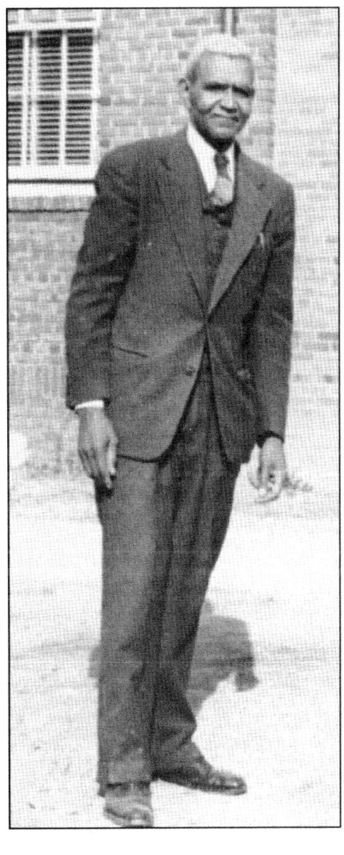

Robert Fields taught masonry at the school for many years. Because of his dedicated service and his unique teaching style, Fields was honored posthumously by the naming of the Fields-Sims-Wright Vocational Center in 1980. Mr. Fields died in 1963. (Courtesy of Burke High School.)

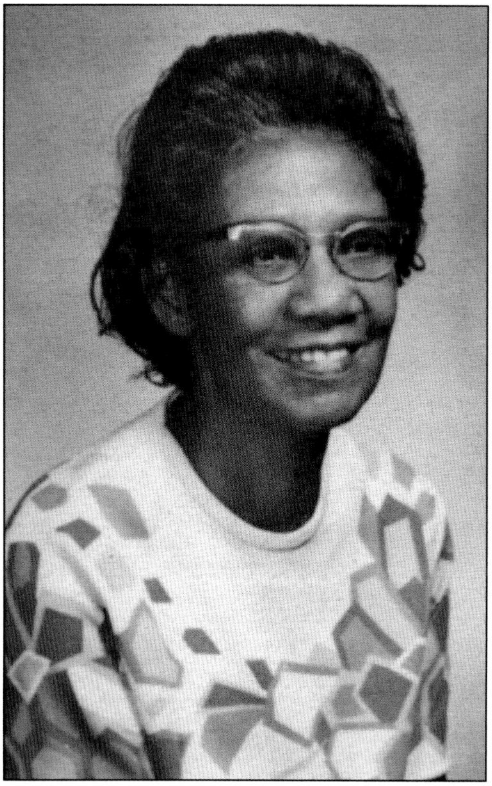

Marjorie H. Howard, a mathematics teacher, was assigned by the principal to reorganize the student newspaper during the 1940–1941 school year. The newspaper was renamed the *Parvenue*. During the 1941–1942 school year, students published their first yearbook under the leadership of Howard. (Courtesy of Burke High School.)

This group was responsible for nearly 2,000 students. Several of these teachers came from Avery High School after the school was closed in 1954. (Courtesy of the Avery Research Center.)

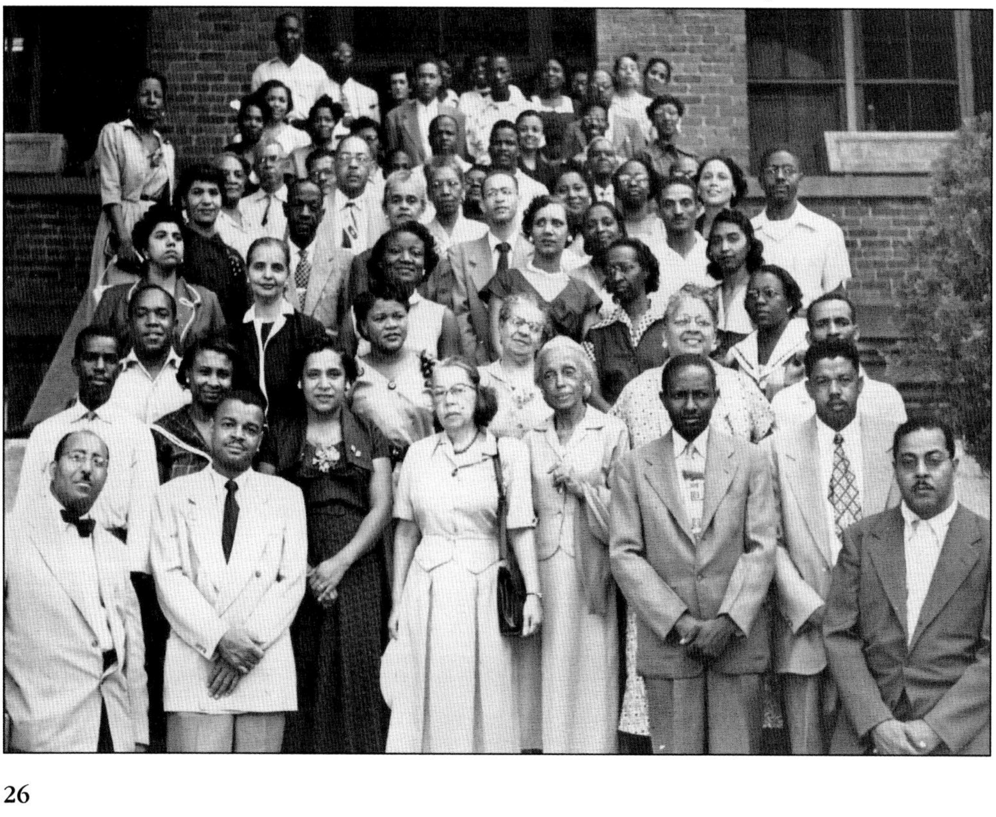

W. R. Meriwether brought stability to the position of principal from 1962 until 1982. His son, Delano (class of 1960), became the first African American to integrate Duke's School of Medicine. (Courtesy of Burke High School.)

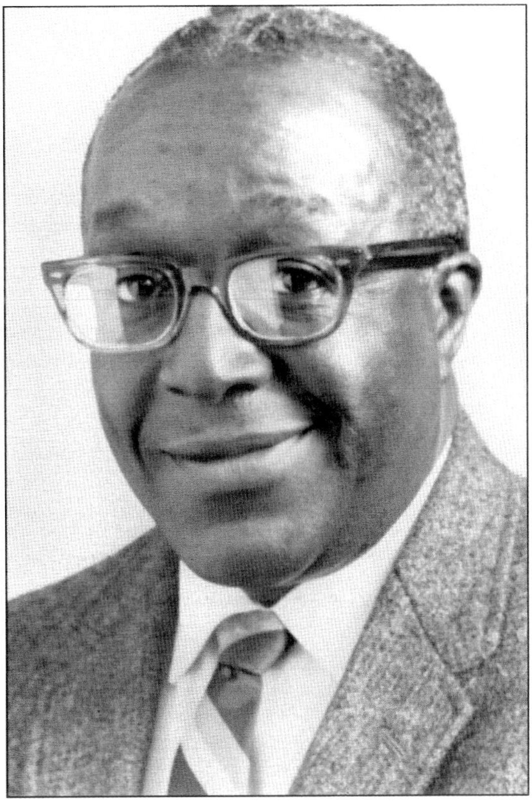

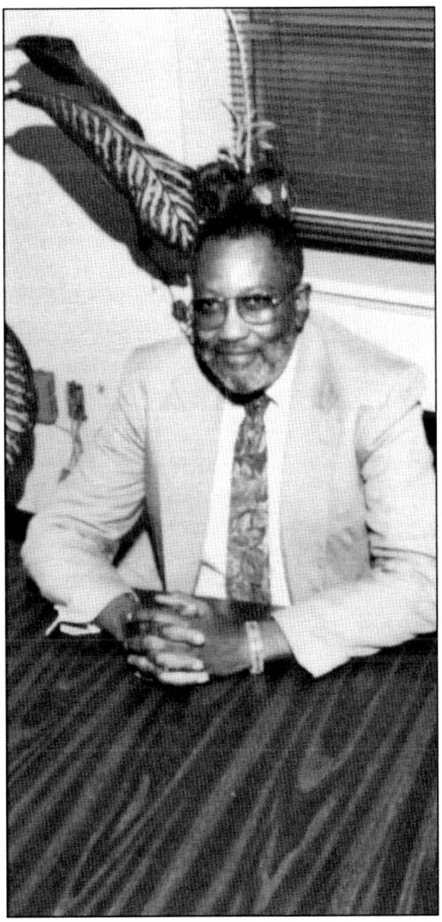

Leckyler Gaillard was appointed principal in 1982. He brought about a smooth transition to the faculty, now including teachers from the defunct Charles A. Brown and Charleston High Schools. Also, in 1988, he was called upon to organize the logistics for placing the Academic Magnet High School on Burke's campus. Gaillard remained in the position until 1995. (Courtesy of Burke High School.)

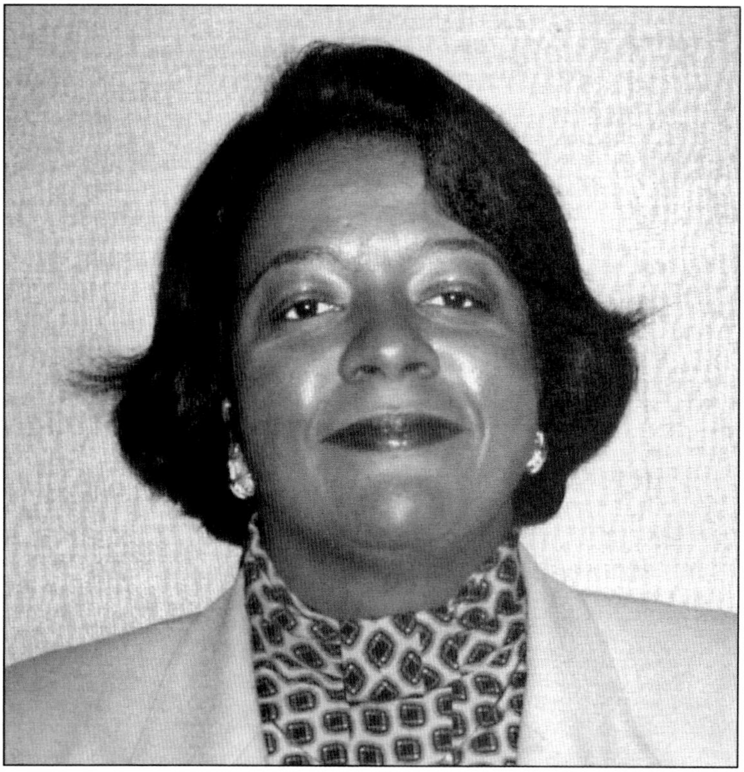

Jeannetta Scott became the first female principal to hold that position. Scott was principal from 1995 to 1998. (Courtesy of Burke High School.)

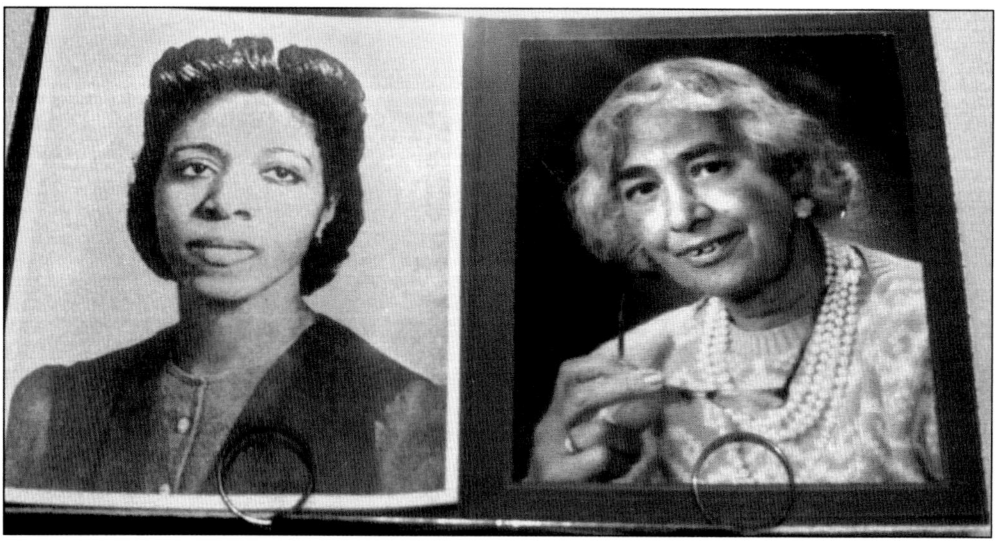

Malissa Smith Burkhalter (left) and Viola Duvall Stewart (right) played a significant role by eradicating unequal pay between white and African American teachers. In 1943, with the support of the NAACP, Burkhalter filed a petition with the school board. The petition indicated that unequal pay based on race was unconstitutional. Burkhalter was dismissed from the school district on a technicality. Duvall replaced Burkhalter that same year and filed a suit against the city school board with the federal district court. The court ruled in her favor, but it was not until 1946 that African American teachers in District 20 finally received the same salaries as their white counterparts. (Courtesy of the Avery Research Center.)

"Excuses don't excuse; and explanations don't explain."
Miss A. K. McGriff

"Why the dear God."
Mrs. S. G. Oglesby

"Ah lookee here, we don't have all of that in here, hear?"
Mr. E. B. Shaw

"I think so, don't you agree? Yes, yes, let's go on."
Miss L. Simms

"Wha ya say Tuff."
Mr. L. Anderson

"You students are a mess."
Mr. R. F. Perry

"Ya'll funny talking people ought to be quiet."
Mr. L. Byrd

"Lord Help!"
Miss L. E. Heyward

"Come on children, please, we don't have much time."
Mrs. L. Sims

"You must be ten men cause one man can't be so dum."
Mr. M. Risher

". . .and I mean that thing, honey."
Miss J. L. Richardson

"Children you just don't study, you just don't study!"
Mrs. F. S. Grant

"Don't fool yourself. Everybody knows what's going on."
Mr. W. R. Meriwether

"It's always better to be able to say that 'I'm glad I did;
than to have to say 'I wished I had."
Mr. E. A. Roper

These quotes of some of the faculty members were taken from the 1965 yearbook. It was a senior class tradition to express their views about the faculty and their fellow classmates upon graduating. (Courtesy of the Avery Research Center.)

ONE may think that Burke High School is just another school with ordinary buildings, ordin students and classes, ordinary lunch periods; but not so ordinary teachers.

Just by looking at some of our teachers at Burke, one would not believe that they would hav phrases that would charm the husk into trying to grow another husk over itself.

Take one abnormal day at Burke. You can just about hear the melodious voice of Miss Mc-Griff singing a tune of "Excuse don't excuse, explanations don't explain." Or something just a tuneful as "Feshie" (I wonder who she could have been talking to). Of course, we all know whc she was talking to when she said, "Time is passing are you?"

Get this, right across the hall is the wonderful Miss Simms, whispering her ever famous "Don't wait until the deadline students". And when the students meet the deadline, she would probably say, "Isn't that something" but we know who agrees with that.

Let's go over to the Administration building to eavesdrop on a few of our really great teachers.

Just as we walk up the stairs, we hear Mr. Taylor give his typing students a not so encour ing word, "Stop typing, stop typing, stop typing."

Right next to Mr. Taylor is Mrs. Blackman agreeing as always "O.K."

Now going further down the hall we find Mrs. Harrison saying in her most dramatic voice "You will be penalize for this!" But Mrs. Simmons sympathizes with the students by saying "Que Lastimal."

Let us return to the Annex building, but just before we enter the building we can hear Mr. Cook yell "Didn't you see that stop sign."

We should not forget Mrs. R. B. Brown, because as she says I'm from the "Now Generatio Keep doing your thing Mrs. Brown.

Let us go upstairs, but as we approach we can hear Mrs. Hutchinson say "Don't wait until the deadline." With that thought in mind, we return downstairs and out of the door.

Just as we pass the Library building we can hear Mr. Miller say softly "Just shut your mo

Suddenly we find ourselves in front of the Science building where all of the Mad Scientists dwell. Such arch-scientists as Miss F. B.Campbell, who says "I don't know what to say about people." And another is our illustrous Mr. Graves who agrees with Miss Campbell, but as he says "I won't say it."

Well as we have seen, most of these teachers really care (?) But there are times when they can get just a tiny bit unconcerned about where we go. As Miss L. A. Williams says "I am not going in the bathroom to look for you Seniors."

This testimony reflects the sentiments of the senior class of 1970 and how they viewed certain members of the faculty. (Courtesy of Burke High School.)

Three

CAMPUS SCENES

Burke was like a home away from home.

—Stephen Graham III (Class of 1954)

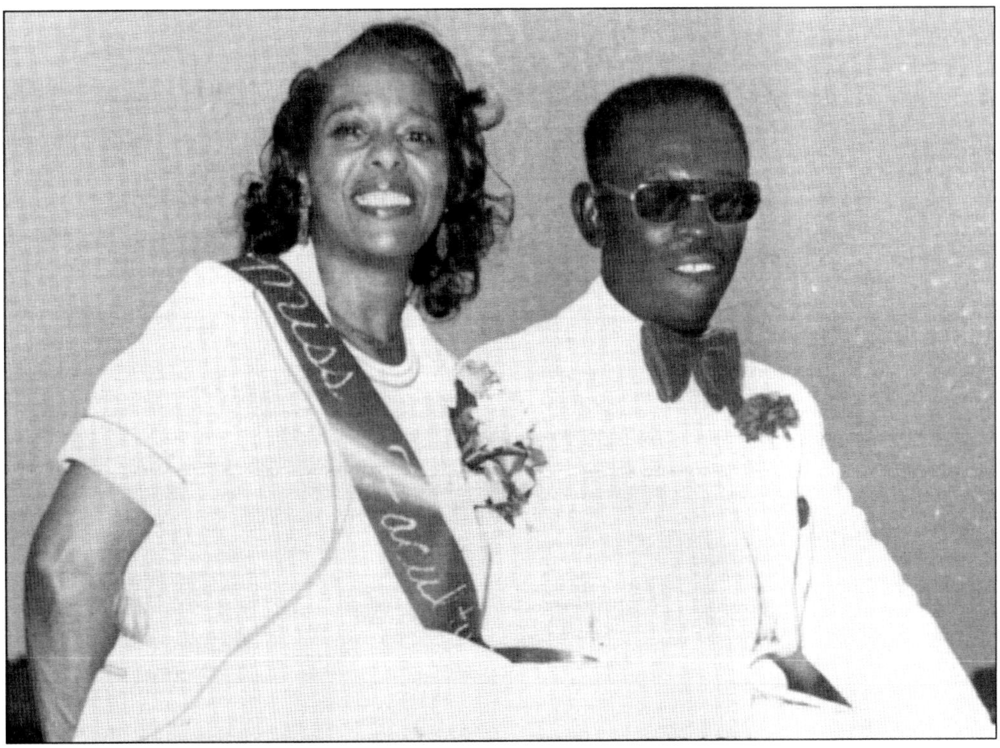

Popular in the late 1970s was the selection of Mr. and Miss Faculty. Pictured in 1978 are Mildred E. Carr and L. Anderson. They were participants in the Homecoming Parade. (Courtesy of Burke High School.)

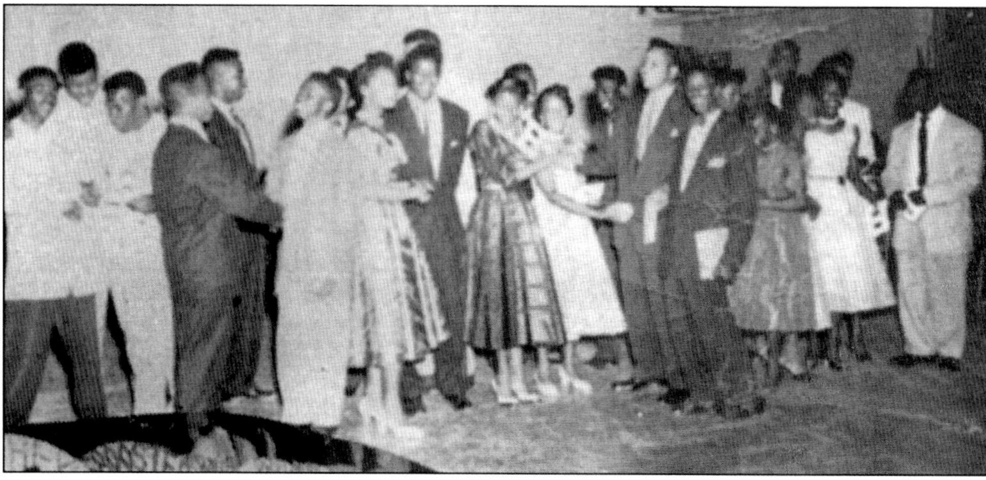

Pictured above are students at the homecoming dance. Below are other activities at the homecoming game in 1954. (Courtesy of the Avery Research Center.)

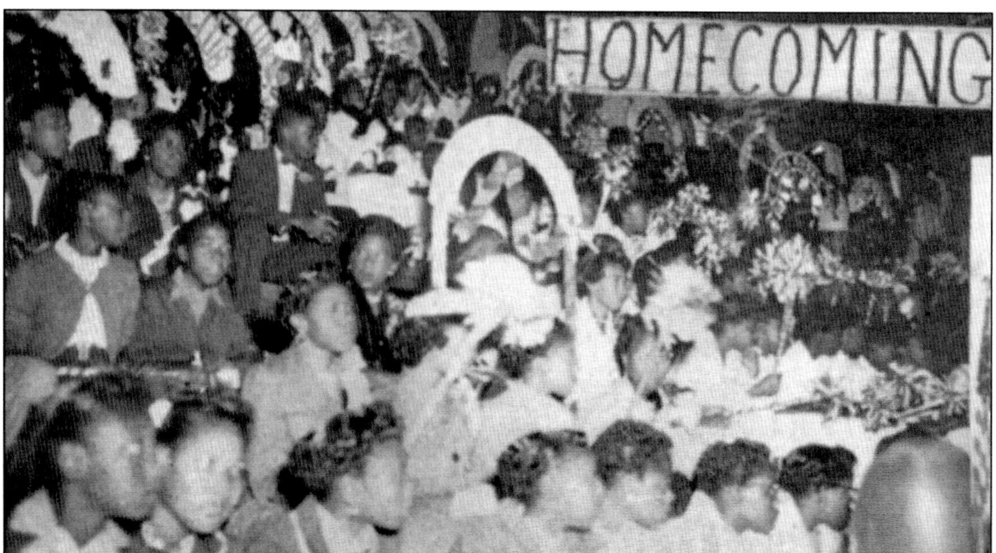

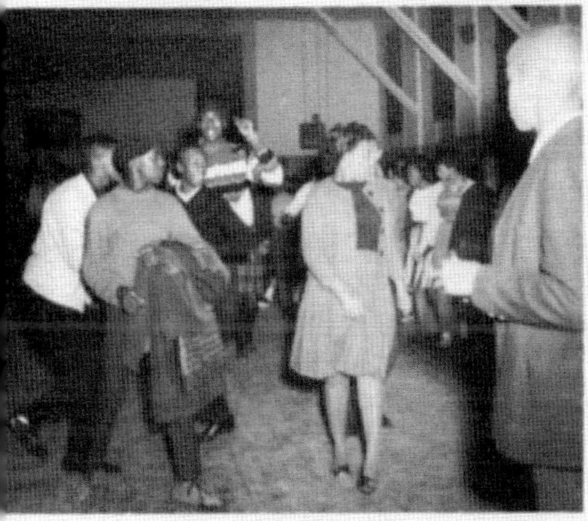

"Dig dis boss step!"

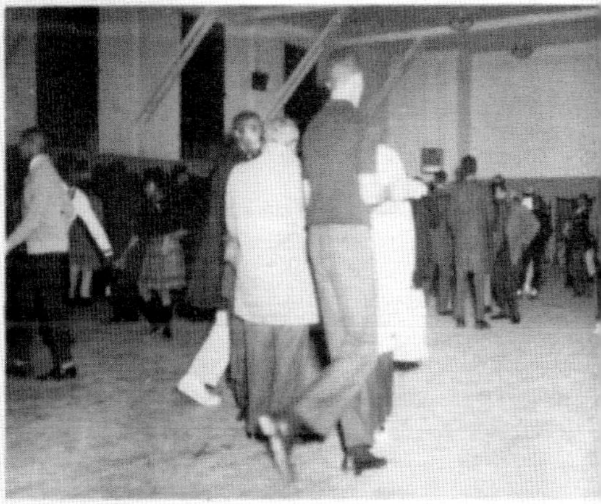

"Ah, there's nothing to the Watusi. I'll show you h
it's done . . . . some other time."

Members of the student body enjoy themselves at a dance sponsored by the yearbook staff in 1963. This event was held in order to raise funds to help support the publishing of the yearbook. (Courtesy of the Avery Research Center.)

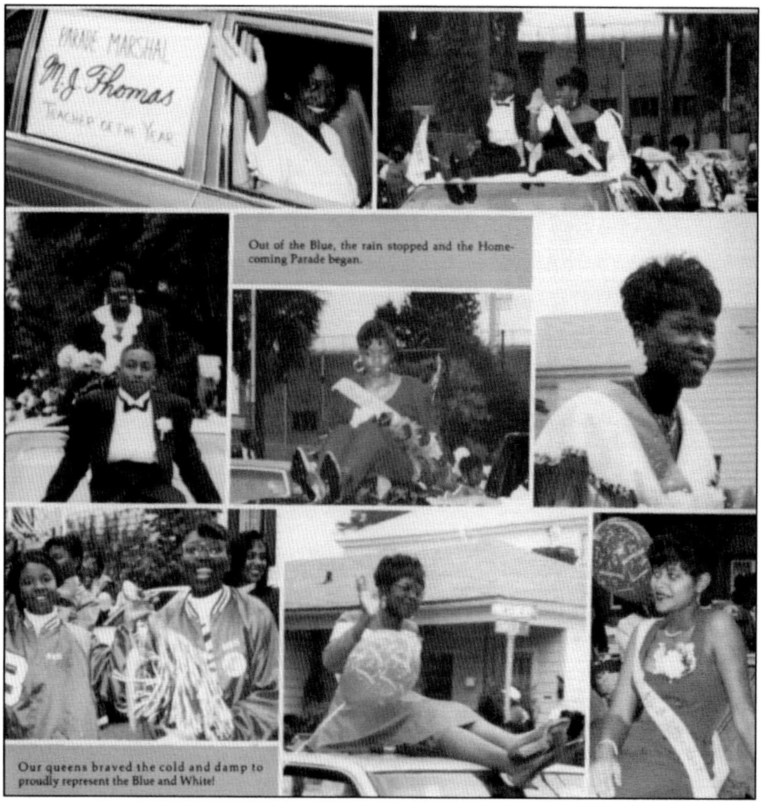

One of the most exciting events of student life at Burke was homecoming, as seen in this 1994 image. (Courtesy of Burke High School.)

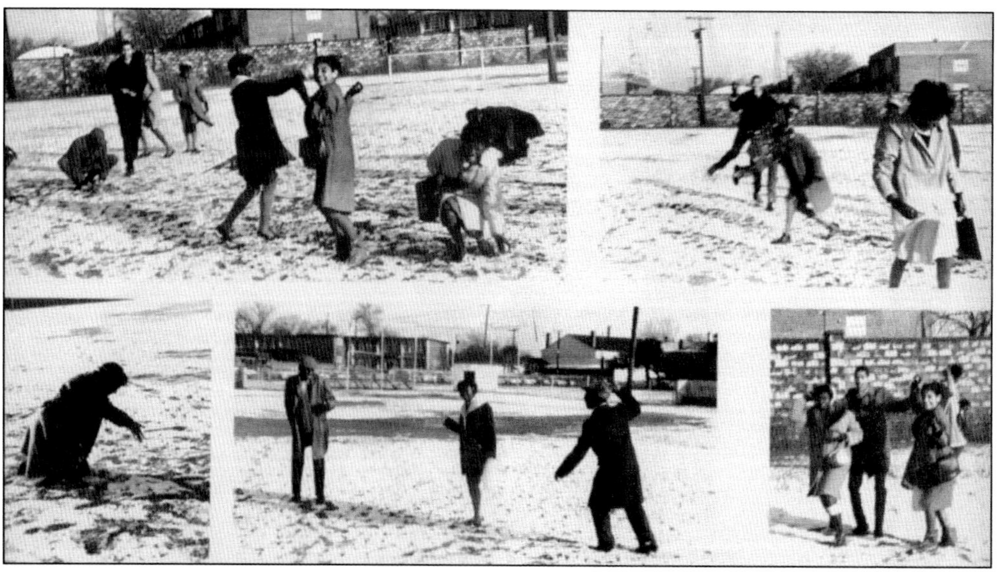

Several members of the senior class enjoyed a rare snow-day occurrence on Harmon Field *c.* 1966. In the background to the left is the administration building, and to the right is the gymnasium. (Courtesy of the Avery Research Center.)

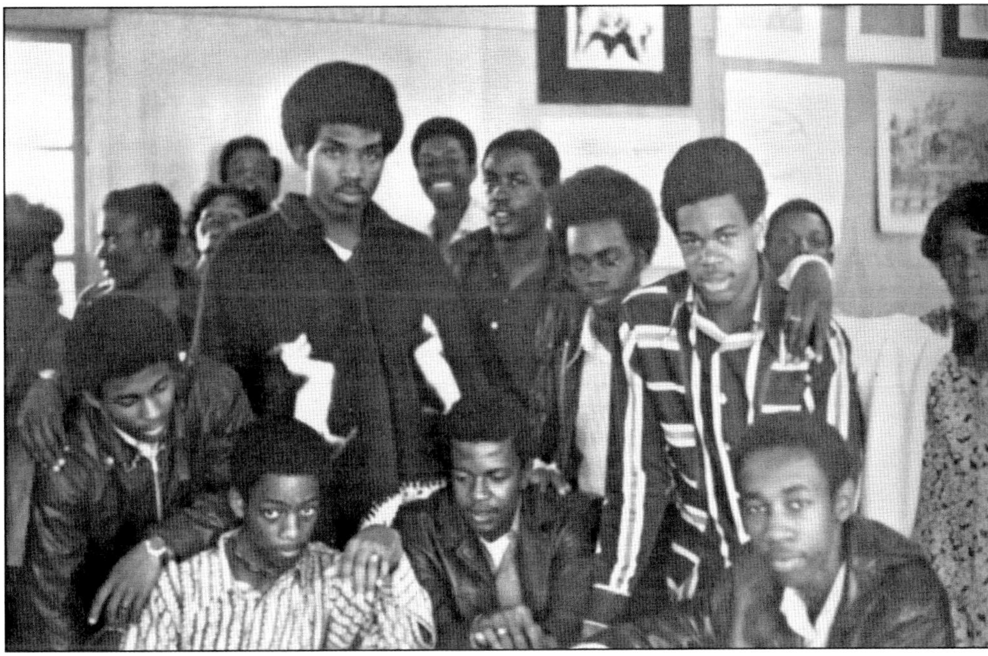

Members of the senior class revealed the style of dress and hairstyles that were adorned during the early 1970s. Several of the students were shown wearing their hair natural, which was commonly referred to as an afro. (Courtesy of Burke High School.)

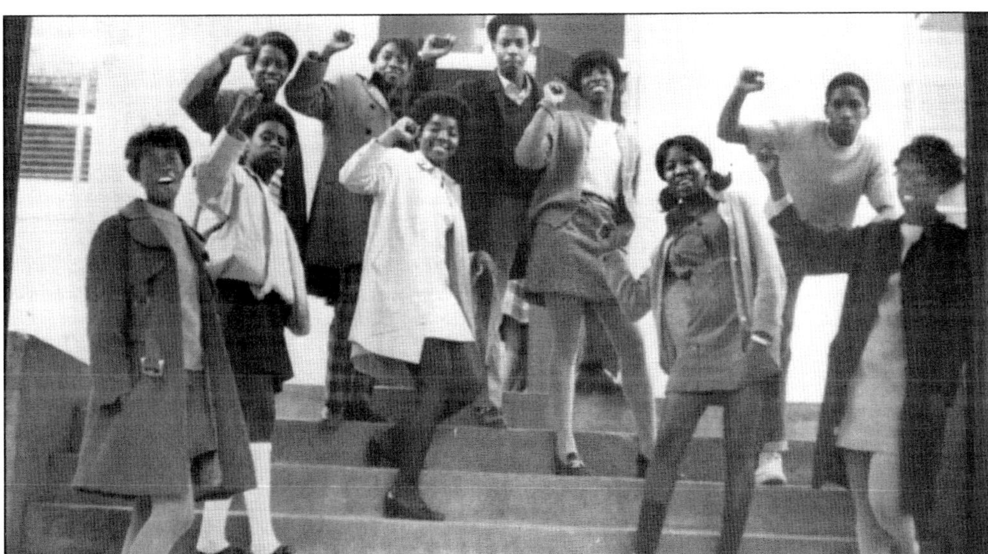

By the early 1970s, the "Black Power Movement" had spread across the country, as evidenced by members of the student council as they displayed the black power sign in 1971. (Courtesy of the Avery Research Center.)

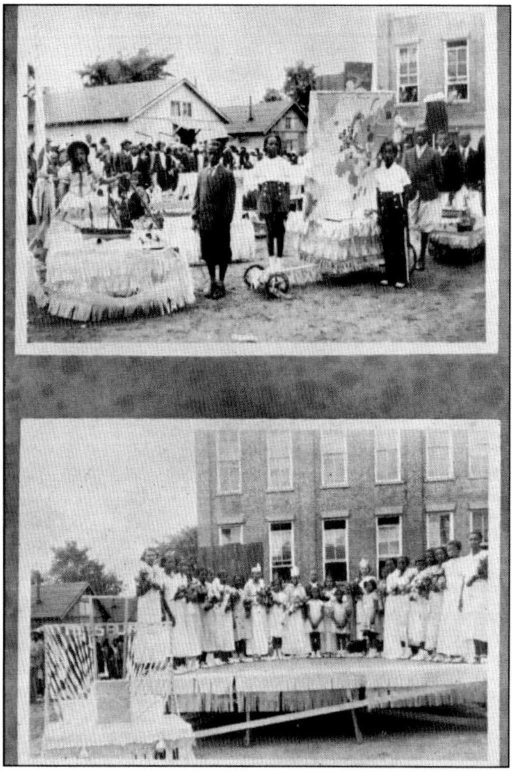

Before there was a marching band and football games played on Friday nights, students participated in what was known as Field Day *c.* 1937. (Courtesy of the Avery Research Center.)

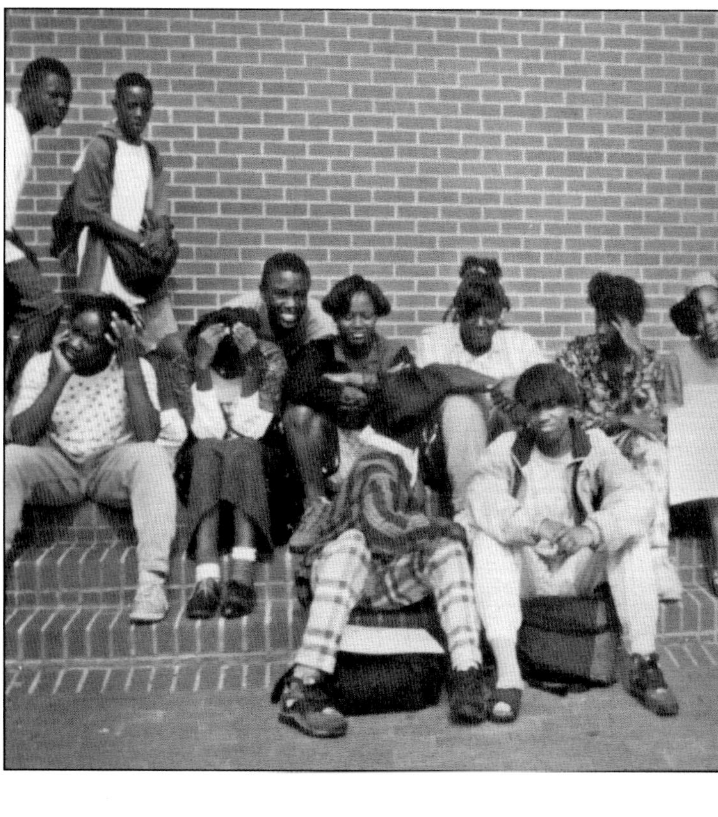

A long-standing tradition at Burke was seniors sitting on the senior steps (the steps leading to the annex building). By the 1990s, the steps were no longer in existence, and seniors had no designated area for themselves. Pictured are students sitting in front of the fine arts building in 1994. (Courtesy of Burke High School.)

Four

Clubs and Organizations

The school was well organized to include academics, music, and extracurricular activities.

—Alice A. Pyatt (Class of 1955)

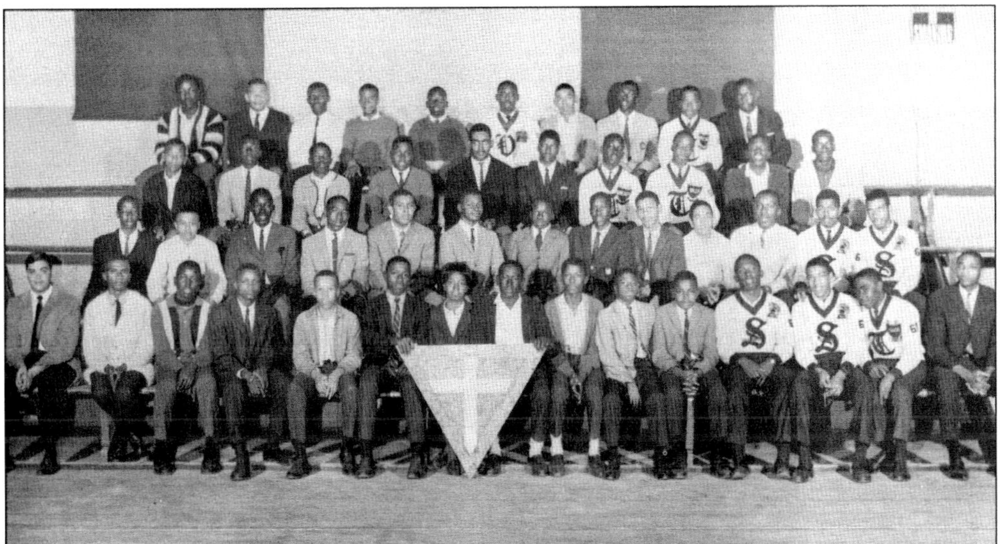

The purpose of the Hi-Y Club was to create, maintain, and extend throughout the home, school, and community, high standards of Christian character. The organization was composed of young men from the 9th though the 12th grades. The club was organized in 1944. (Courtesy of the Avery Research Center.)

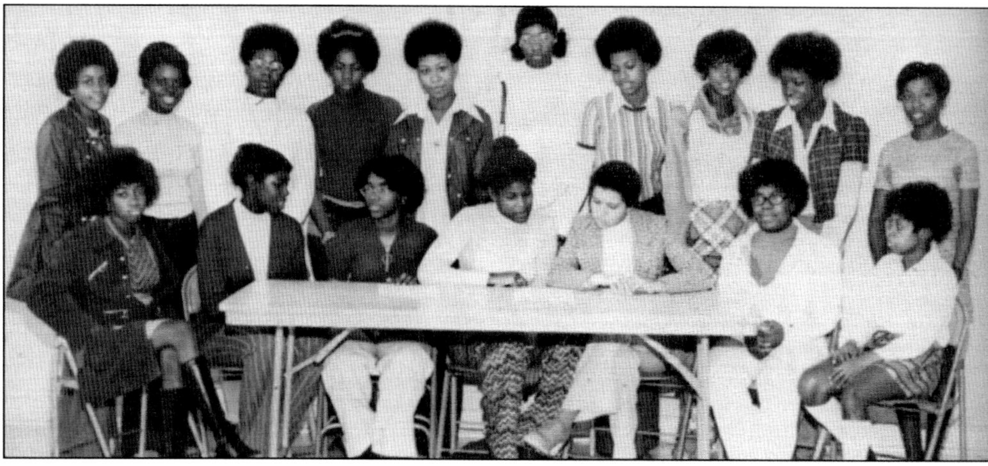

Above are members of the Tri-Hi-Y Club in 1973. The organization still had a sizeable membership, as viewed in the image. (Courtesy of Burke High School.)

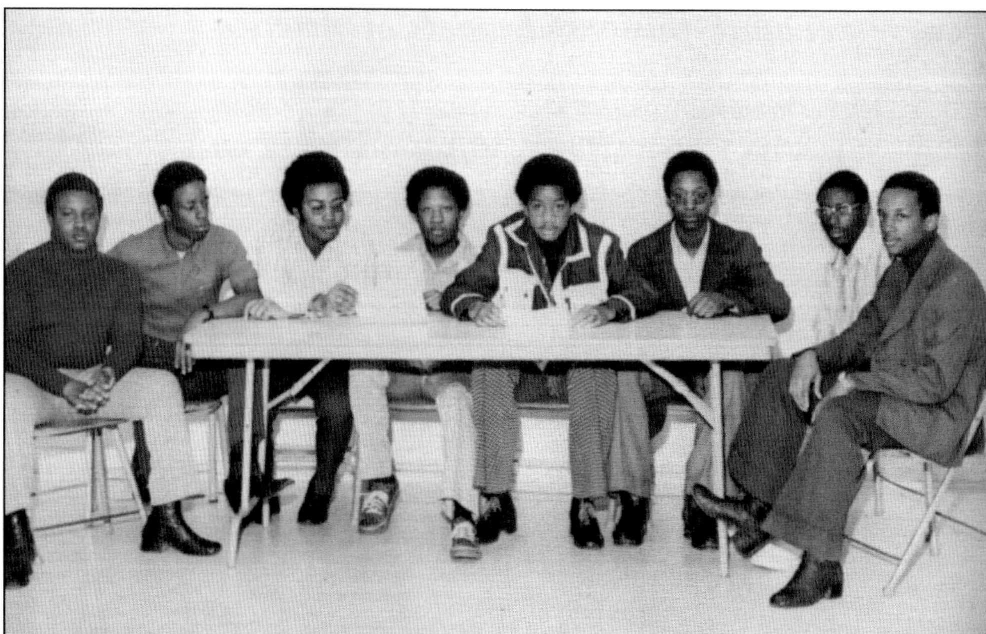

The membership in the Hi-Y Club had dropped significantly since its inception in 1944. By the late 1990s, the club was not listed as an organization on the campus. This photograph was taken in 1973. (Courtesy of Burke High School.)

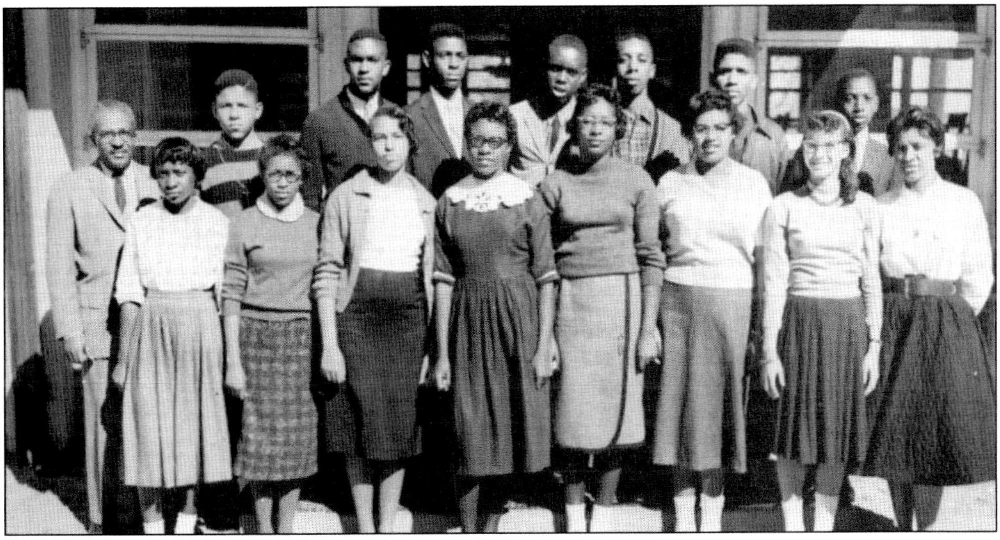

The purpose of the Science Club was to create an interest in science. In this photograph taken in 1959, each member was required to have at least one project to be entered in the science fair. Two members of the club, Delano Meriwether and Andrea Jones, received high recognition at the science fair in 1959. (Courtesy of the Avery Research Center.)

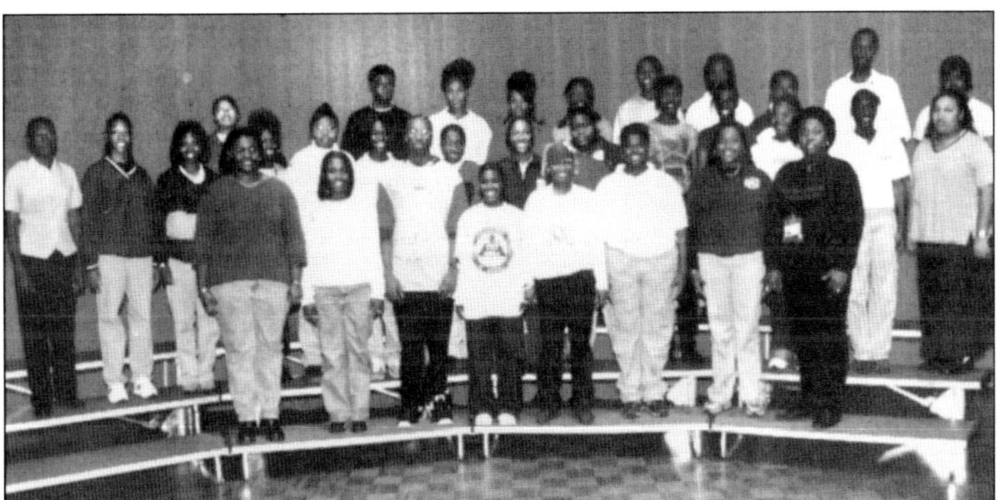

By the 1990s, the Forensic, Nurses, and Physician Clubs were grouped under one cluster. This image of the health occupational students shows those students who had expressed an interest in pursuing health-related careers in 2001. (Courtesy of Burke High School.)

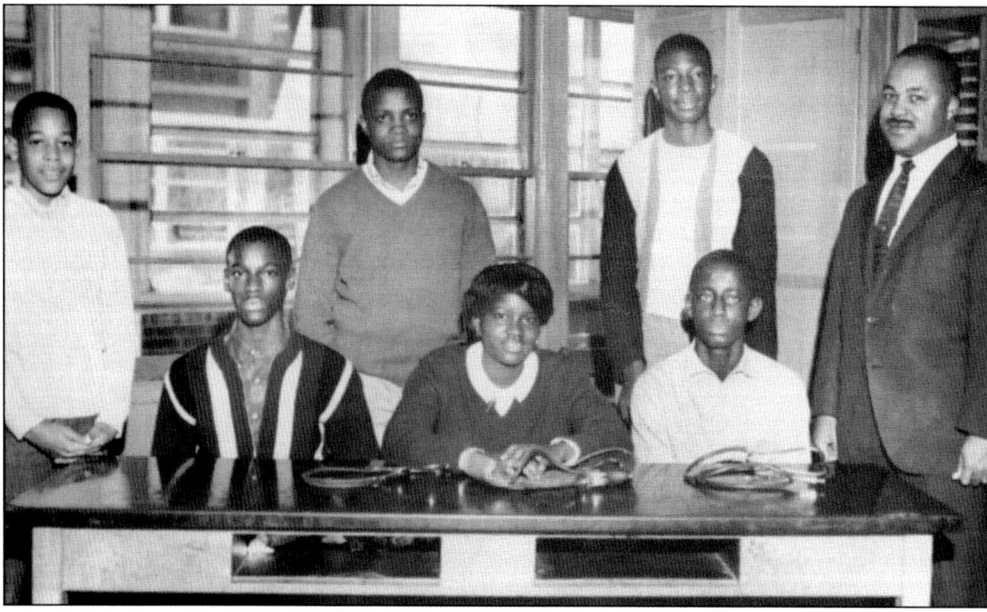

Taken in 1966, these image reveals an awareness by the faculty to encourage students to consider other occupations, specifically in relation to the health fields. Pictured are members of the Physicians Club. (Courtesy of the Avery Research Center.)

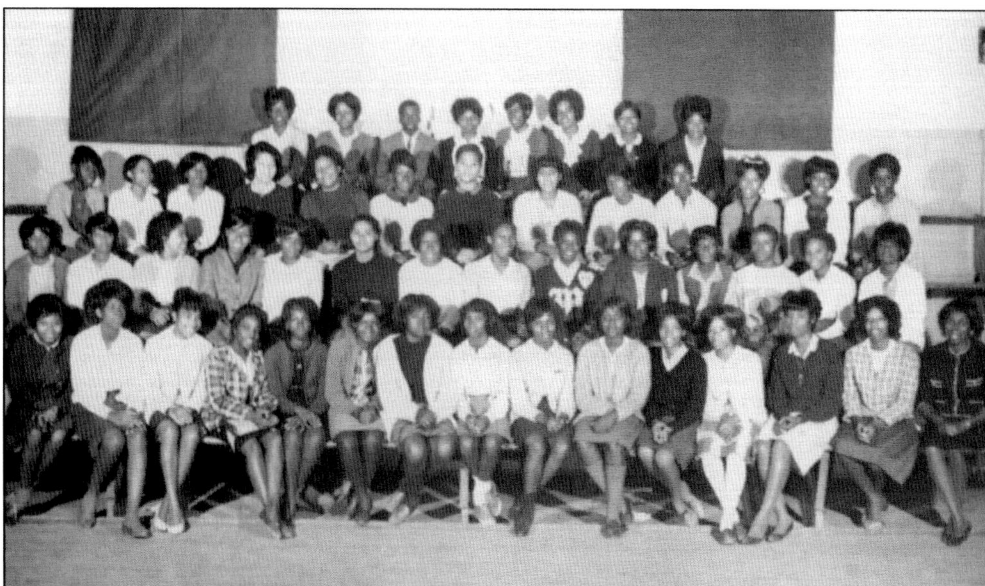

The members of the Future Nurses Club are pictured above. Included in the 1968 image was one male student. The picture revealed that there was a high level of interest in the area of nursing as a profession. (Courtesy of Burke High School.)

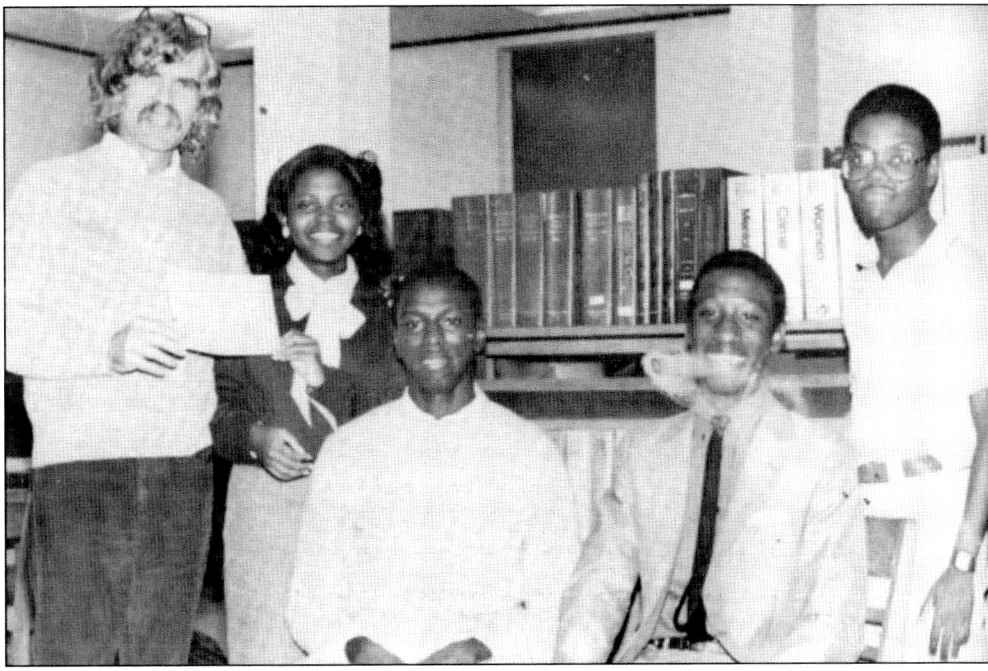

By the 1980s, the students at Burke were exposed to various laboratory sciences. Members were allowed to explore the intricacies of forensic science as a career path. Pictured from left to right in 1984 are M. Gallagher, Caroline Wright, Craig Miller, Keith Douglas, and Alfred Brown. (Courtesy of Sherman Pyatt.)

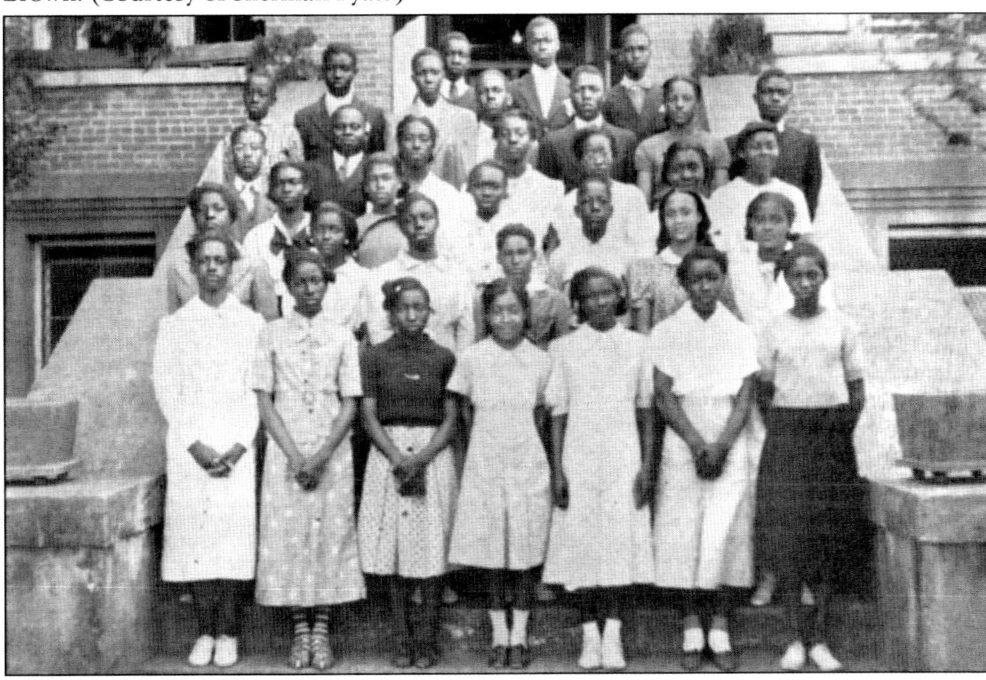

There was early participation by the students in school affairs, as evident in this image from 1937. A key component of the student council was to increase student interest in school affairs. (Courtesy of the Avery Research Center.)

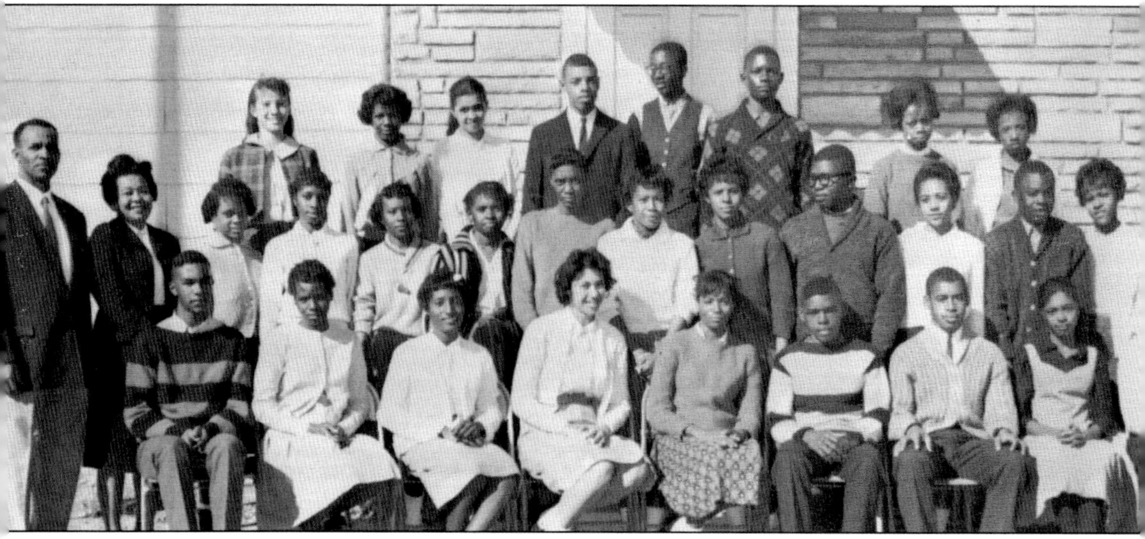

Among the many purposes of the student council, pictured here in 1960, were to better the relationship between the administration, faculty, and student body; to prepare the students for active life in a democracy; to make them self-directive; to teach social cooperation; to increase student interest in school; and to foster respect for law and order. (Courtesy of the Avery Research Center.)

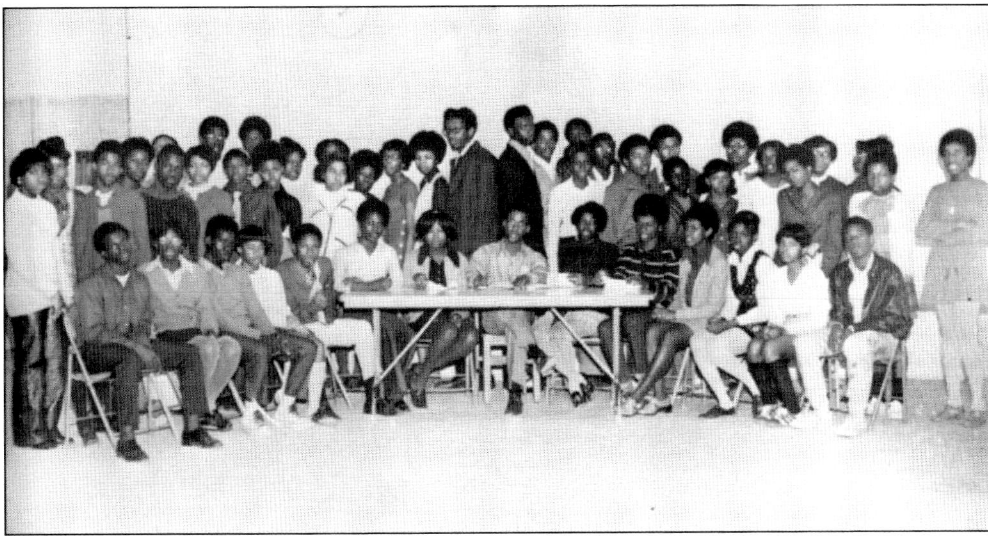

The mission of the student council was to organize the school so as to preserve the rights of students and to provide character training for future citizens in a democratic society. The photograph above is of the council for 1971. Pictured below is the council in 1980. (Courtesy of Burke High School.)

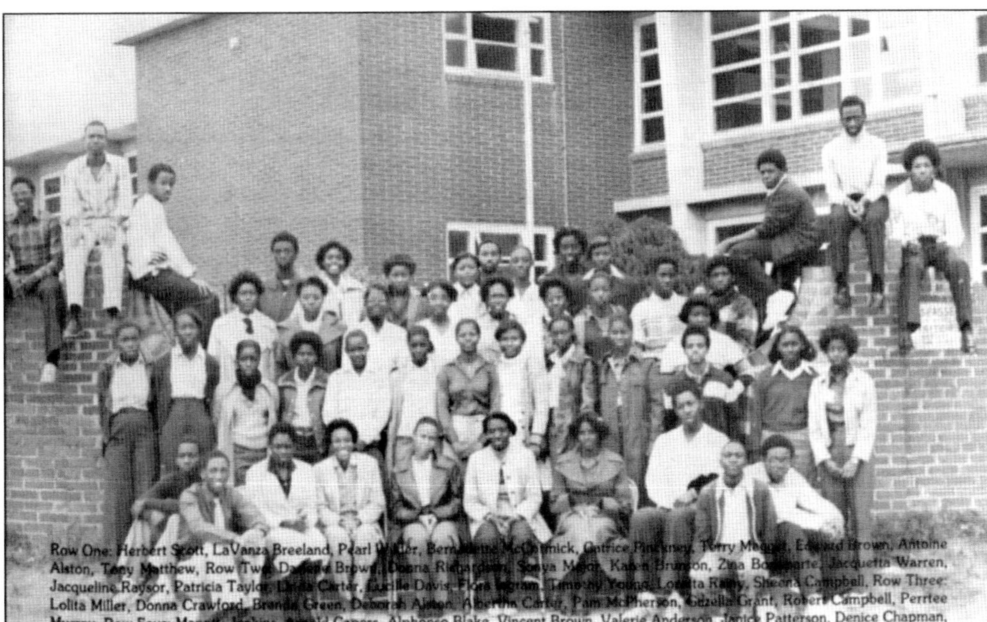

Row One: Herbert Scott, LaVanza Breeland, Pearl W[illegible]er, Bernadette McCormick, Gatrice Pinckney, Terry M[illegible], Edward Brown, Antoine Alston, Tony Matthew, Row Two: Darlene Brown, Donna Richardson, Sonya Major, Karen Brunson, Zina Bonaparte, Jacquetta Warren, Jacqueline Raysor, Patricia Taylor, Linda Carter, Lucille Davis, Flora Ingram, Timothy Young, Loretta R[illegible], Sheena Campbell, Row Three: Lolita Miller, Donna Crawford, Brenda Green, Deborah Alston, Albertha Carter, Pam McPherson, Gezella Grant, Robert Campbell, Perrtee Murray, Row Four: Manotti Jenkins, Arnold Capers, Alphonso Blake, Vincent Brown, Valerie Anderson, Janice Patterson, Denice Chapman, Tyrone Smalls, Eleena Geathers, Angela Goff, Sabena Scott, Raue Martinez, John Green, Alfred Sheppard

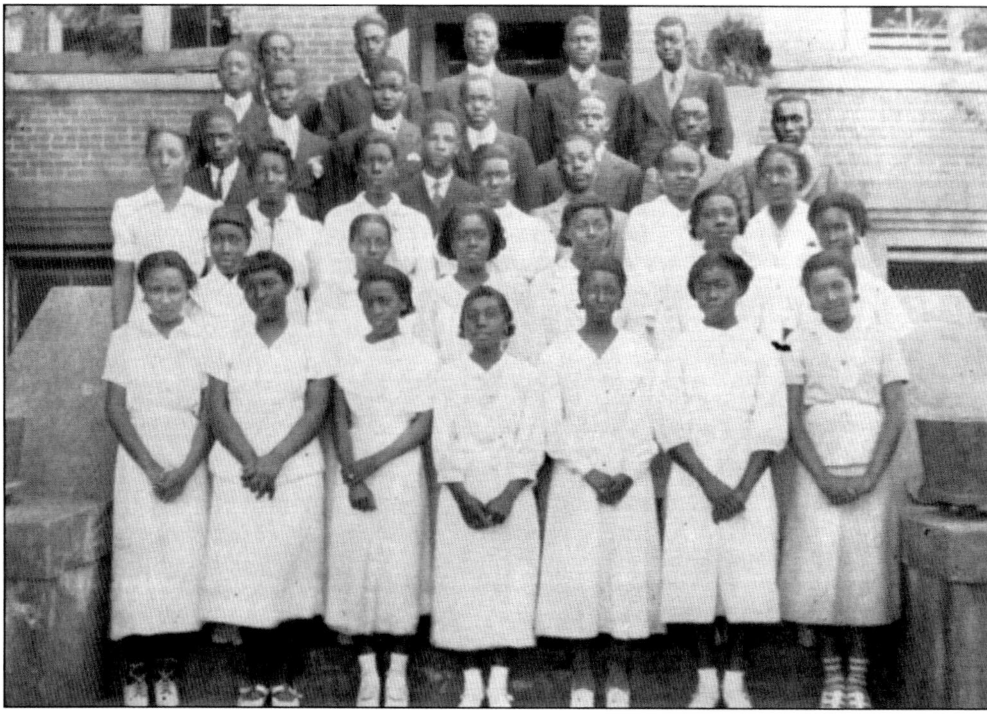

Prior to the arrival of Eugene Hunt, there was a musical group in existence, as shown in this image in 1937. The members were known as the Glee Club. (Courtesy of the Avery Research Center.)

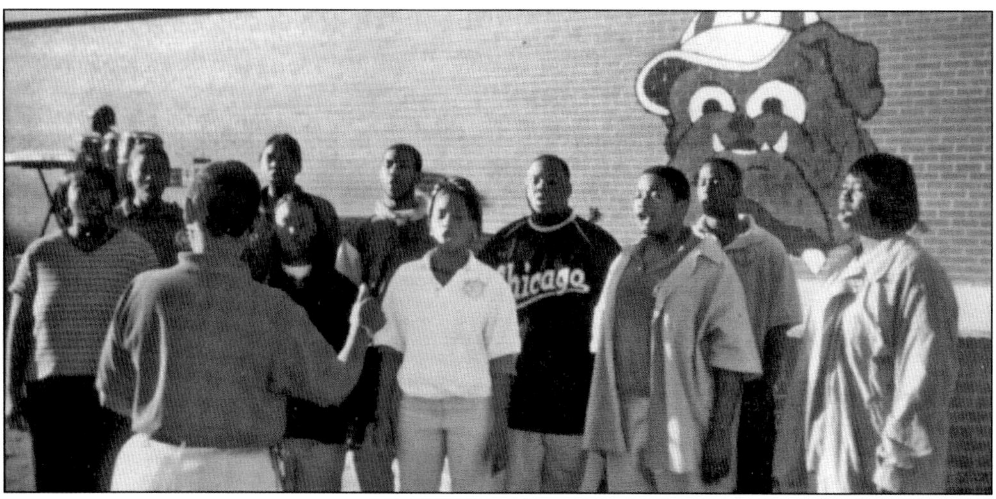

By the 1990s, the choir, under the direction of Vivian Jones, changed their name to the Blue Notes. In June 1999, this choir traveled to Africa to participate in the Second Annual Choral Festival of Accra, Ghana. (Courtesy of Burke High School.)

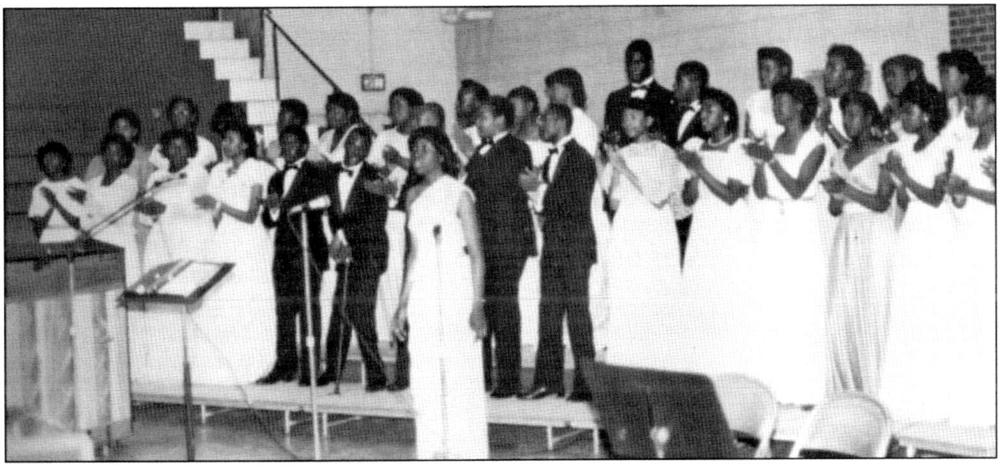

The senior choir is shown during their annual spring concert held in the gymnasium in 1984. The concert band would accompany the choir during the spring and Christmas concerts. (Courtesy of Burke High School.)

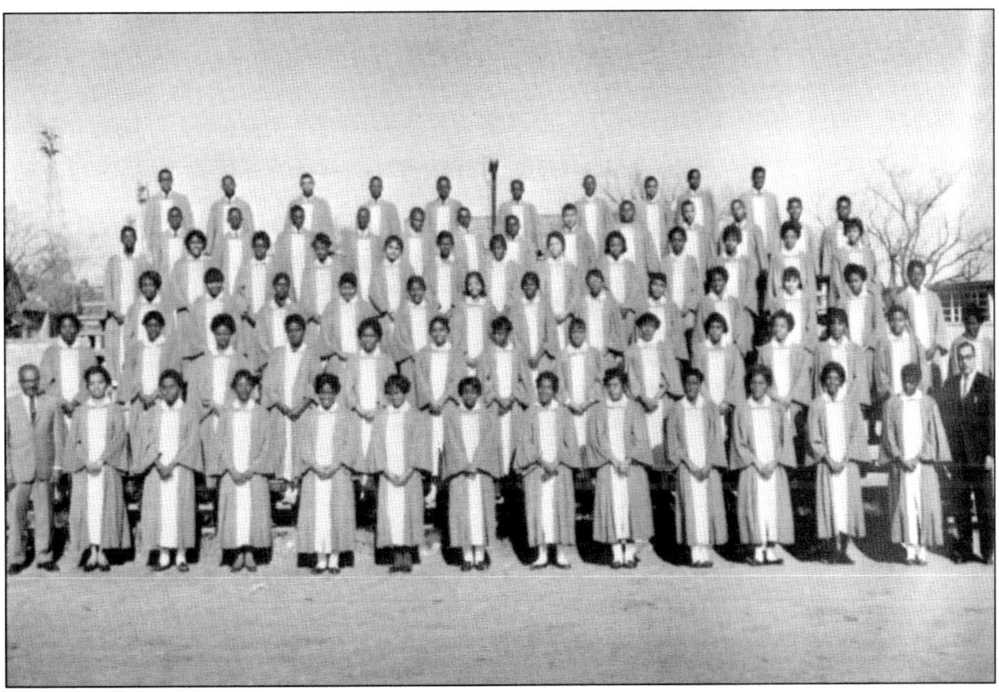

Under the direction of H. H. Fleming, the Senior Choir presented the annual Christmas and spring concerts in 1960. (Courtesy of the Avery Research Center.)

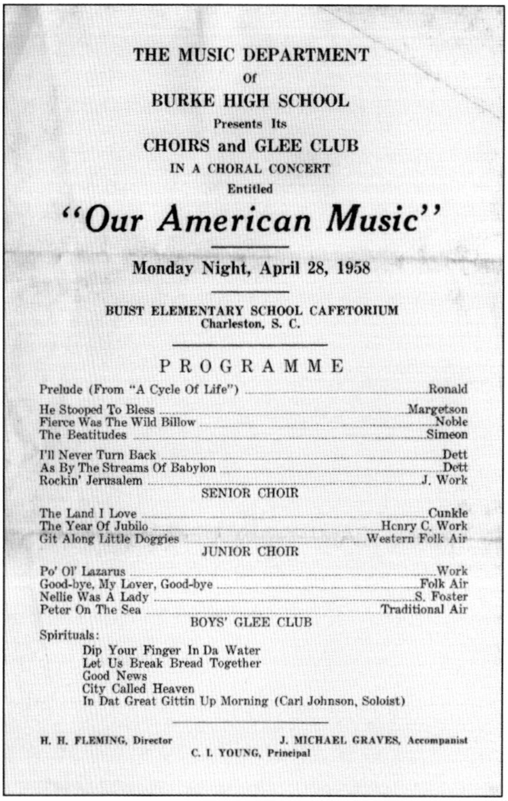

THE MUSIC DEPARTMENT
Of
BURKE HIGH SCHOOL
Presents Its
CHOIRS and GLEE CLUB
IN A CHORAL CONCERT
Entitled

"Our American Music"

Monday Night, April 28, 1958

BUIST ELEMENTARY SCHOOL CAFETORIUM
Charleston, S. C.

PROGRAMME

Prelude (From "A Cycle Of Life") .... Ronald

He Stooped To Bless .... Margetson
Fierce Was The Wild Billow .... Noble
The Beatitudes .... Simeon

I'll Never Turn Back .... Dett
As By The Streams Of Babylon .... Dett
Rockin' Jerusalem .... J. Work

SENIOR CHOIR

The Land I Love .... Cunkle
The Year Of Jubilo .... Henry C. Work
Git Along Little Doggies .... Western Folk Air

JUNIOR CHOIR

Po' Ol' Lazarus .... Work
Good-bye, My Lover, Good-bye .... Folk Air
Nellie Was A Lady .... S. Foster
Peter On The Sea .... Traditional Air

BOYS' GLEE CLUB

Spirituals:
Dip Your Finger In Da Water
Let Us Break Bread Together
Good News
City Called Heaven
In Dat Great Gittin Up Morning (Carl Johnson, Soloist)

H. H. FLEMING, Director — J. MICHAEL GRAVES, Accompanist
C. I. YOUNG, Principal

Concerts were held twice a year by the music department. This 1958 program included the senior and junior choirs. There was a boy's Glee Club that performed as well. (Courtesy of the Avery Research Center.)

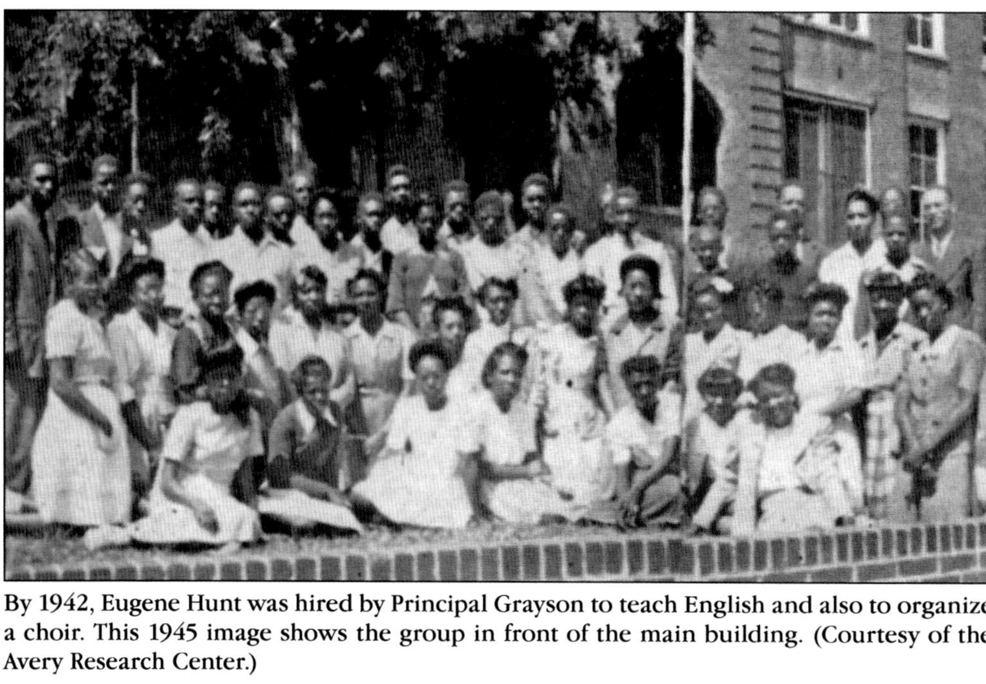

By 1942, Eugene Hunt was hired by Principal Grayson to teach English and also to organize a choir. This 1945 image shows the group in front of the main building. (Courtesy of the Avery Research Center.)

Holland "Toby" Daniels was credited with organizing the first Burke band in 1941. During the first year of its inception, the band was comprised of 10 students. Daniels remained director of bands until 1955. (Courtesy of Burke High School.)

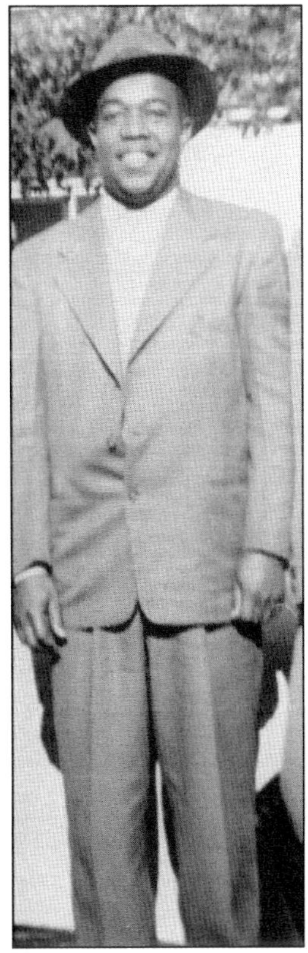

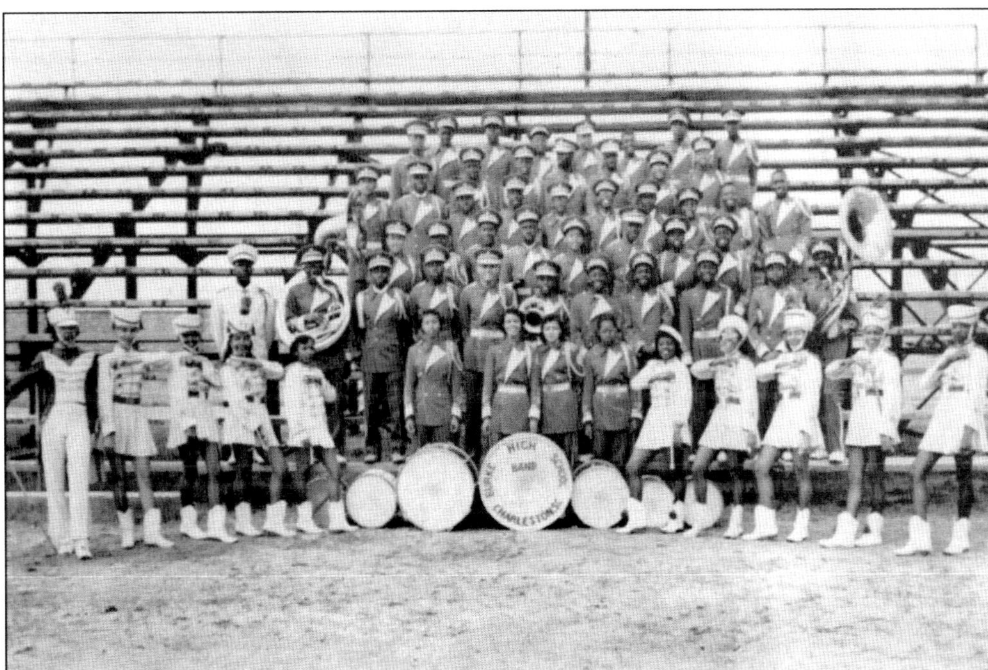

In 1955, the band raised nearly $8,000 to purchase new uniforms and instruments as seen in this 1958 image. (Courtesy of Burke High School.)

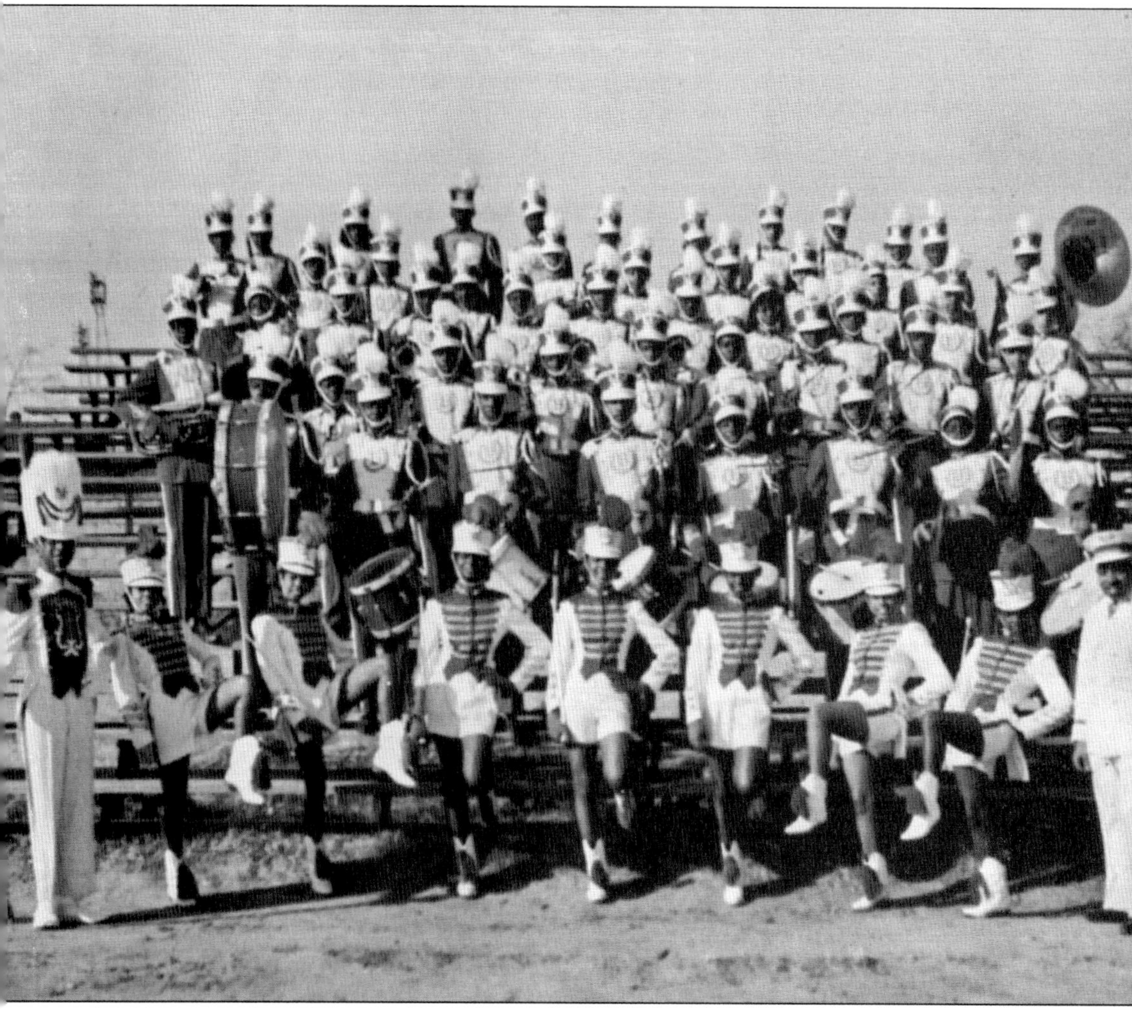

By 1963, the band showcased their new uniforms, made possible through the efforts of the Parent Teacher Association and the student body. (Courtesy of the Avery Research Center.)

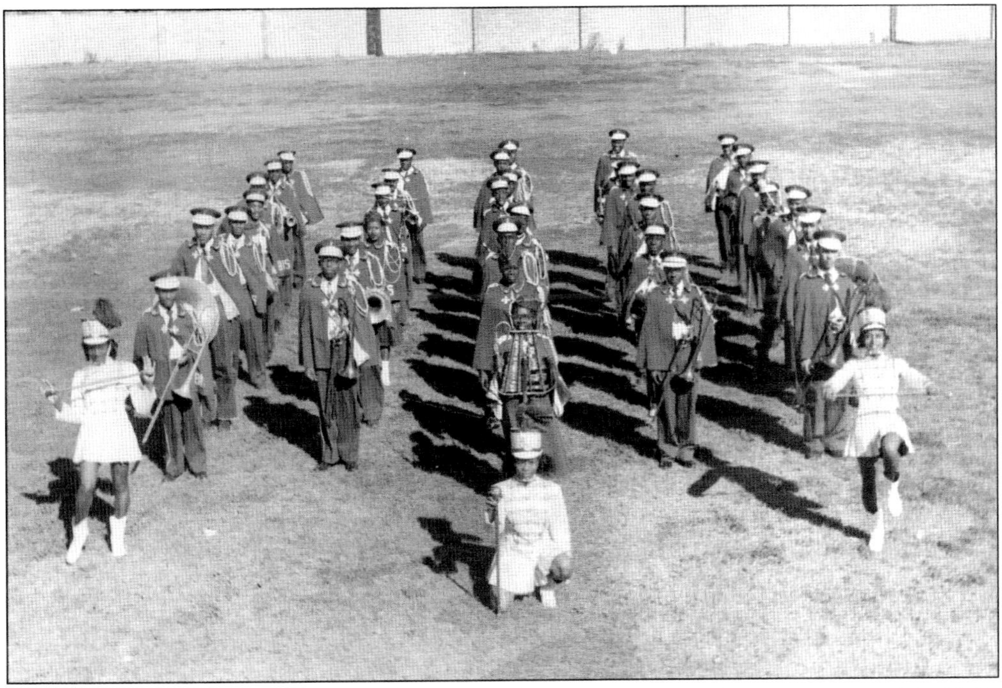

In 1948, the band appeared in uniforms for the first time since it was organized in 1941. During the first seven years of its inception, the band performed in standard black and white clothing. (Courtesy of the Avery Research Center.)

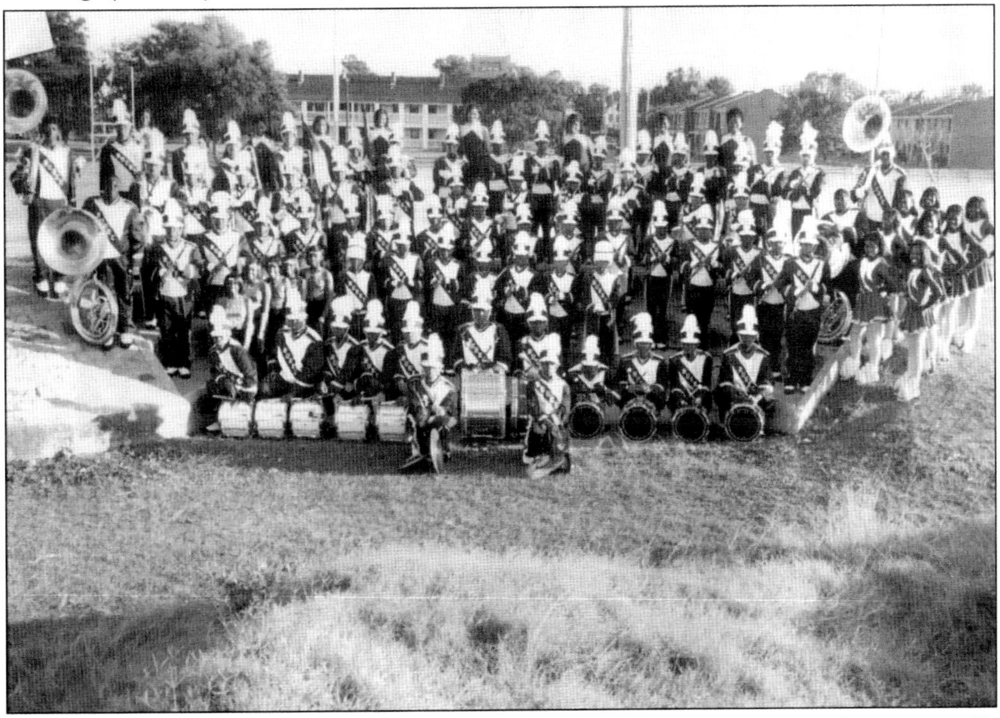

By 2000, this group, under the direction of Linard McCloud, became nationally and internationally known. They performed as far away as Canada. (Courtesy of Burke High School.)

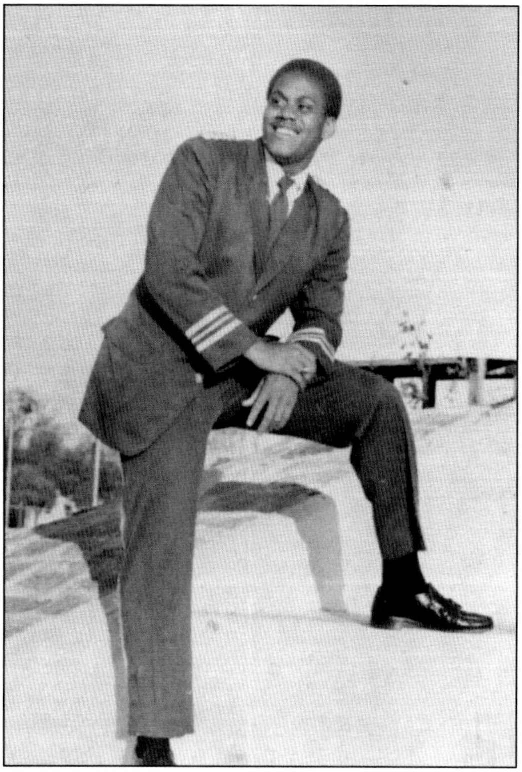

Linard McCloud became director of bands in 1978. A 1972 graduate, McCloud has held the position longer than any director in the school's history. Beginning in 1941 with Toby Daniels, there would be six directors before McCloud assumed the helm. In 1983, McCloud and George Kenny held the position of co-band directors. (Courtesy of Burke High School.)

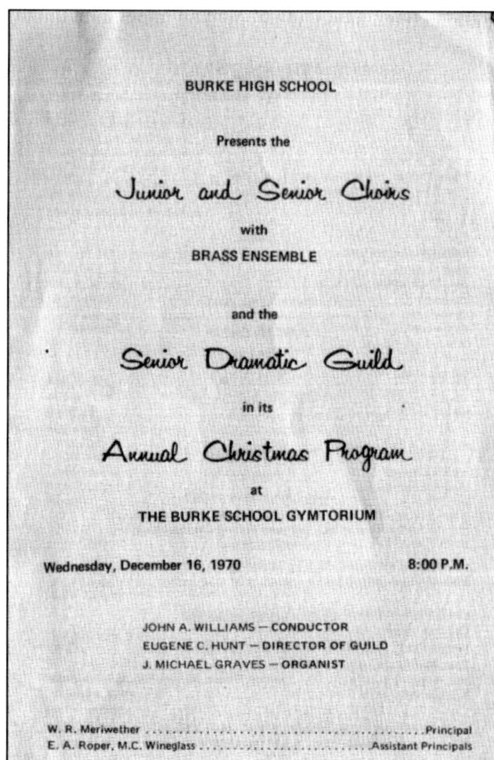

BURKE HIGH SCHOOL

Presents the

Junior and Senior Choirs

with

BRASS ENSEMBLE

and the

Senior Dramatic Guild

in its

Annual Christmas Program

at

THE BURKE SCHOOL GYMTORIUM

Wednesday, December 16, 1970 8:00 P.M.

JOHN A. WILLIAMS – CONDUCTOR
EUGENE C. HUNT – DIRECTOR OF GUILD
J. MICHAEL GRAVES – ORGANIST

W. R. Meriwether .... Principal
E. A. Roper, M.C. Wineglass .... Assistant Principals

This 1970 program shows both choirs, along with the brass ensemble and the senior dramatic guild, in a performance at the annual Christmas concert. These programs began in the early 1940s. (Courtesy of the Avery Research Center.)

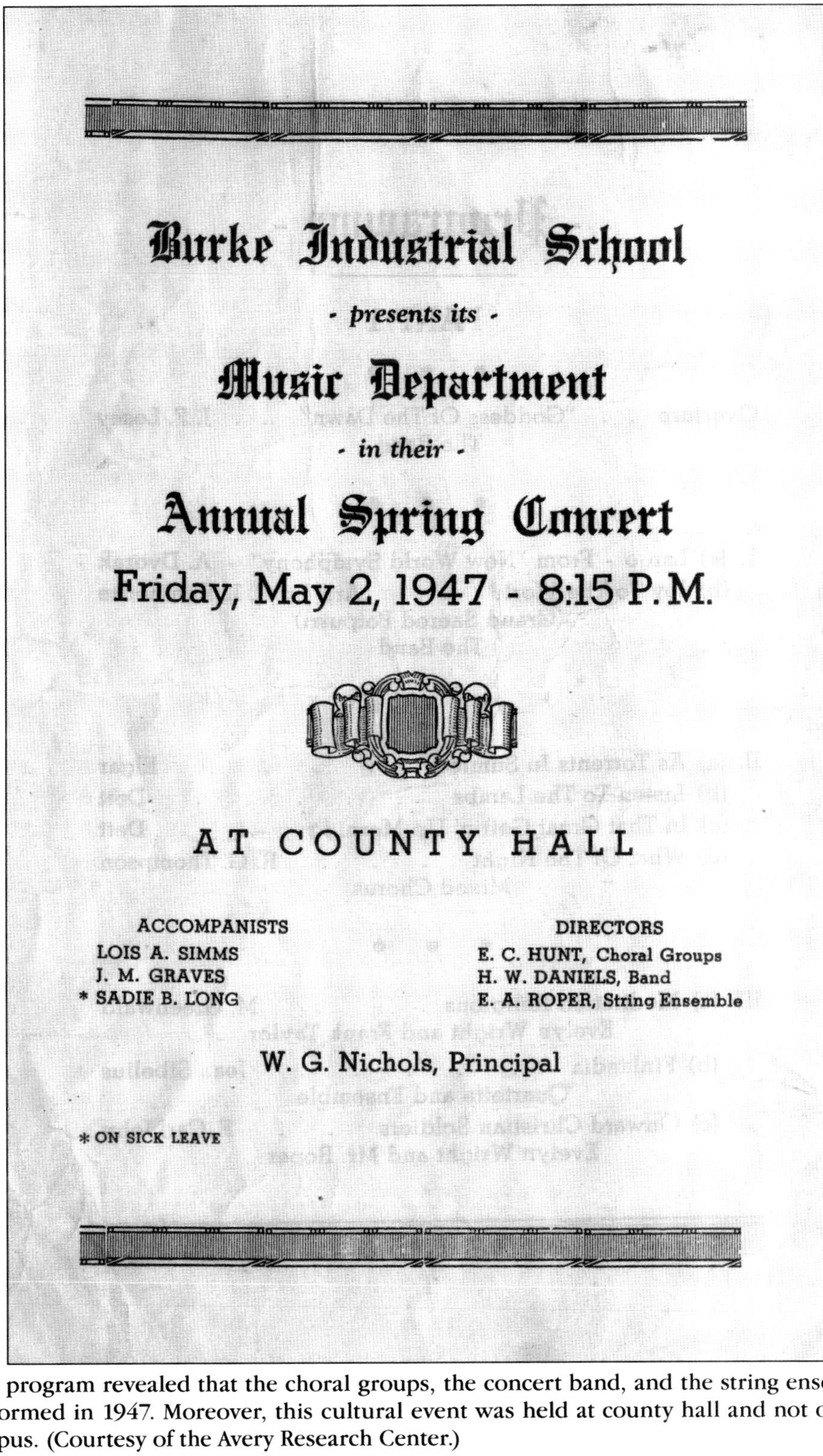

Burke Industrial School

- presents its -

Music Department

- in their -

Annual Spring Concert

Friday, May 2, 1947 - 8:15 P.M.

AT COUNTY HALL

ACCOMPANISTS	DIRECTORS
LOIS A. SIMMS	E. C. HUNT, Choral Groups
J. M. GRAVES	H. W. DANIELS, Band
* SADIE B. LONG	E. A. ROPER, String Ensemble

W. G. Nichols, Principal

* ON SICK LEAVE

This program revealed that the choral groups, the concert band, and the string ensemble performed in 1947. Moreover, this cultural event was held at county hall and not on the campus. (Courtesy of the Avery Research Center.)

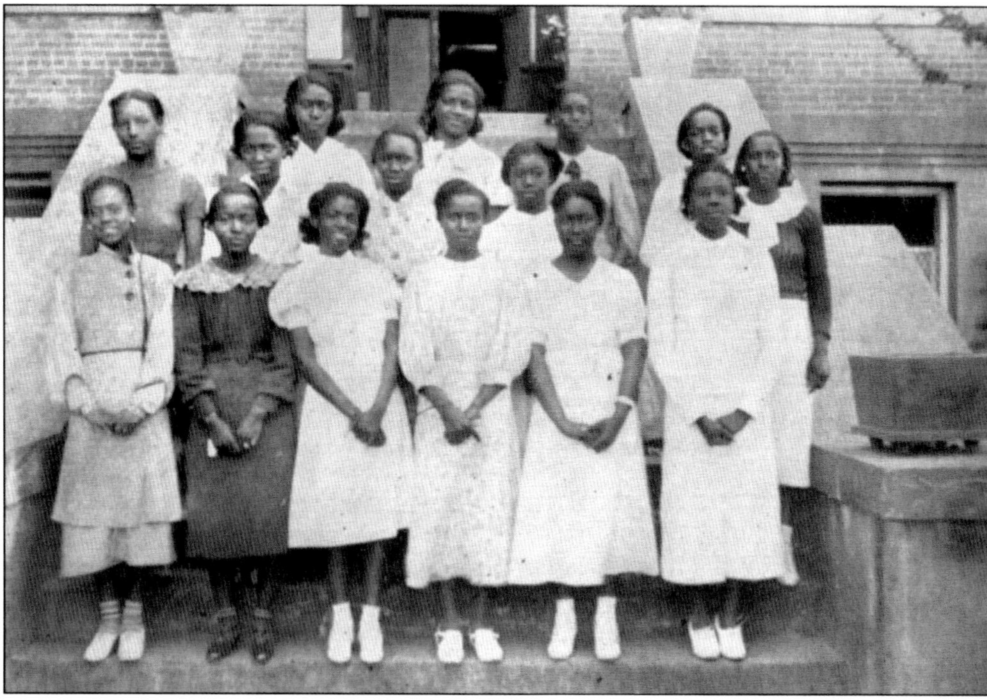

The Domestic Science Club was the precursor to the New Homemakers Club and the Future Homemakers of America in 1937. During the 1930s, domestic science consisted of laundry, cooking, and sewing. (Courtesy of the Avery Research Center.)

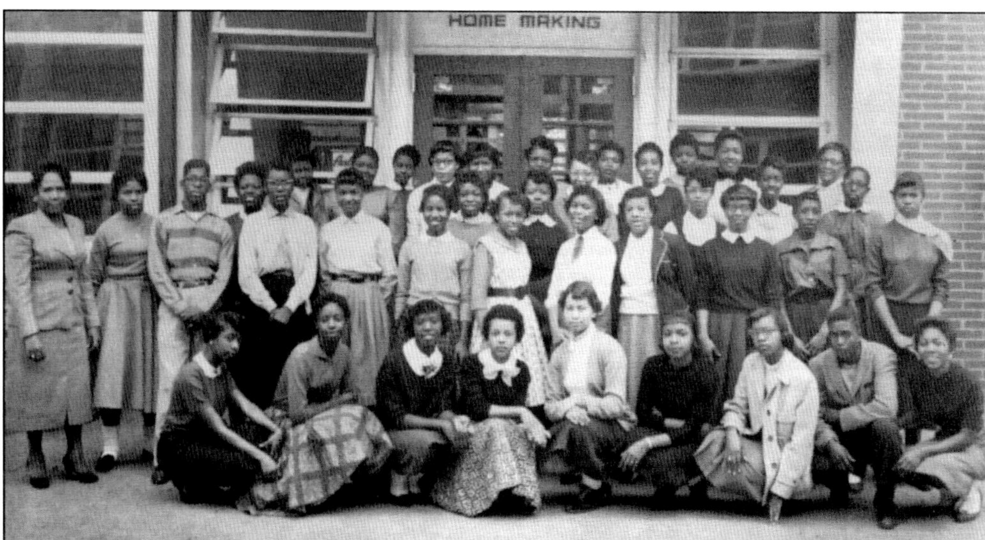

This 1958 image of the New Homemakers Club was composed of boys and girls of the home economics department. The purpose of the organization was to train students for useful citizenship, efficient leadership skills for home and community, and to participate in cooperative efforts. (Courtesy of the Avery Research Center.)

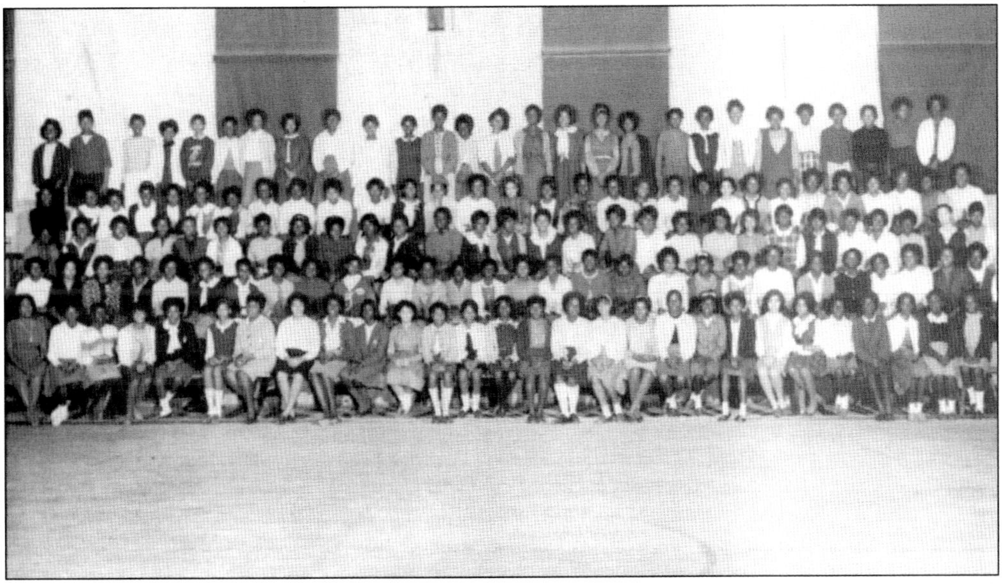

This 1968 image of New Homemakers of America shows very few young men, even though the organization was opened to boys and girls of the home economics department. (Courtesy of the Avery Research Center.)

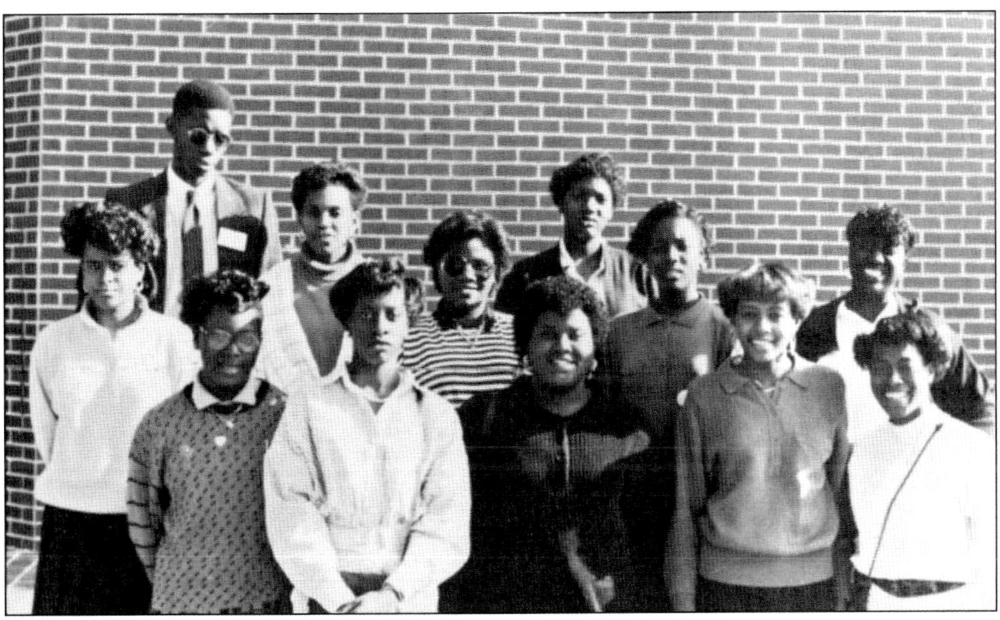

By 2000, this club was known as Future Homemakers of America, a group made up of students from the consumer home economics class. This organization consisted of boys and girls and trained in the area of culinary arts and consumer service. (Courtesy of Burke High School.)

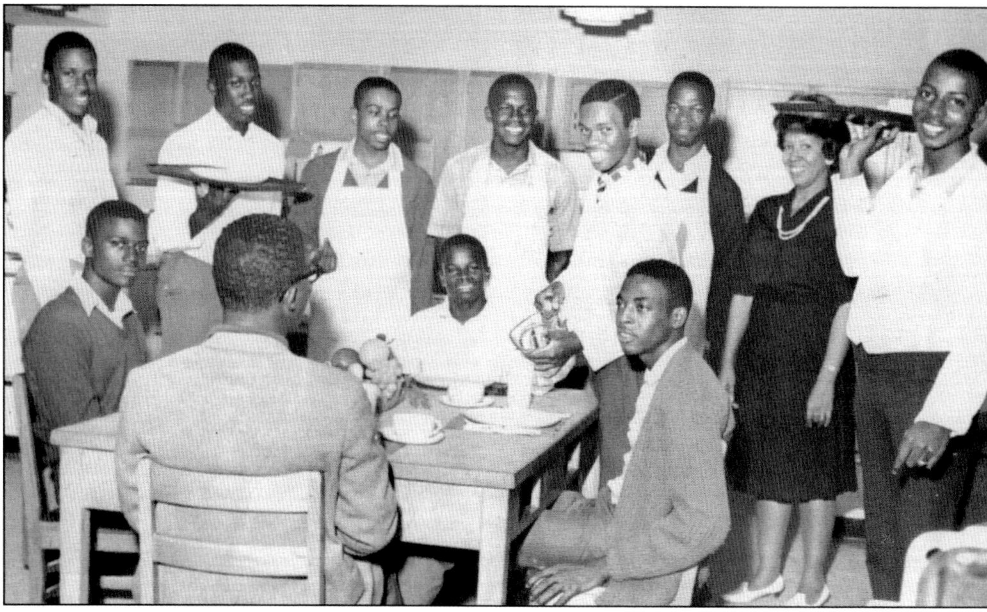

This 1966 photograph reveals a class established for the male students enrolled in a home economics class. There were 25 young men who made up the boys' home economics class. (Courtesy of the Avery Research Center.)

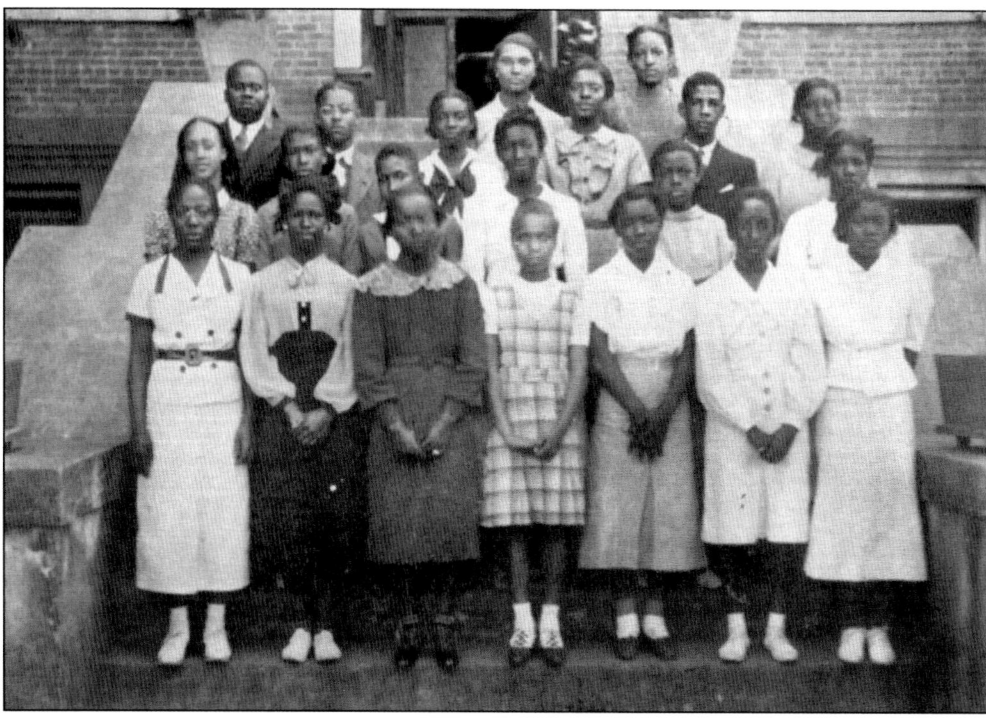

In 1937, the Scholastic Club was started, along with what would later become known as the National Honor Society. The members at that time consisted of 10th and 11th graders. (Courtesy of the Avery Research Center.)

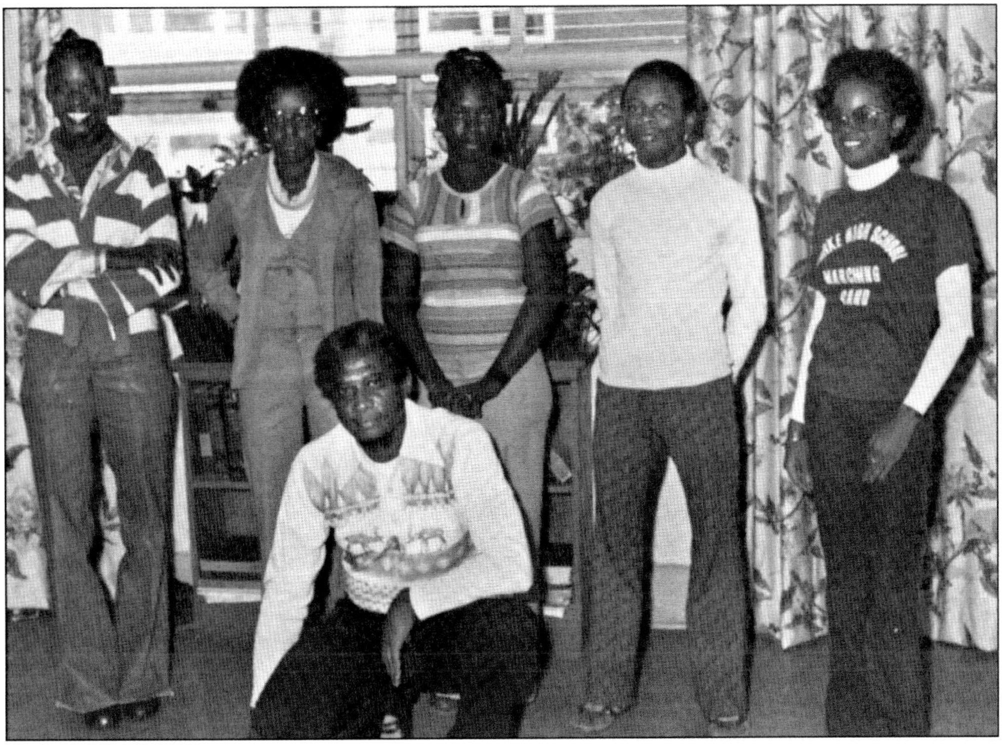

The members of the 1978 National Honor Society were relatively small in numbers as compared to the Scholastic Club in 1937. (Courtesy of Burke High School.)

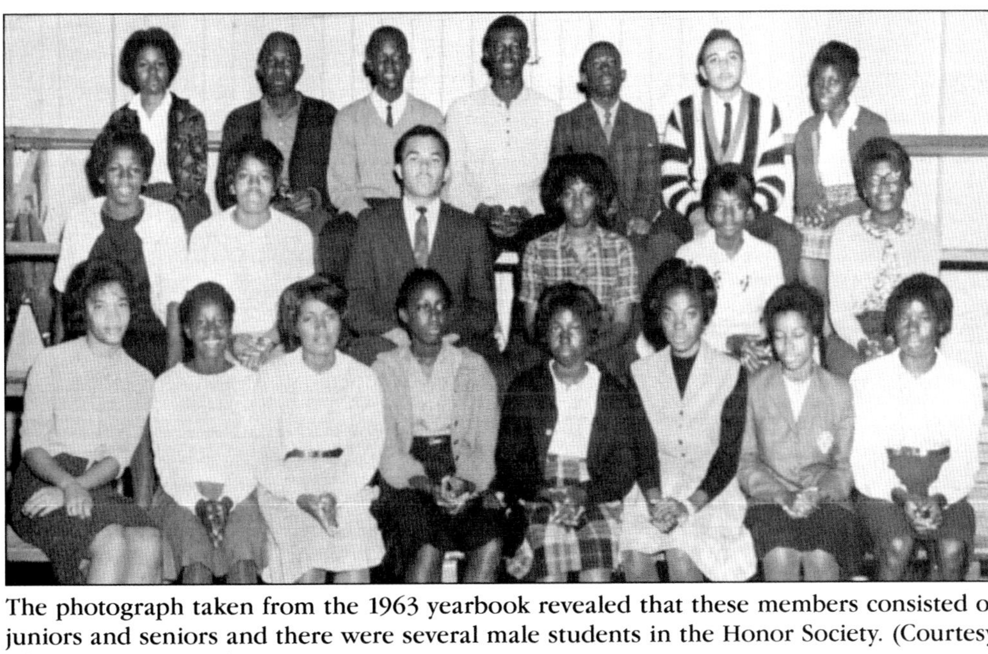

The photograph taken from the 1963 yearbook revealed that these members consisted of juniors and seniors and there were several male students in the Honor Society. (Courtesy of the Avery Research Center.)

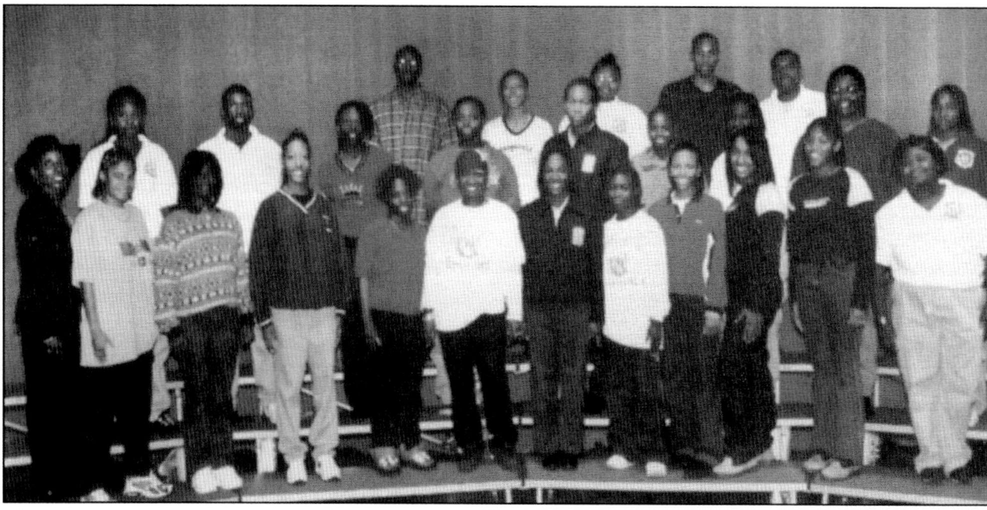

The National Honor Society of Secondary Schools was organized at Burke in 1952. Students in 2001 were elected for membership on the basis of leadership, scholarship, service, and character. Shown above are members of the National Honor Society in 2001. (Courtesy of Burke High School.)

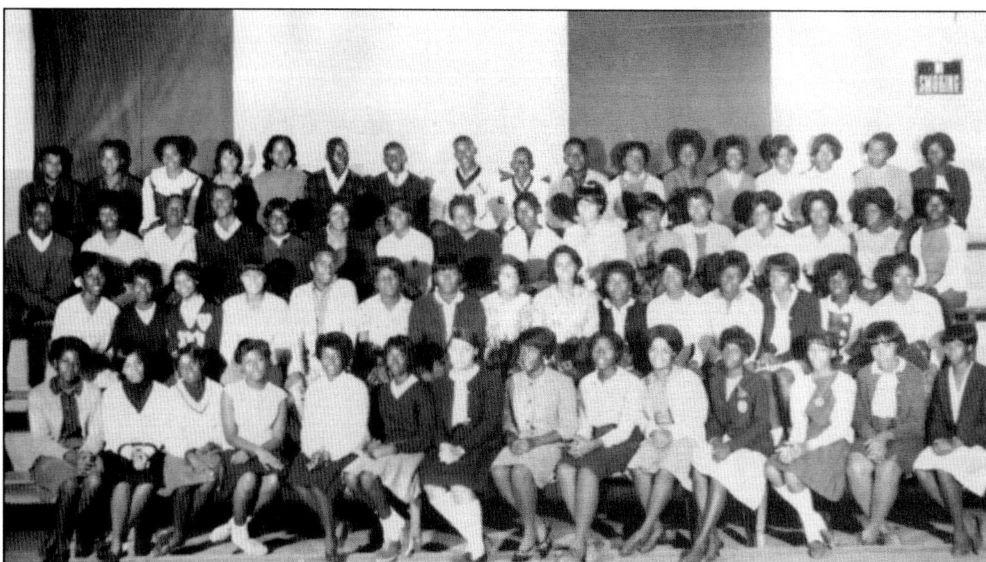

During the 1960s, the career path for many African American students was teaching. This 1966 image of Future Teachers of America was indicative of the noble profession that many students sought. (Courtesy of Burke High School.)

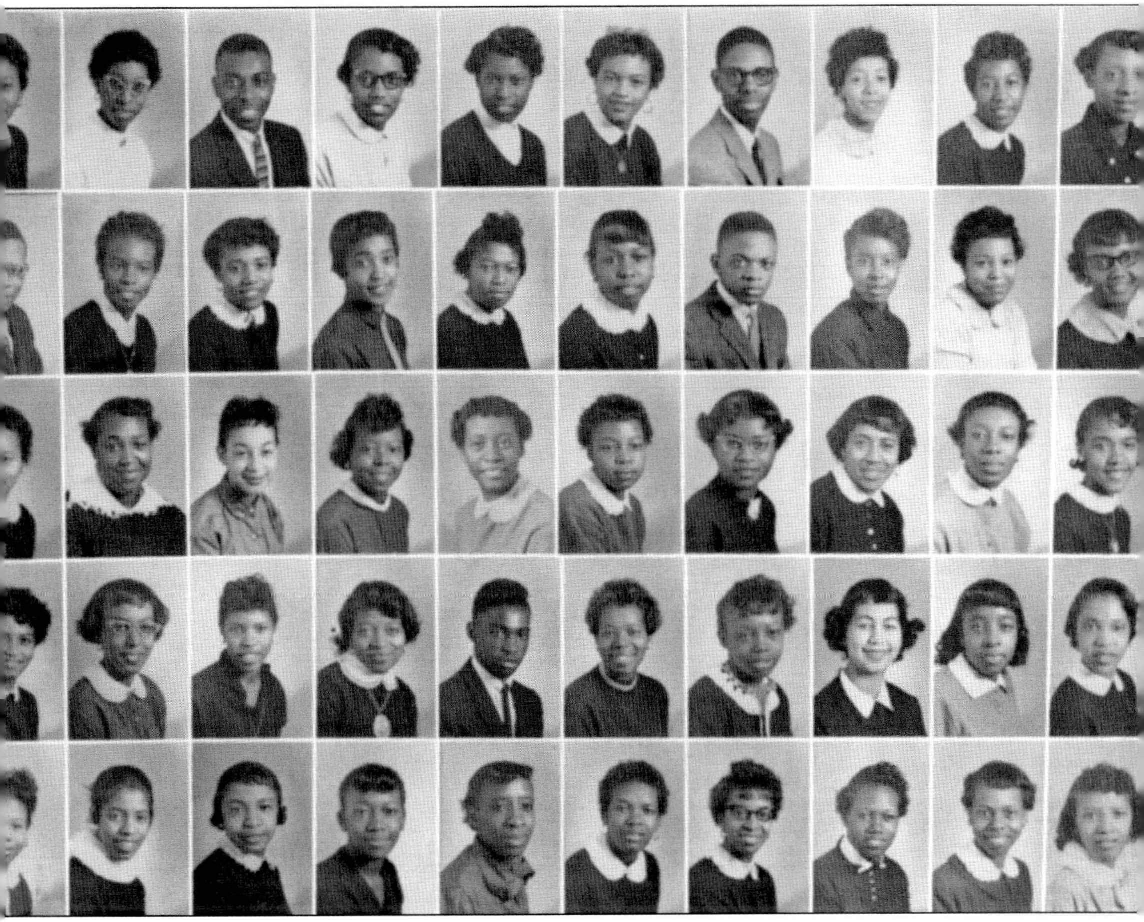

As seen in this 1958 photograph, the Future Teachers of America was then known as the Mary McLeod Bethune Future Teachers of America Club. This club was comprised of approximately 60 sophomores, juniors, and seniors. Besides exploring the teaching profession as a career, these students studied the lives of great teachers and developed student leadership through worthwhile service. (Courtesy of the Avery Research Center.)

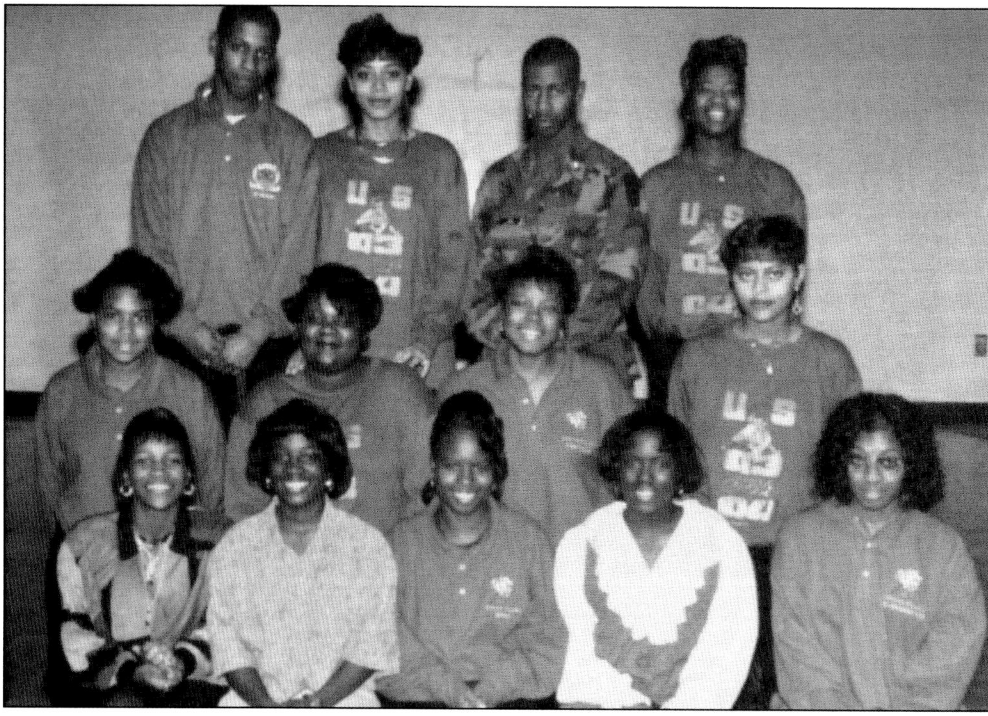

The Teacher Cadet Program was designed to acquaint students with the teaching profession. Those who participated received college credit from the Citadel Military College. The students spent about one month in 1994 working in schools at a grade of their choosing. (Courtesy of Burke High School.)

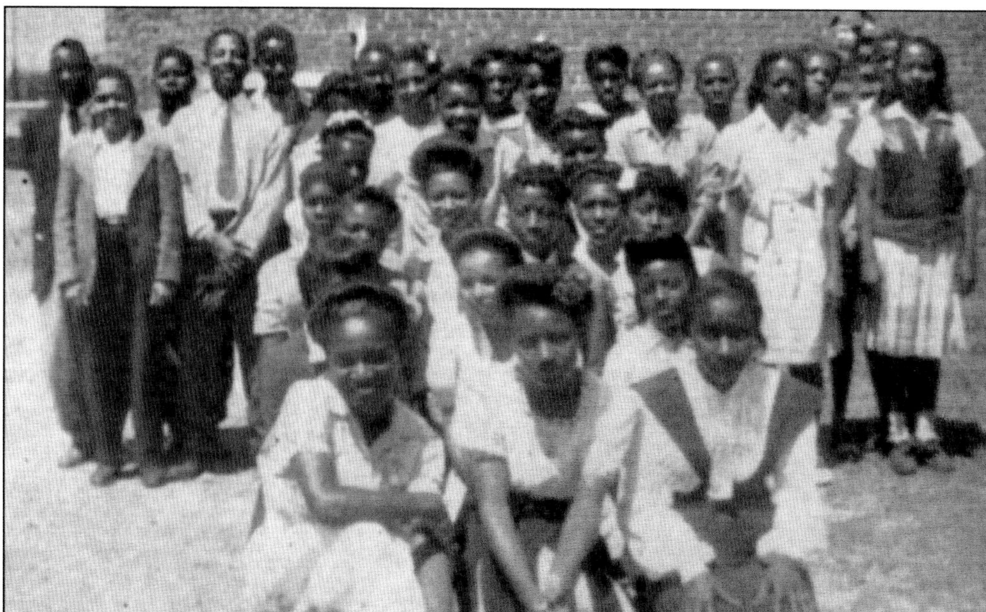

Sarah Green Oglesby became the drama coach in 1943. The Thespians Club, pictured here in 1945, would later change their name to the Drama Club. (Courtesy of the Avery Research Center.)

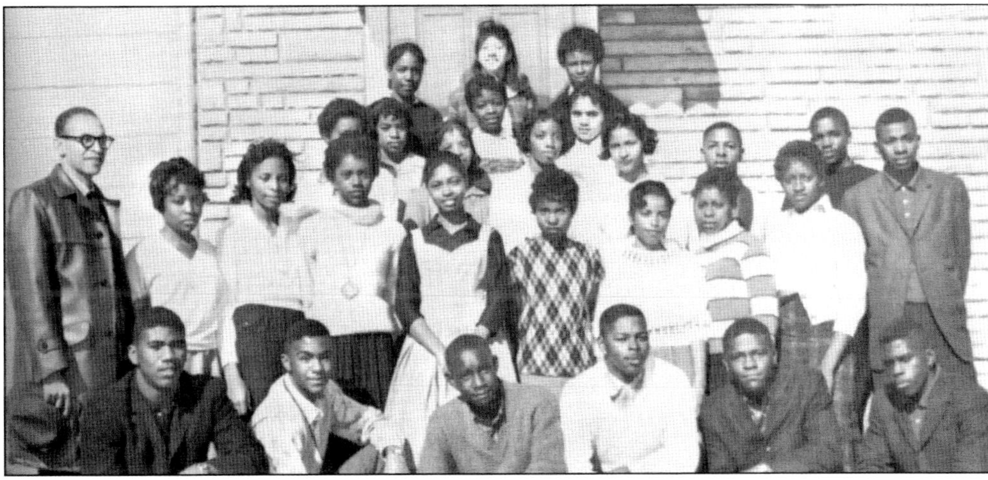

The Senior Dramatic Guild was organized to broaden the educational and cultural background of the students at Burke and to develop their dramatic potential. It also aimed to present to the general public the highest caliber of dramatic entertainment. (Courtesy of the Avery Research Center.)

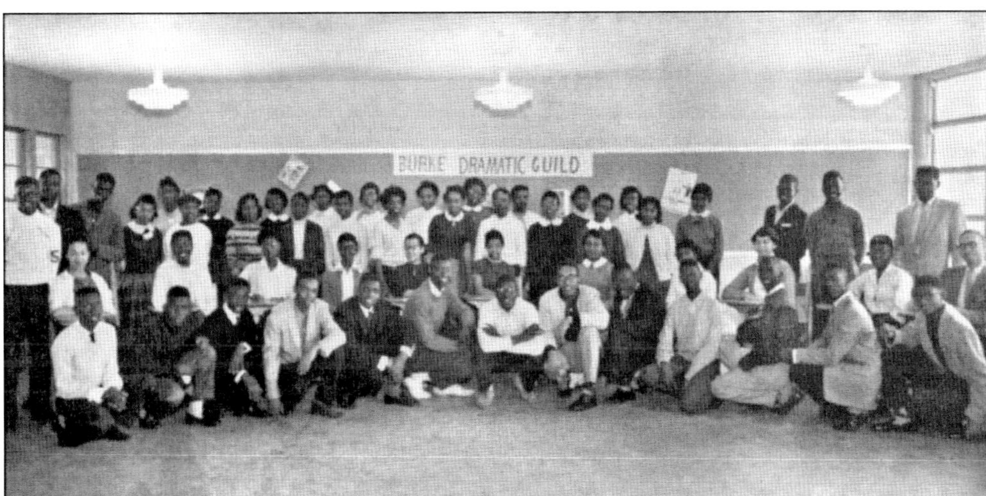

The Drama Guild had it first appearance in 1945. It was then called the Thespian Dramatic Club. By the late 1950s, it was called the Dramatic Guild and consisted of students from the sophomore, junior, and senior classes. The aim of the organization was to develop an interest in theater. (Courtesy of the Avery Research Center.)

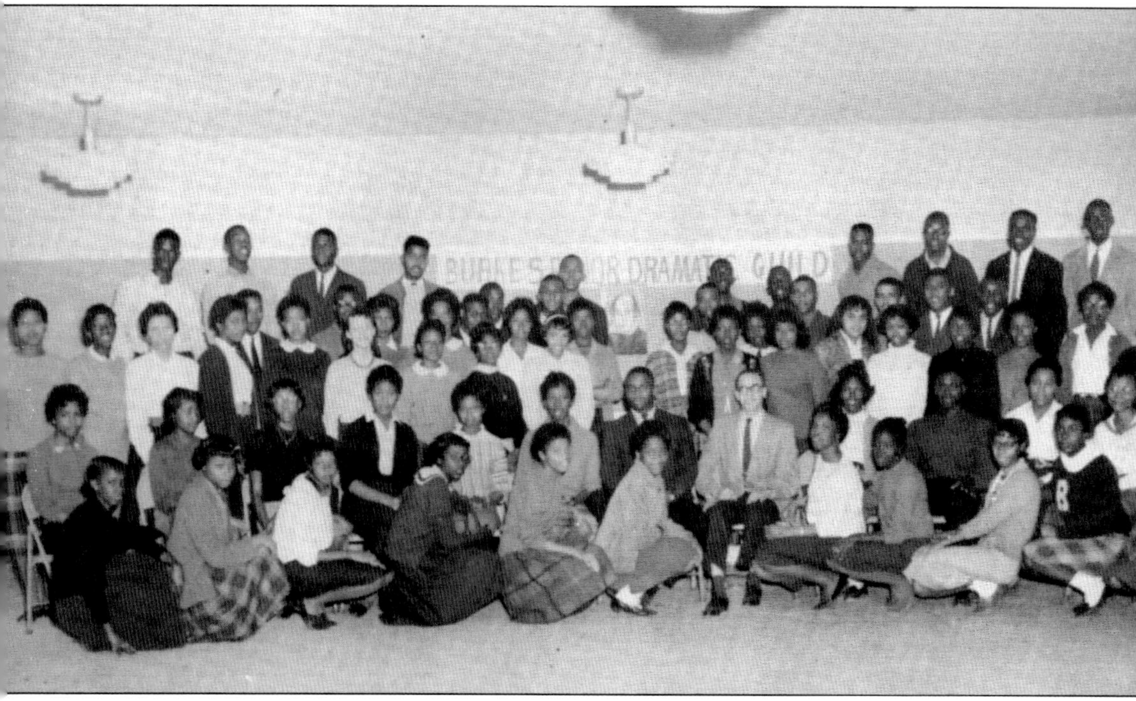

The Dramatic Guild presented *Antigone*, one of the great Greek classical plays, during the school year of 1960. This group was made up of members from the junior and senior grades. (Courtesy of the Avery Research Center.)

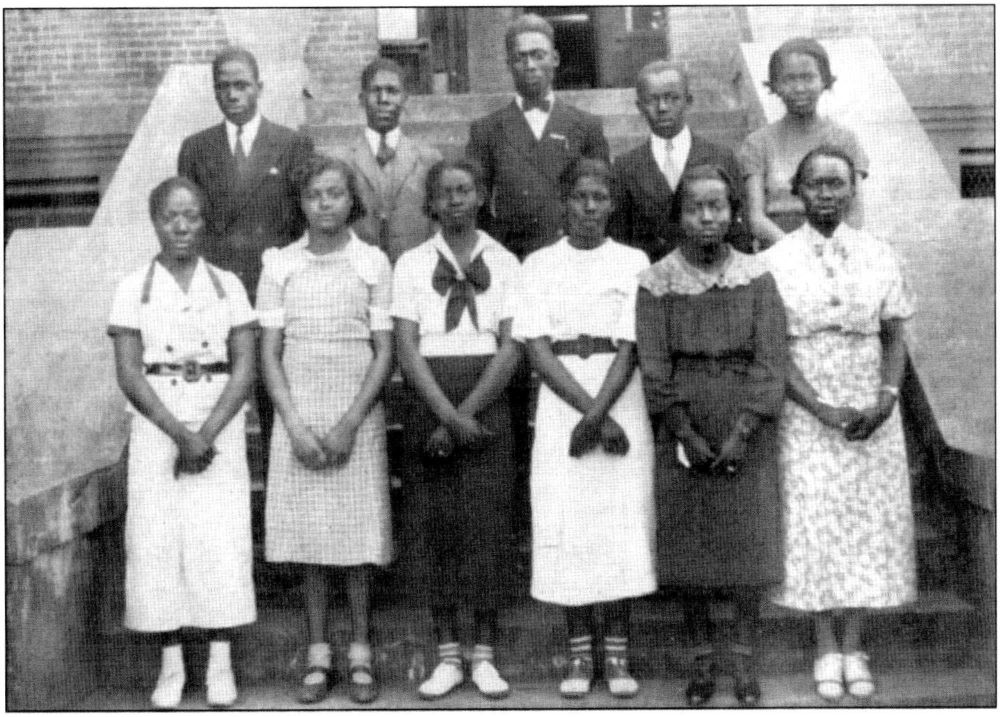

The students displayed in this 1937 image were responsible for the school newspaper, called the *Spotlight*. The staff consisted of an editor in chief, assistant editor, social editor, sports editor, and a literary editor. In 1940, the name of the paper was changed to the *Parvenue*. (Courtesy of the Avery Research Center.)

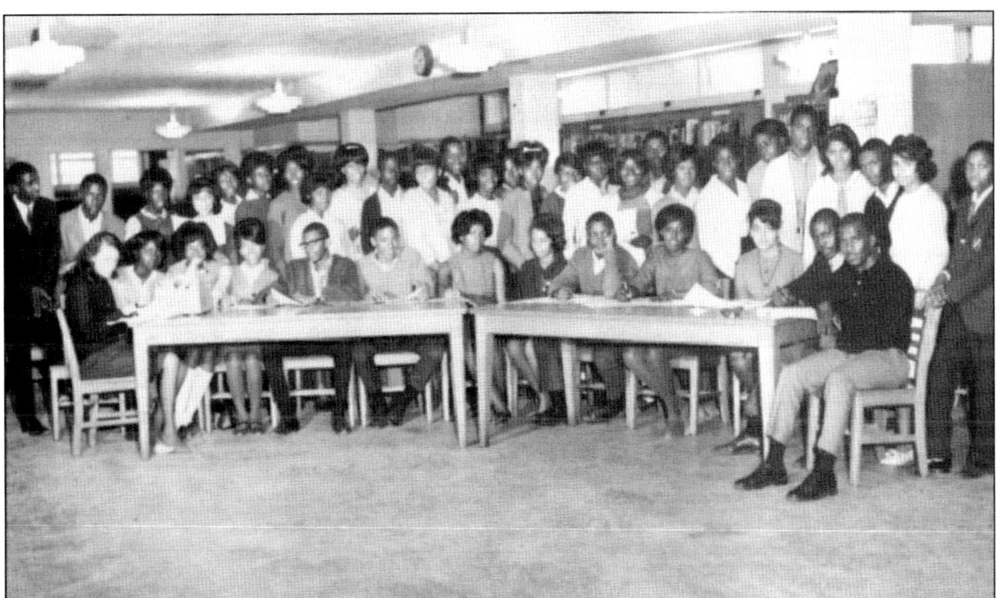

Here is a group shot of the *Parvenue* staff in 1966. This was one of the largest groups in the history of the school's newspaper. Clyde Johnson was the faculty advisor. (Courtesy of Burke High School.)

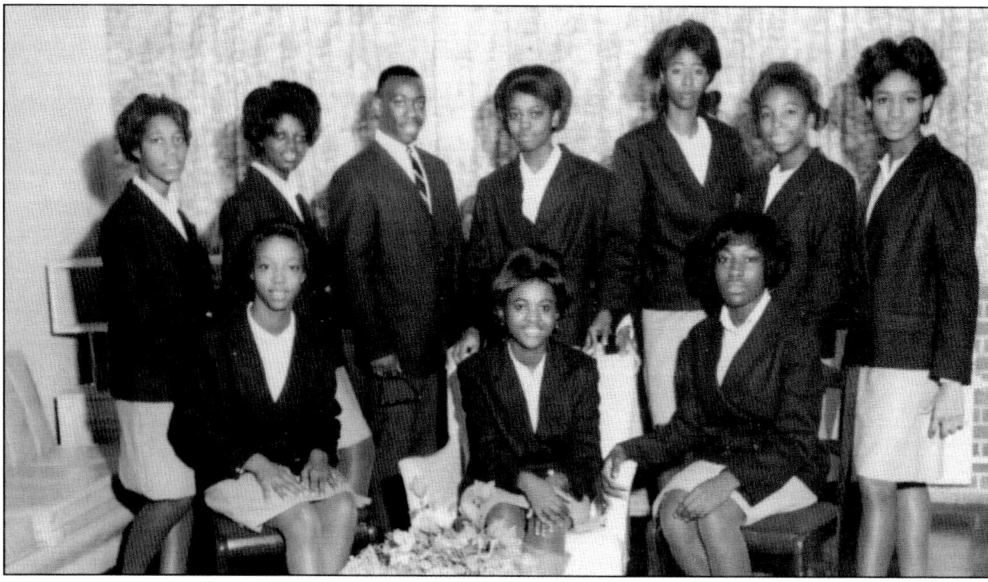

By the mid-1960s, several social clubs were organized for young men and young ladies. These clubs became an integral part of student life through the late 1970s. Pictured are (above) La-Norias, a 1965 social club, and the Celestians Club of 1971, shown below. (Courtesy of Burke High School.)

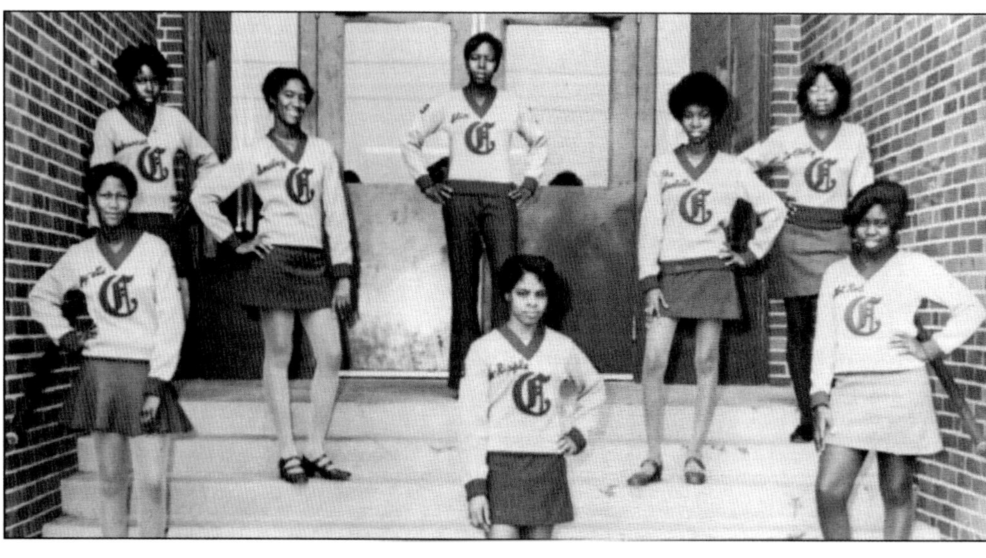

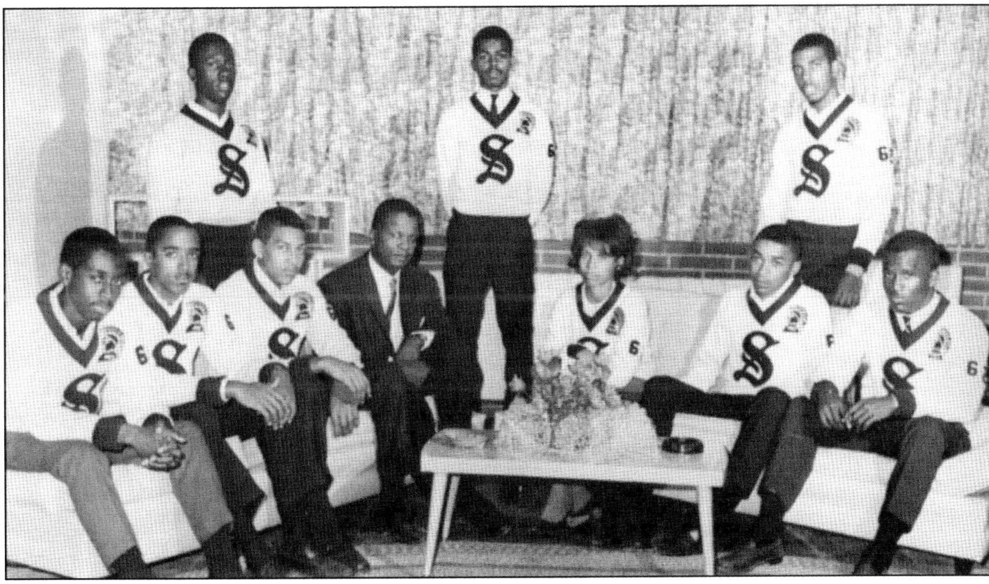

Pictured above are the gentlemen of the Spartans in 1965. Below are the ladies of Lespetite Mademoisells' in 1968. Each of the clubs had a faculty advisor, and the male clubs had an unofficial queen. (Courtesy of the Avery Research Center.)

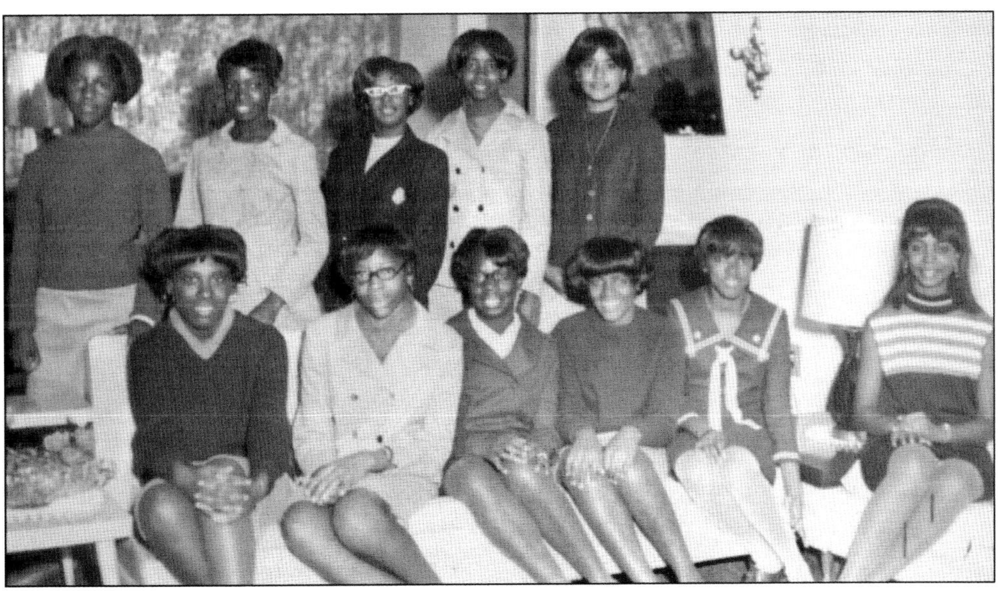

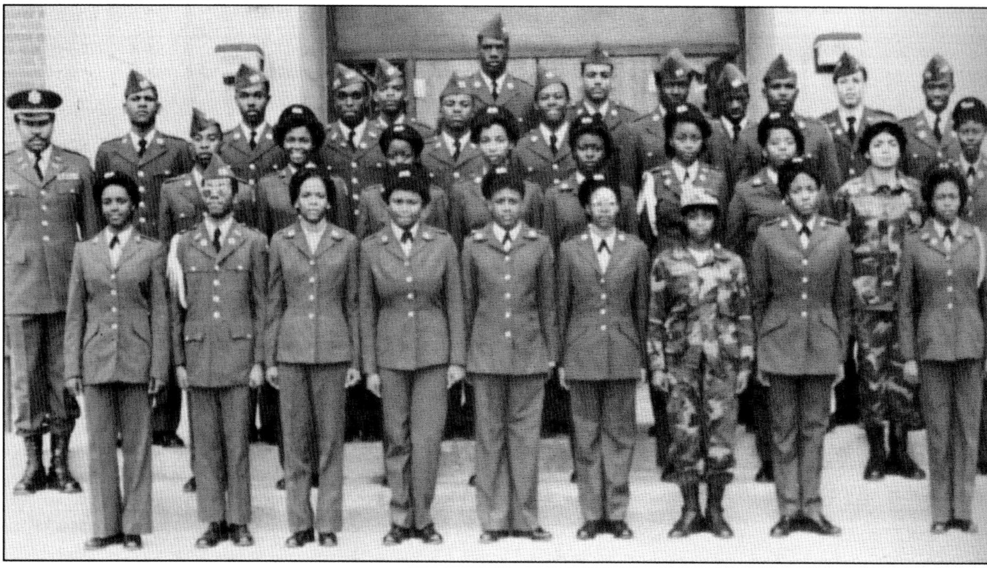

The ROTC program began on the campus in 1983. It is evident from this photograph taken in 1984 that there was an overwhelming regard by the students for structure and discipline in their lives. In 1997, the Junior ROTC participated in the inauguration parade for Pres. Bill Clinton in Washington, D.C. (Courtesy Burke High School.)

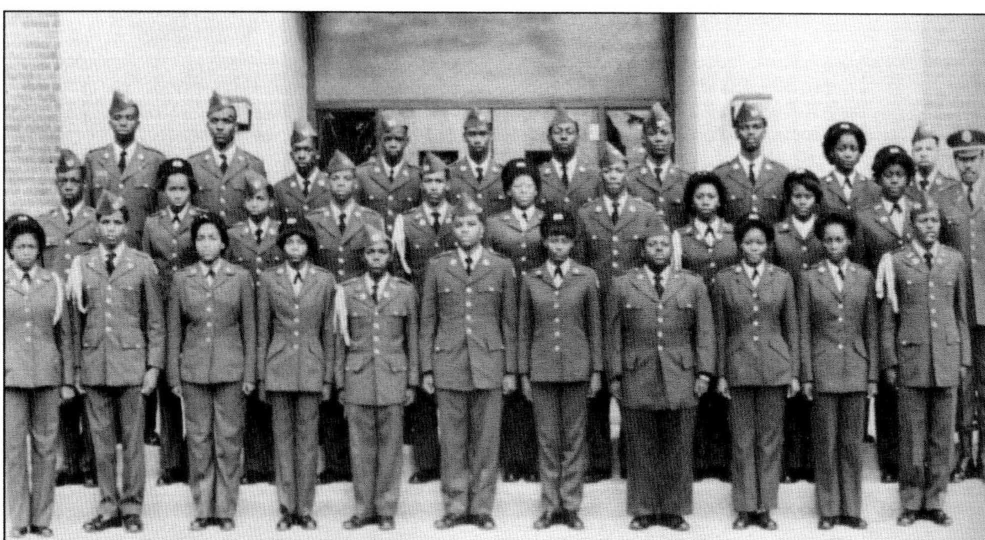

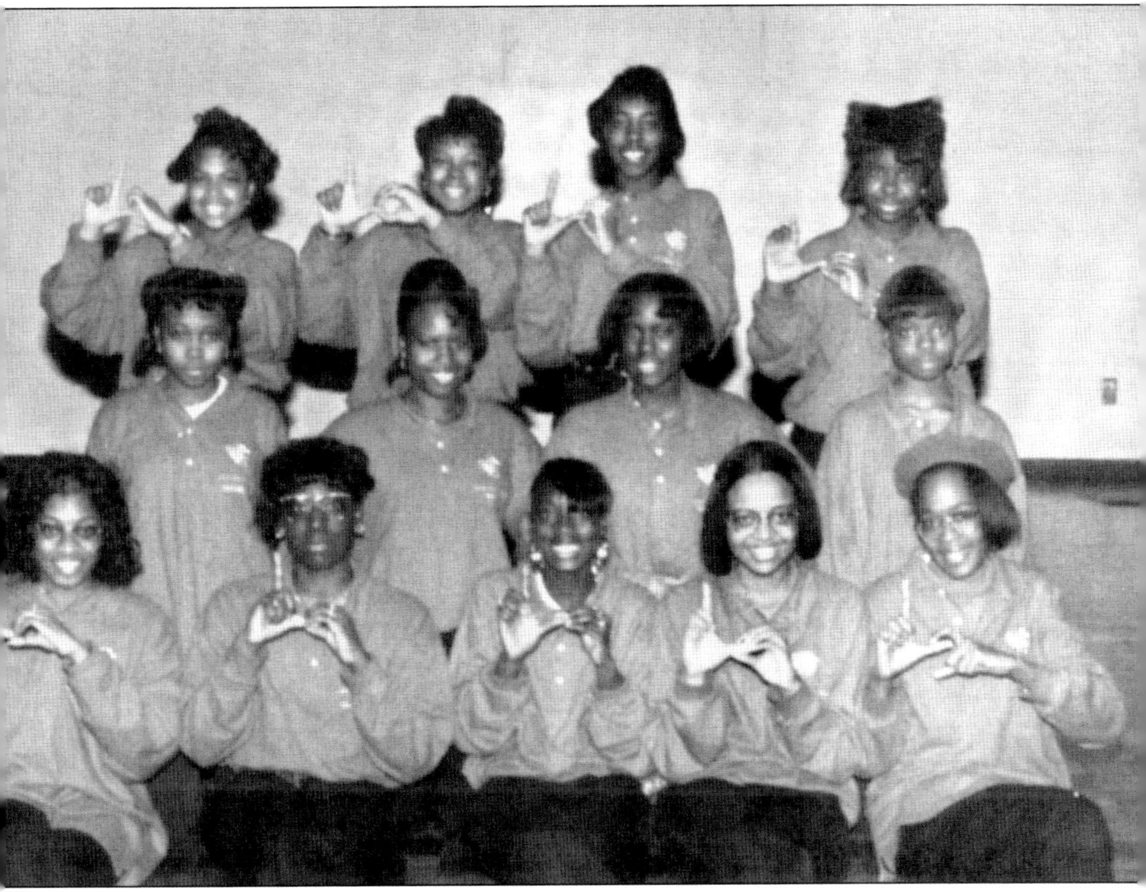

By the 1990s, many of the social clubs from the 1960s were no longer in existence. They were replaced by clubs that mirrored several Greek fraternities and sororities. Members of the Llambda Quizzettes are seen here in 1994. (Courtesy Burke High School.)

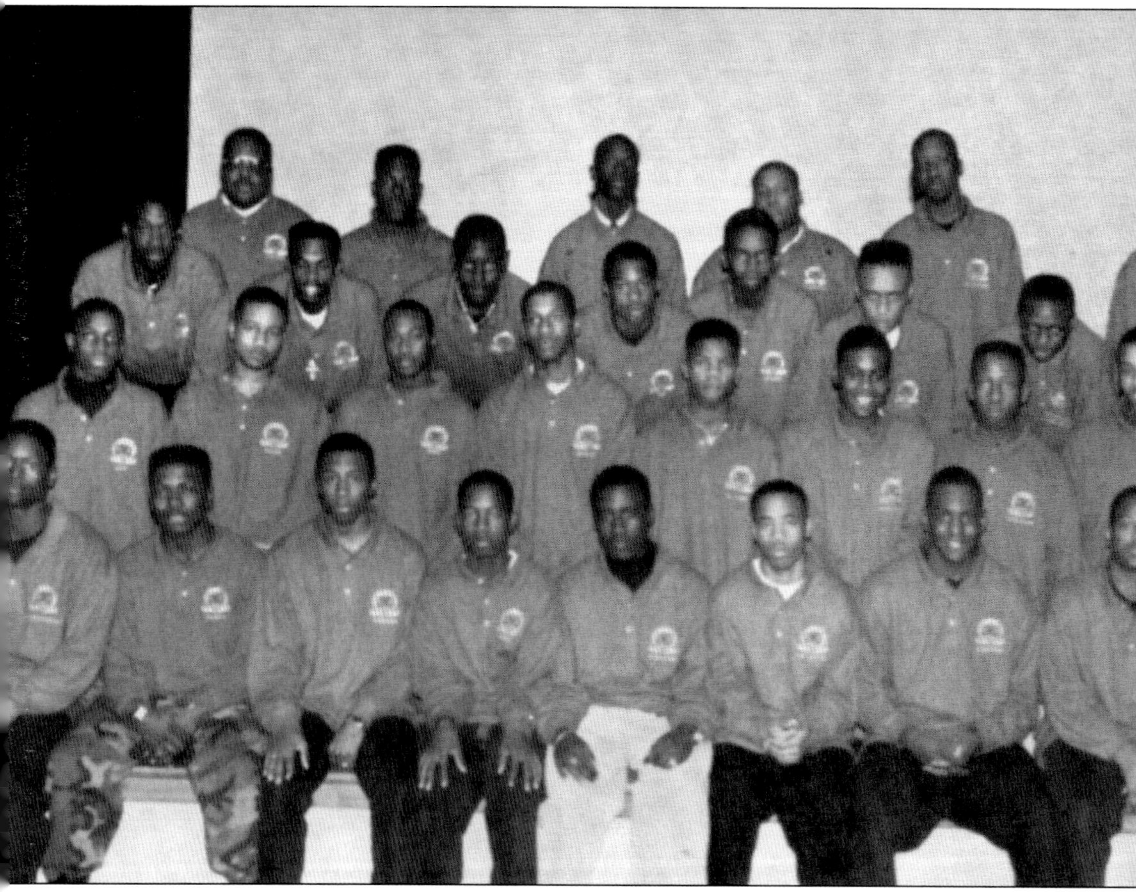

The members of the Omega Fly Brothers, pictured here in 1994, were under the tutelage of Omega Psi Phi fraternity. The faculty advisor was usually a member of this fraternity. (Courtesy Burke High School.)

Five

ATHLETICS

For the first time in the history of the school, the team is self supporting.

—William G. Wright, teacher (1935)

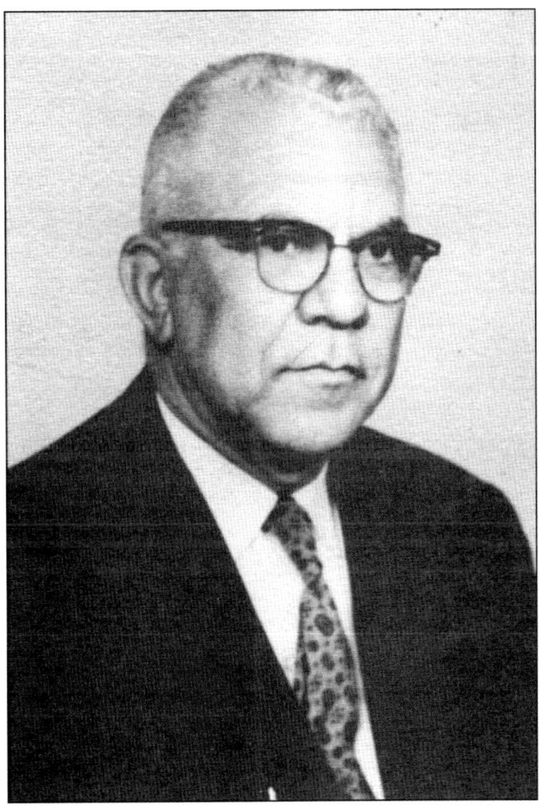

William G. Wright, a carpentry teacher, organized the boys' football and basketball teams in 1934. A vocational building was named for him, as well as two other faculty members. This graduate of Burke was considered the "father of athletics" at Burke. In order to support the teams, he used his personal money and solicited funds from the faculty and staff to purchase equipment. Wright collected the used uniforms from the Citadel Military College and Porter Academy (Porter Gaud) for the football team. Also in 1936, he proposed an annual Thanksgiving Day football game between Burke and Avery Normal Institute as a means to raise funds for equipment and uniforms for team. (Courtesy of the Avery Research Center.)

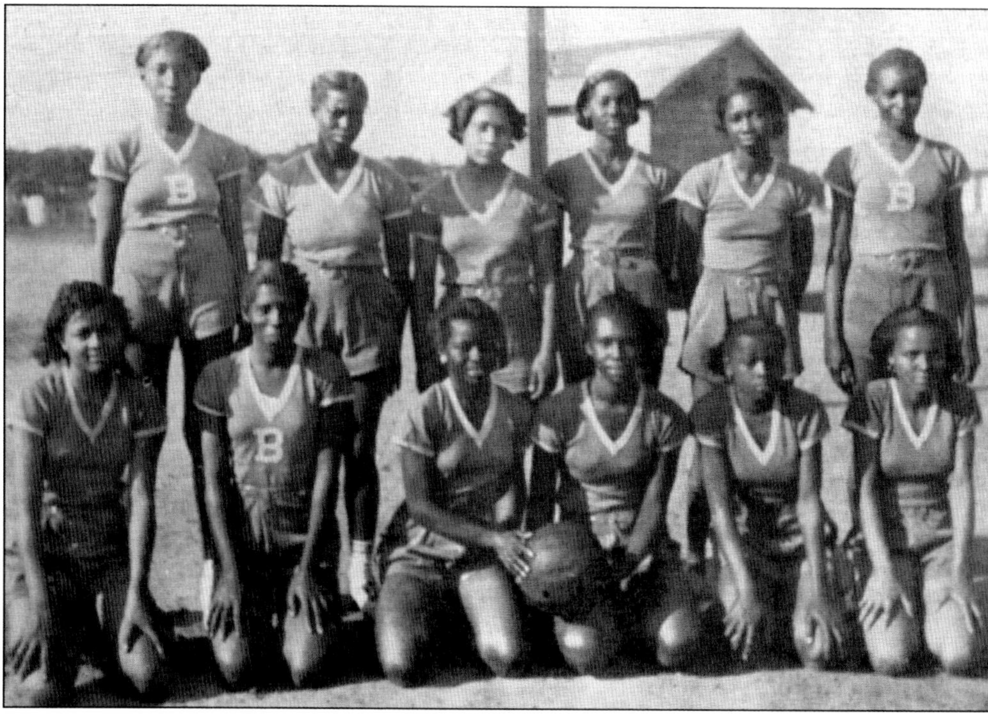

Pictured are members of the girls' basketball team around 1936. The team was organized by J. L. Pearson and Ms. Hare in 1935. (Courtesy of Burke High School.)

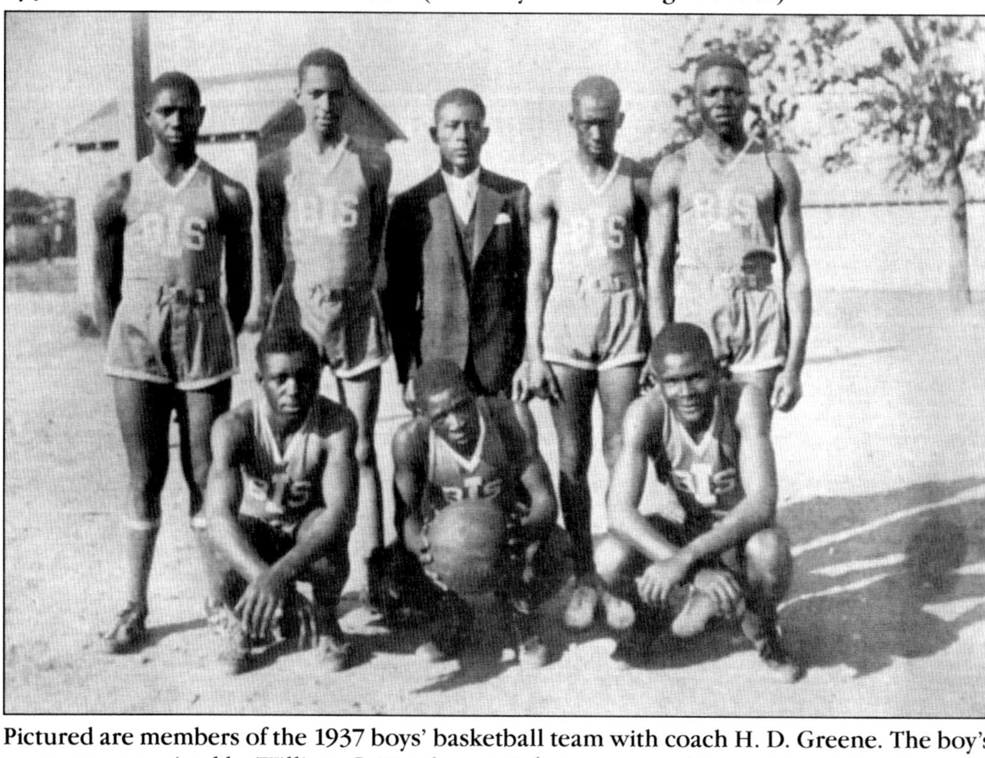

Pictured are members of the 1937 boys' basketball team with coach H. D. Greene. The boy's team was organized by William G. Wright in 1936. (Courtesy of Burke High School.)

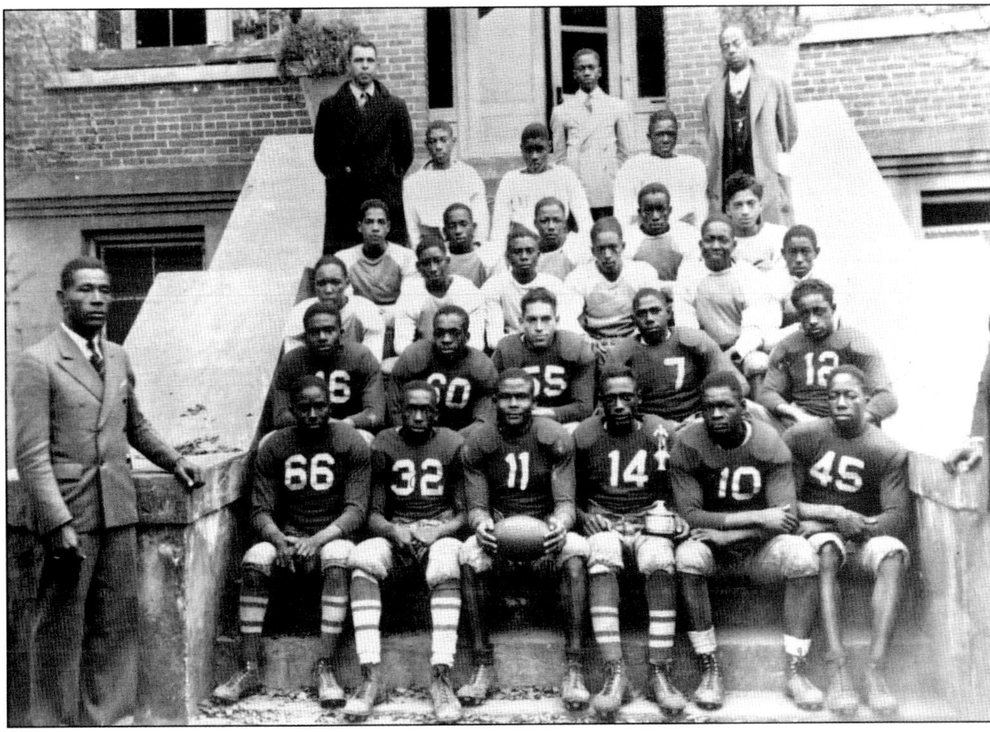

In 1938, the school produced its first championship under the coaching of A. D. Greene, pictured at far left. They won the lower and state championship. The championship game was played in Orangeburg. (Courtesy of the Avery Research Center.)

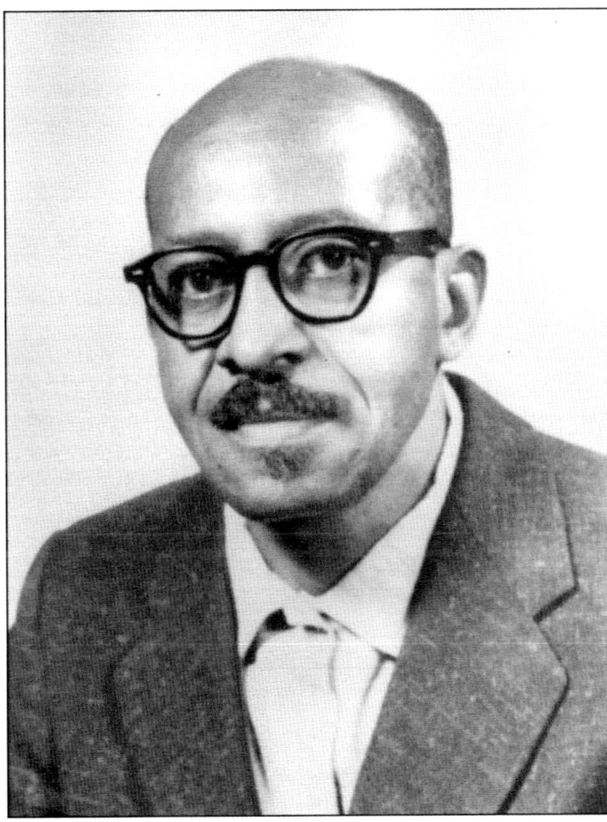

Beginning in 1941, coach J. A. Moore led the football team to an unprecedented four consecutive undefeated seasons. With the assistance of coach "Buck" Lesesne, Moore guided the boys' basketball team to state championships from 1948 to 1950. (Courtesy of the Avery Research Center.)

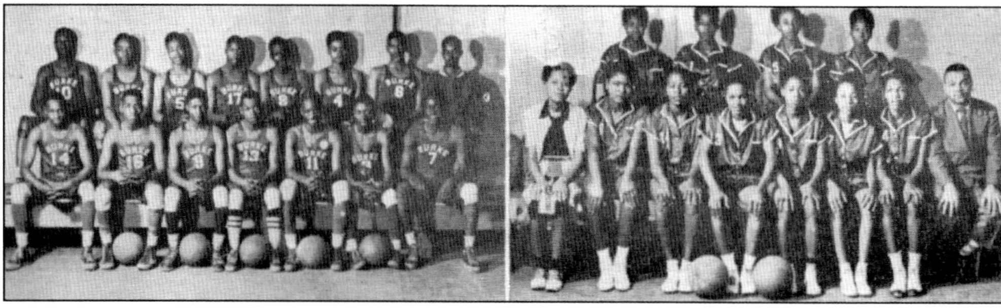

Pictured is a 1948 photograph of the boys' and girls' basketball teams, who won their conference titles and captured the South Carolina Athletic Conference tournament. The tournament was held in Charleston, March 4–6, 1948. (Courtesy of the Avery Research Center.)

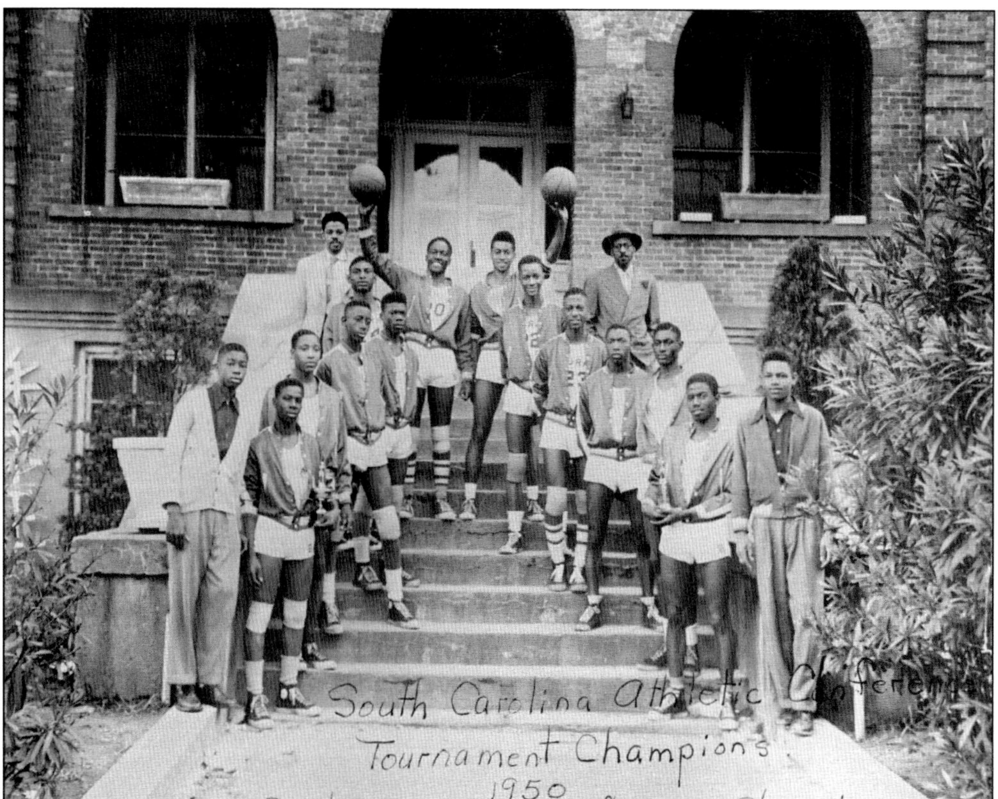

This team won the South Carolina Athletic Conference Championship in 1950. It marked the first time in the history of the conference that a team had repeated three times in a row as champions. The team was coached by Joseph A. Moore. (Courtesy of the Avery Research Center.)

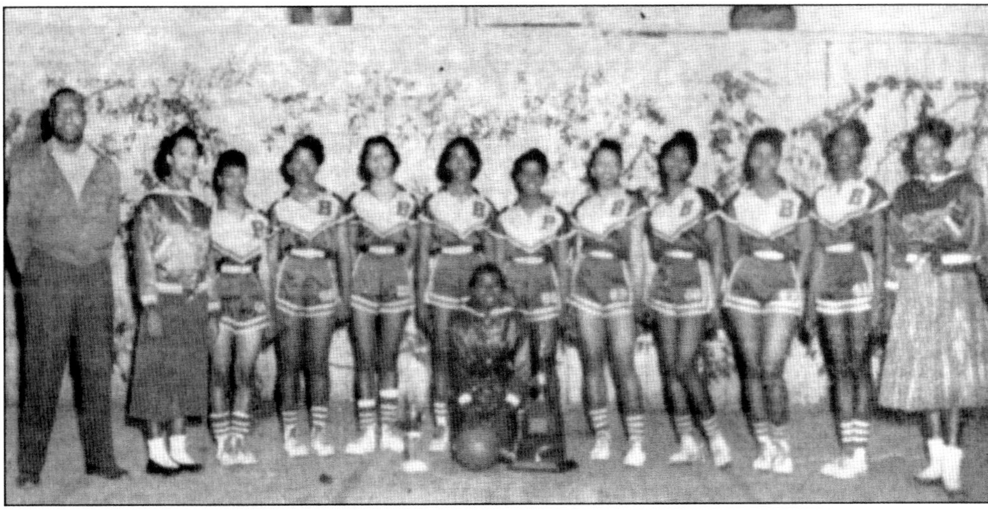

The girls' basketball team won the city and state championships in 1955. Henry Mack was the head coach. (Courtesy of the Avery Research Center.)

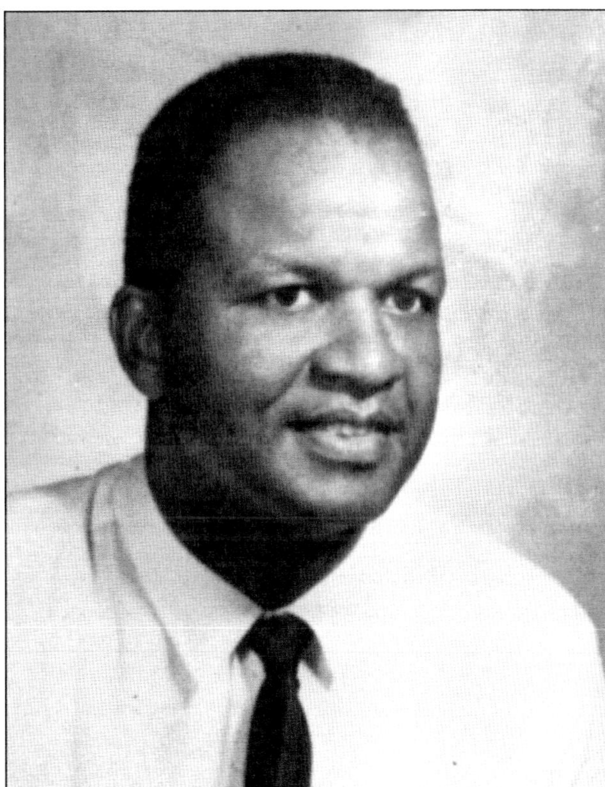

Modie Risher, better known as "Fess," was a graduate of Burke in 1946. He became head football coach in 1955 and led the team to a state championship that same year. Risher coached for 25 years, chaired the physical education department for 23 years, and served as athletic director for 15 years. He coached basketball, baseball, football, and track teams, winning eight lower state titles. Coach Risher retired in 1983. For his dedication and service to the students at Burke and the City of Charleston, the new gymnasium at his alma mater was named in his honor in 2005. (Courtesy of Burke High School.)

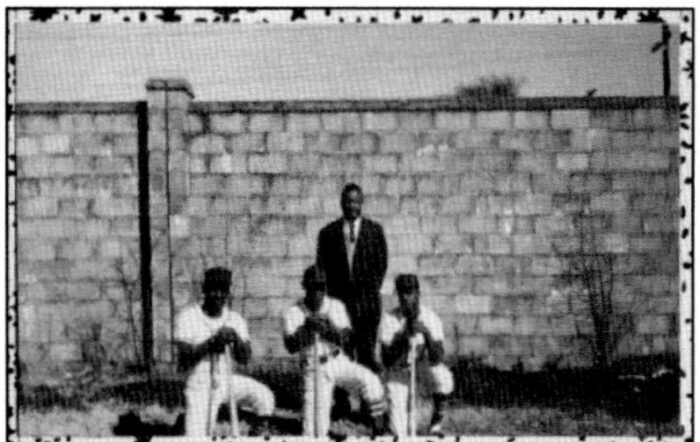

STAR HITTERS
Oran Wright, Rodney Washington, Bernard Keels and Coach M. Risher

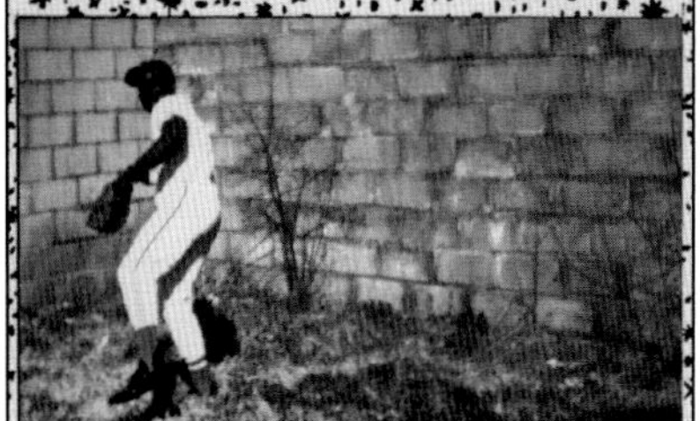

TOP HURLERS
Mack Drayton

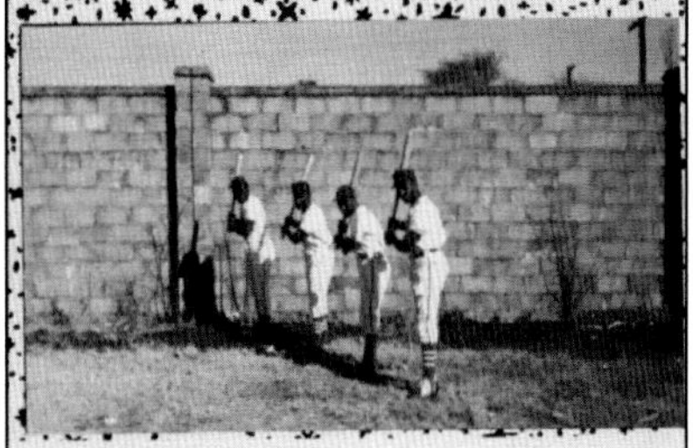

Ready for Next Season
Front to back: Bernard Keels, Rodney Washington, Oran Wright and Mack Drayton

The baseball program began at Burke in 1951 with Modie Risher as the coach. There were approximately 25 students who tried out for the team. They had no equipment and no uniforms. Coach Risher was able to secure some uniforms and equipment from other teams in the area. Below is the roster for the 1965 baseball team. This *c.* 1965 photograph shows some of the members of the team from that school year. (Courtesy of the Avery Research Center.)

TEAM

Pitchers
Mack Drayton
Edward Wine

Catchers
Clinton Dilligard
Dan Washington
Alexander Chisolm

1st Basemen
Vernon Scott
Alexander Hamilton

2nd Basemen
Bernard Keels
Arthur Pezant

Shortstop
Luther Bligen
Danny Jones

3rd Baseman
Oran Wright

Left Fielder
Ronald Turner

Center Fielder
Rodney Washington

Right Fielder
Edward Wine

The track team captured its first state championship in 1970. They were crowned co-state champion with Booker T. Washington High School in Columbia, South Carolina. Pictured at right are the captains of the team displaying a championship trophy. Ronald Simmons is at the left and Horace Hunter at the right. (Courtesy of Burke High School.)

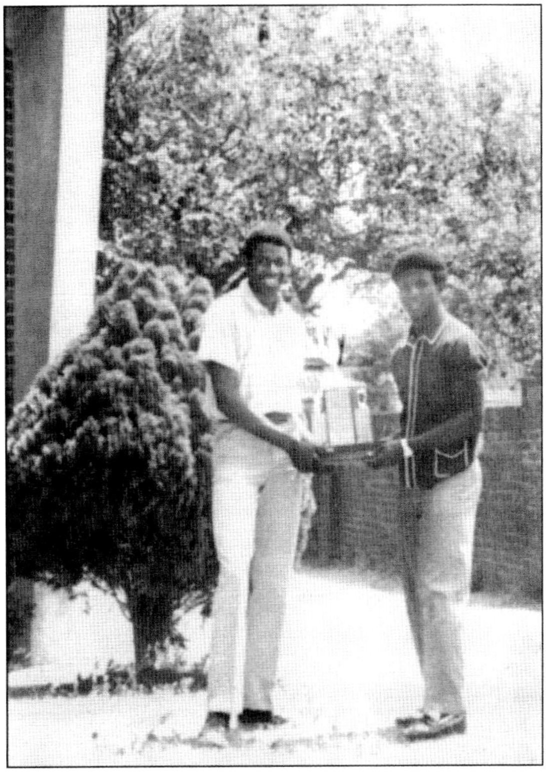

In 1970, this basketball team became the first team to have an undefeated regular season in the school's history. (Courtesy of Burke High School.)

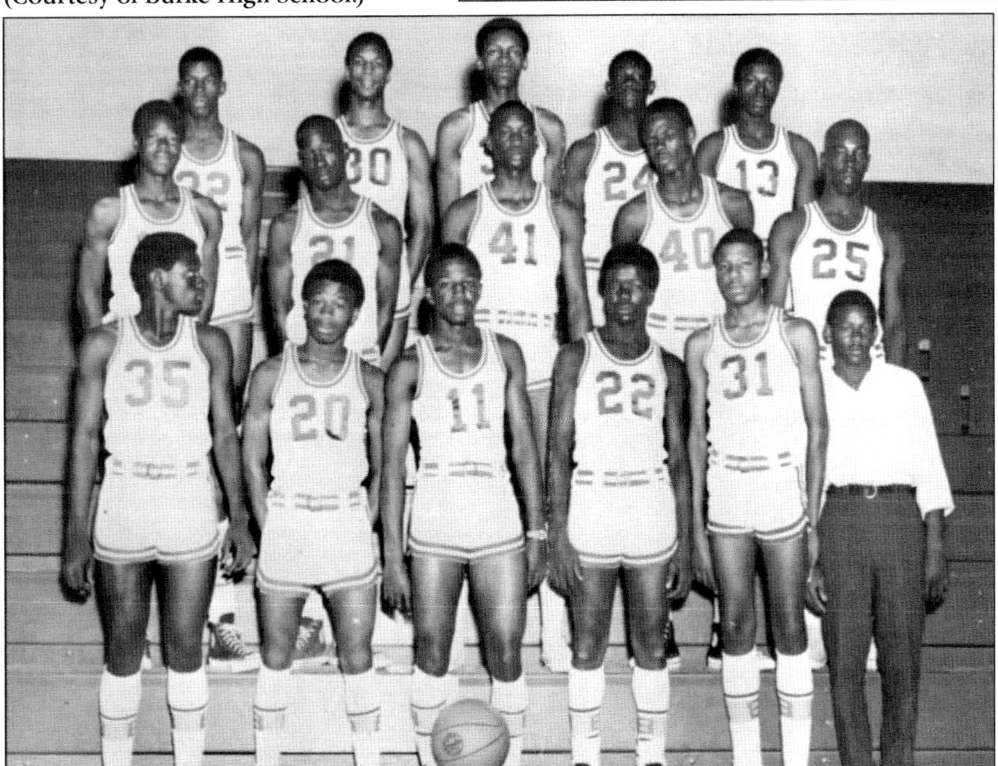

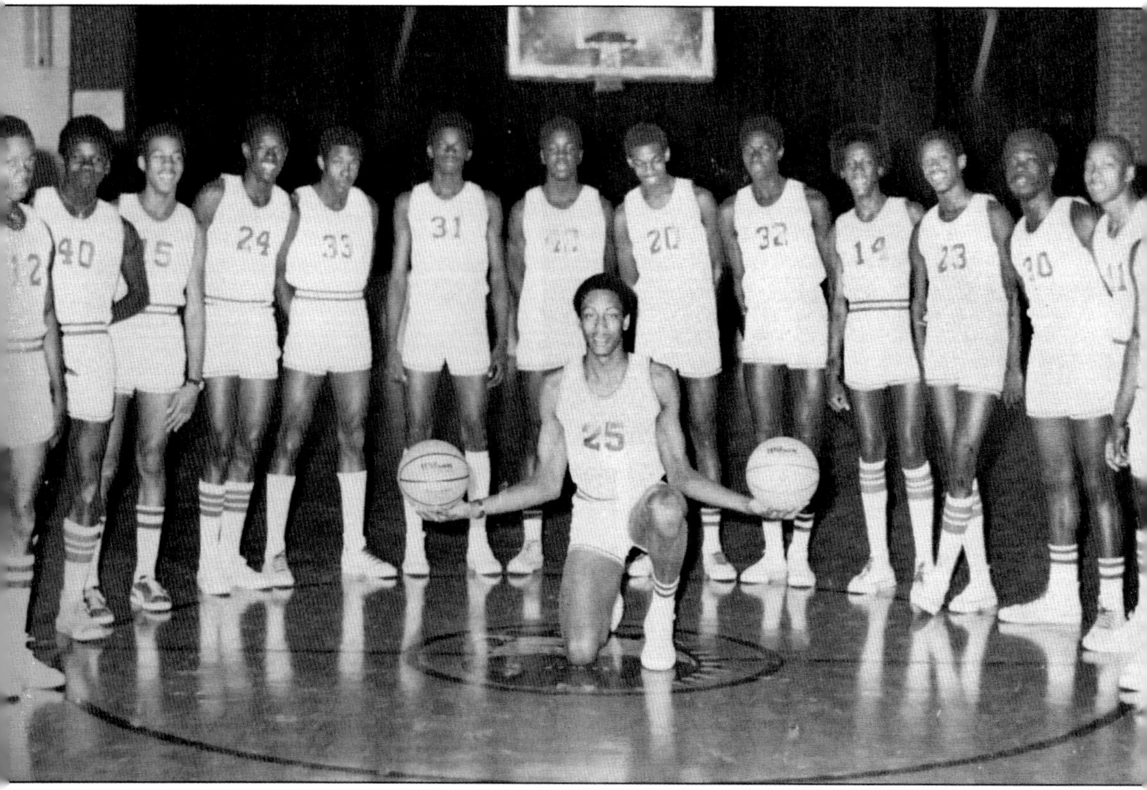

In 1976, this team won the boys' 4A state championship under the direction of coach John Wilford, who was named South Carolina High School Coach of the year. They accomplished that feat again in 1984. (Courtesy of Burke High School.)

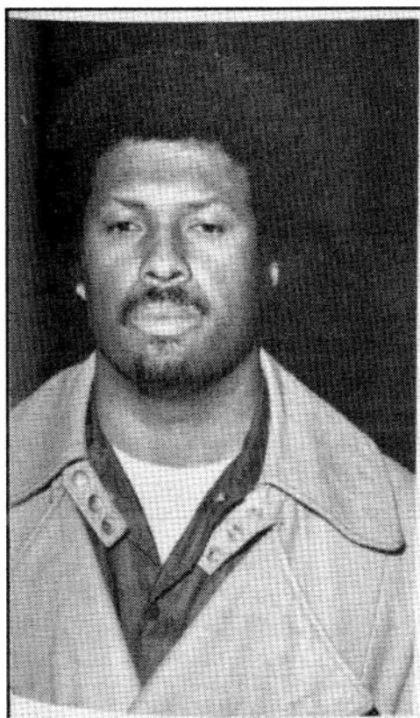

COACH
J. M. Wilford
Coach of the year.

BULLDOG SCHEDULE

Burke	68	Battery Creek	40
”	81	Lincoln	49
”	75	Baptist Hill	47
”	58	C. A. Brown	49
”	88	Baptist Hill	46
”	73	Rivers	36
”	80	C. A. Brown	67
”	70	Baptist Hill	55
”	94	Rivers	76
”	90	Lincoln	63
”	70	Summerville	55
”	79	Middleton	60
”	74	Beaufort	54
”	77	Goose Creek	38
”	57	Middleton	48
”	89	Summerville	58
”	74	Beaufort	48
”	75	Goose Creek	44
”	65	Bonds Wilson	48
”	76	C. A. Brown	65

Pictured above is the 1976 schedule of the boys' basketball team, who had an undefeated season. (Courtesy of Burke High School.)

The Undefeated Record

OPPONENTS		BURKE	OPPONENTS		BURKE
BAPTIST HILL	51	99	ROBERT SMALLS	47	50
BAPTIST HILL	66	96	WILKINSON	81	82
LAING HIGH	54	112	SUMTER HIGH	62	81
LAING HIGH	64	88	WILKINSON	73	91
SUMTER HIGH	55	86	C. A. BROWN	70	97
ROBERTS HIGH	70	98	ROBERTS HIGH	69	103
ROBERT SMALL	58	97	BONDS-WILSON	72	89
COLLETON	47	141	COLLETON	65	130
BONDS-WILSON	70	82	C. A. BROWN	74	89

1969-70 was a RECORD BREAKING year for the BURKE BULLDOGS.

Above is the boys' basketball schedule for 1970, during their undefeated regular season. (Courtesy of Burke High School.)

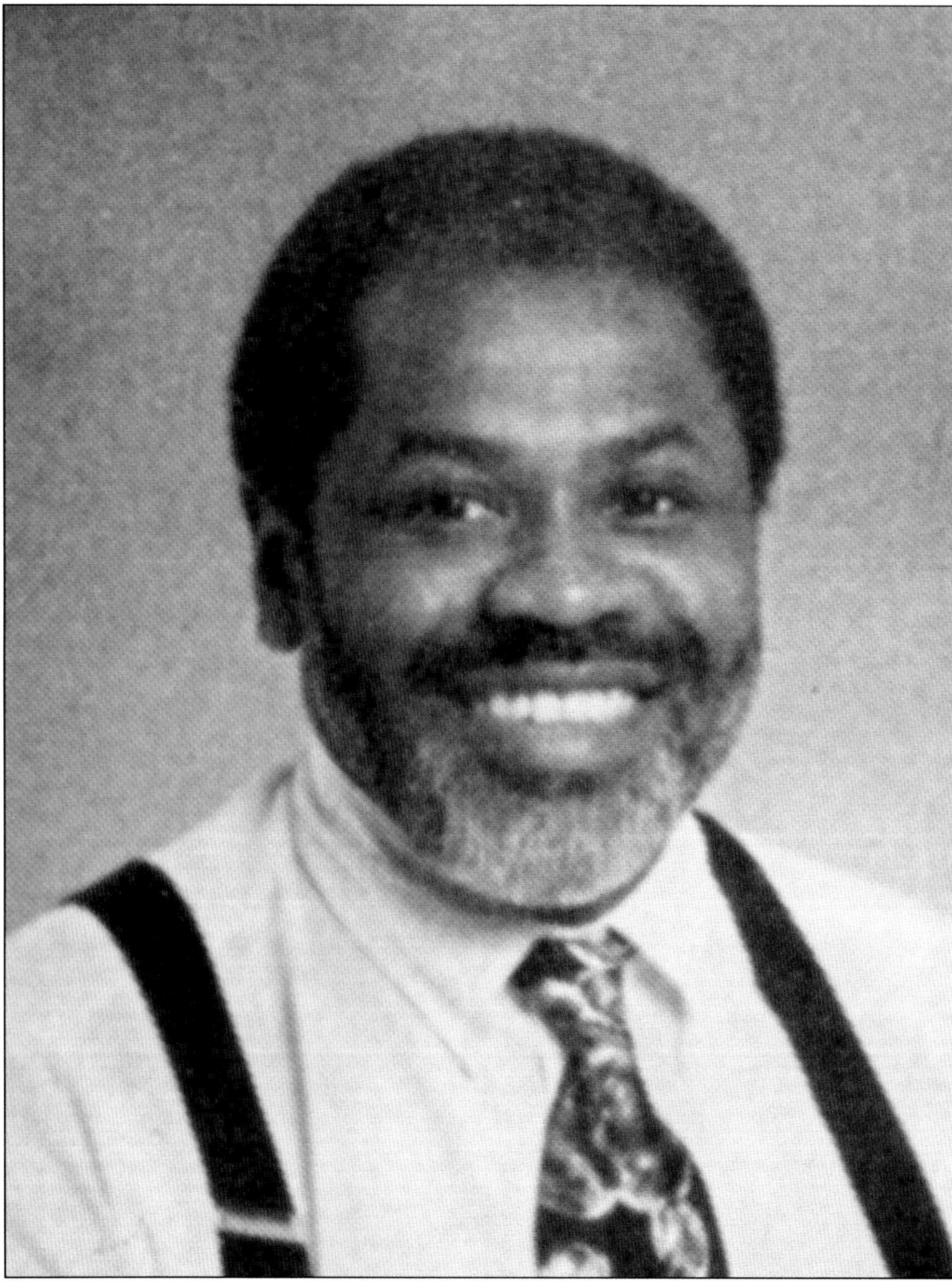

Earl Brown became only the seventh boy's high school coach in South Carolina to reach 500 victories in basketball. He began his coaching career at Alston High School. He also had stints at James Island and Charles A. Brown High Schools. Brown led his 1989 and 1992 teams to state championship games only to lose both games in overtime and double overtime respectively. He has held the post of head basketball coach longer than any other person in the school's history, according to the 2001 yearbook. (Courtesy of Burke High School.)

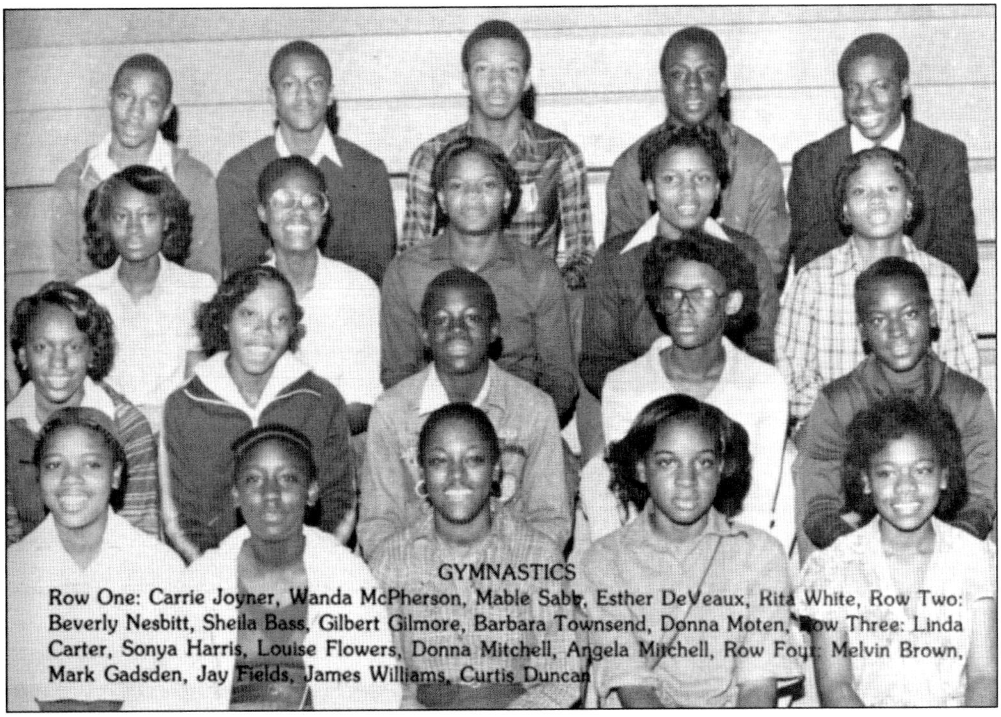

Among Burke's non-traditional sports programs during the past 30 years was gymnastics, pictured above *c.* 1982. Below is the girls' soccer team in 1996. (Courtesy of Burke High School.)

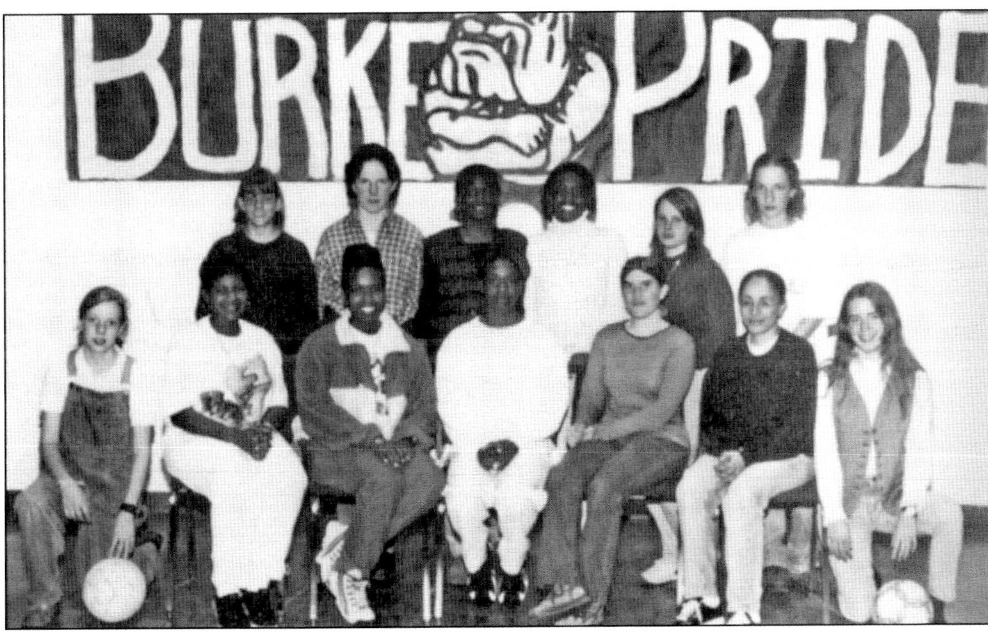

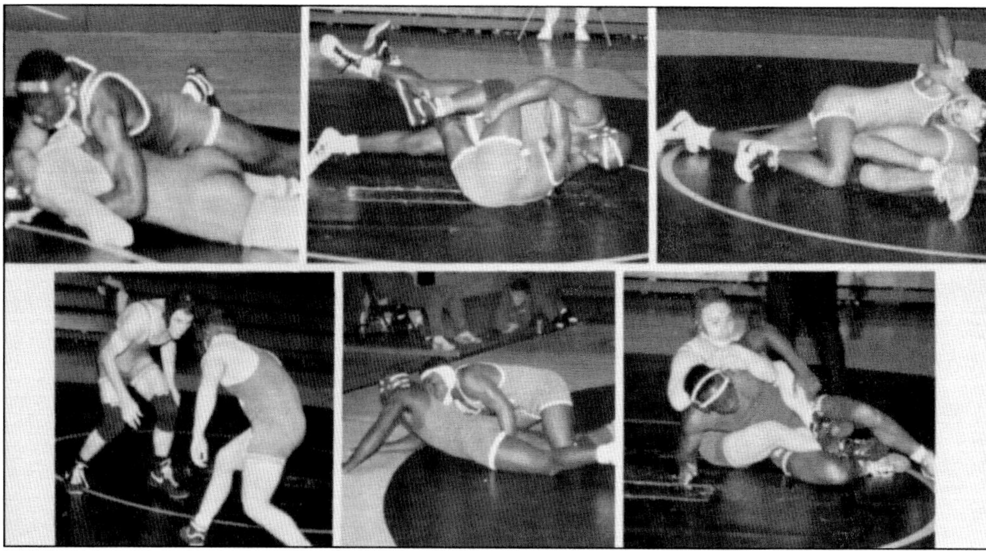

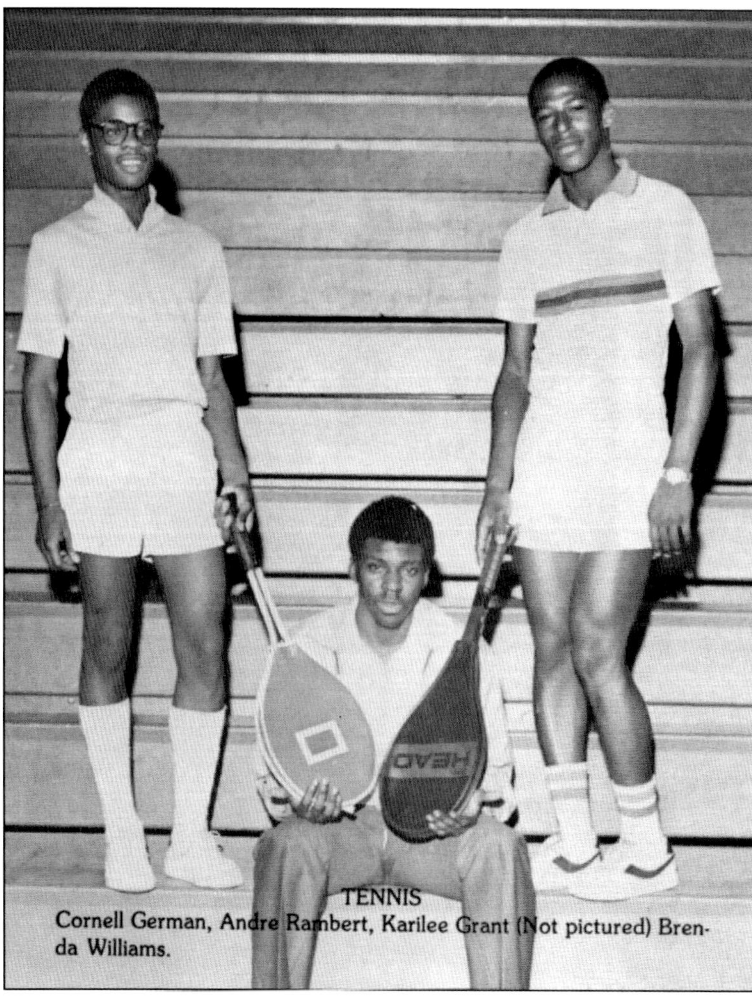

The wrestling team, *c.* 1992, and the tennis team, *c.* 1984, were unable to sustain ongoing programs due to a lack of accessible coaches and student participation. (Courtesy of Burke High School.)

Six

Classes and Students

Burke was more than just a school for blacks. It was, in fact, an institution that transcended its primary mission.

—Rudolph A. Pyatt Jr. (Class of 1951)

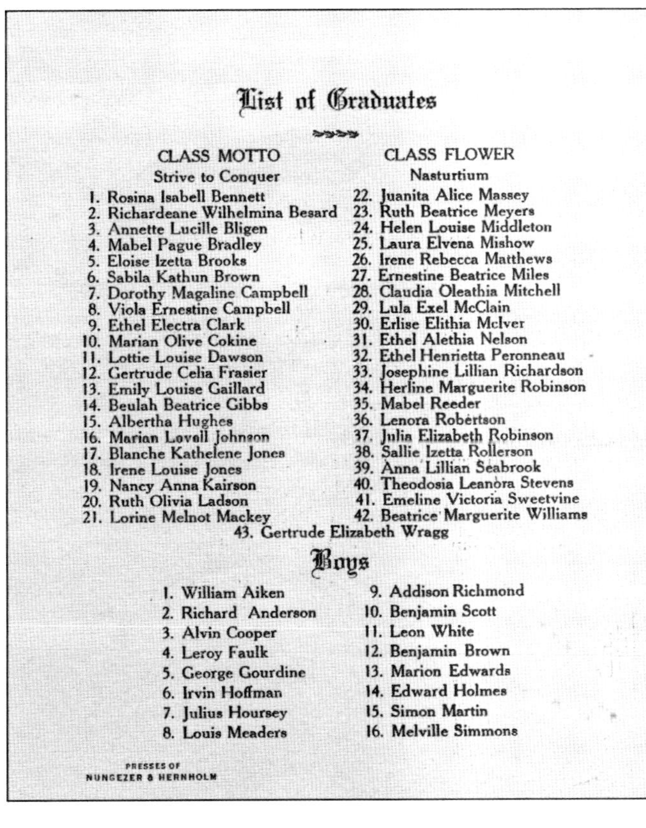

List of Graduates

CLASS MOTTO	CLASS FLOWER
Strive to Conquer	Nasturtium

1. Rosina Isabell Bennett
2. Richardeane Wilhelmina Besard
3. Annette Lucille Bligen
4. Mabel Pague Bradley
5. Eloise Izetta Brooks
6. Sabila Kathun Brown
7. Dorothy Magaline Campbell
8. Viola Ernestine Campbell
9. Ethel Electra Clark
10. Marian Olive Cokine
11. Lottie Louise Dawson
12. Gertrude Celia Frasier
13. Emily Louise Gaillard
14. Beulah Beatrice Gibbs
15. Albertha Hughes
16. Marian Lovell Johnson
17. Blanche Kathelene Jones
18. Irene Louise Jones
19. Nancy Anna Kairson
20. Ruth Olivia Ladson
21. Lorine Melnot Mackey
22. Juanita Alice Massey
23. Ruth Beatrice Meyers
24. Helen Louise Middleton
25. Laura Elvena Mishow
26. Irene Rebecca Matthews
27. Ernestine Beatrice Miles
28. Claudia Oleathia Mitchell
29. Lula Exel McClain
30. Erlise Elithia McIver
31. Ethel Alethia Nelson
32. Ethel Henrietta Peronneau
33. Josephine Lillian Richardson
34. Herline Marguerite Robinson
35. Mabel Reeder
36. Lenora Robertson
37. Julia Elizabeth Robinson
38. Sallie Izetta Rollerson
39. Anna Lillian Seabrook
40. Theodosia Leanora Stevens
41. Emeline Victoria Sweetvine
42. Beatrice Marguerite Williams
43. Gertrude Elizabeth Wragg

Boys

1. William Aiken
2. Richard Anderson
3. Alvin Cooper
4. Leroy Faulk
5. George Gourdine
6. Irvin Hoffman
7. Julius Hoursey
8. Louis Meaders
9. Addison Richmond
10. Benjamin Scott
11. Leon White
12. Benjamin Brown
13. Marion Edwards
14. Edward Holmes
15. Simon Martin
16. Melville Simmons

PRESSES OF
NUNGEZER & HERNHOLM

In 1913, this copy of the commencement program listed all of the graduates for that year. The most striking item about the program was the 42 female graduates as compared to only 16 male graduates. (Courtesy of the Avery Research Center.)

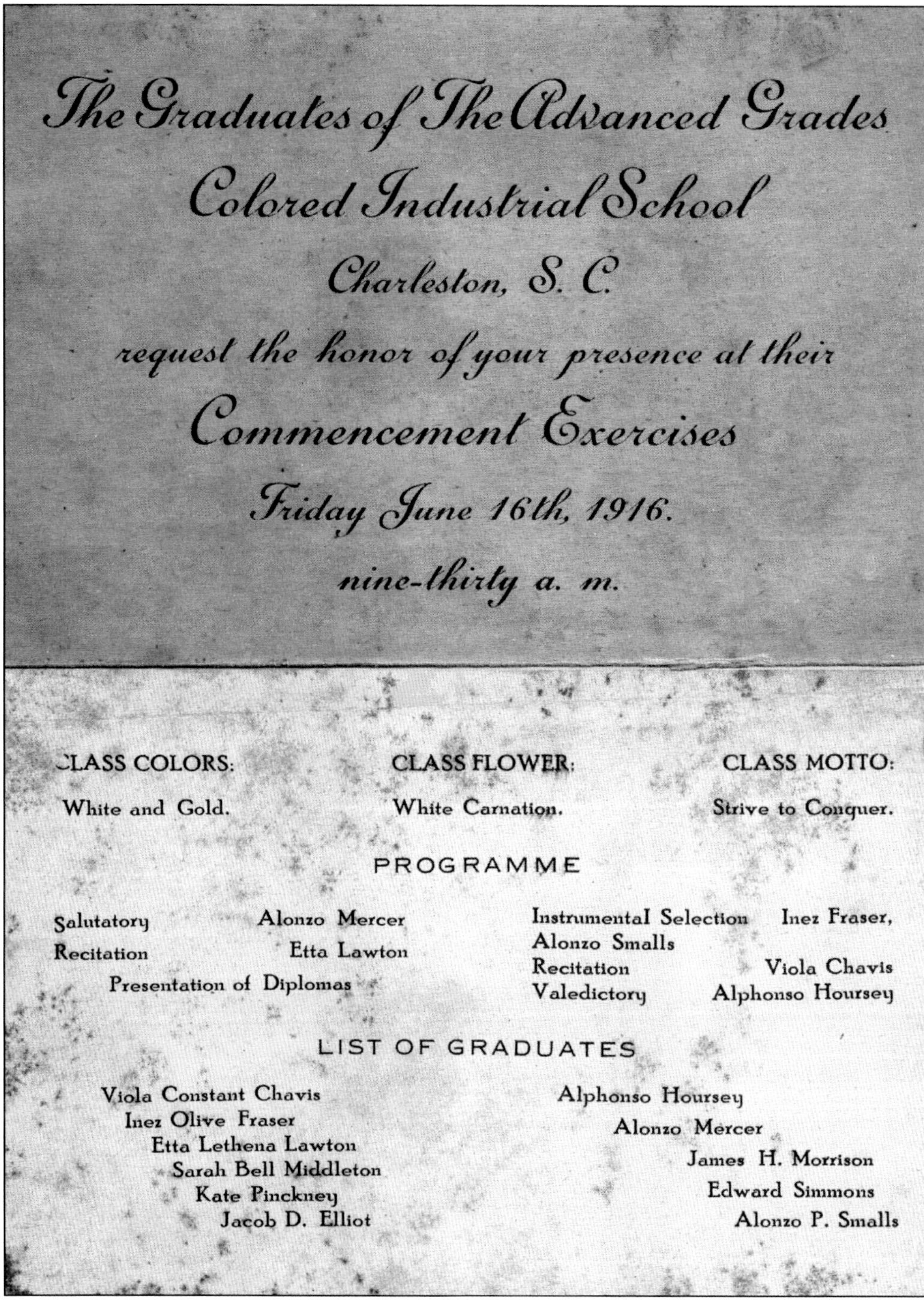

The Graduates of The Advanced Grades
Colored Industrial School
Charleston, S. C.
request the honor of your presence at their
Commencement Exercises
Friday June 16th, 1916.
nine-thirty a. m.

CLASS COLORS: White and Gold.

CLASS FLOWER: White Carnation.

CLASS MOTTO: Strive to Conquer.

PROGRAMME

Salutatory Alonzo Mercer
Recitation Etta Lawton
Presentation of Diplomas
Instrumental Selection Inez Fraser, Alonzo Smalls
Recitation Viola Chavis
Valedictory Alphonso Hoursey

LIST OF GRADUATES

Viola Constant Chavis
Inez Olive Fraser
Etta Lethena Lawton
Sarah Bell Middleton
Kate Pinckney
Jacob D. Elliot
Alphonso Hoursey
Alonzo Mercer
James H. Morrison
Edward Simmons
Alonzo P. Smalls

This 1916 program gave the names of those students who had completed the requirements to graduate from the eighth grade. This was the highest grade at that time. (Courtesy of the Avery Research Center.)

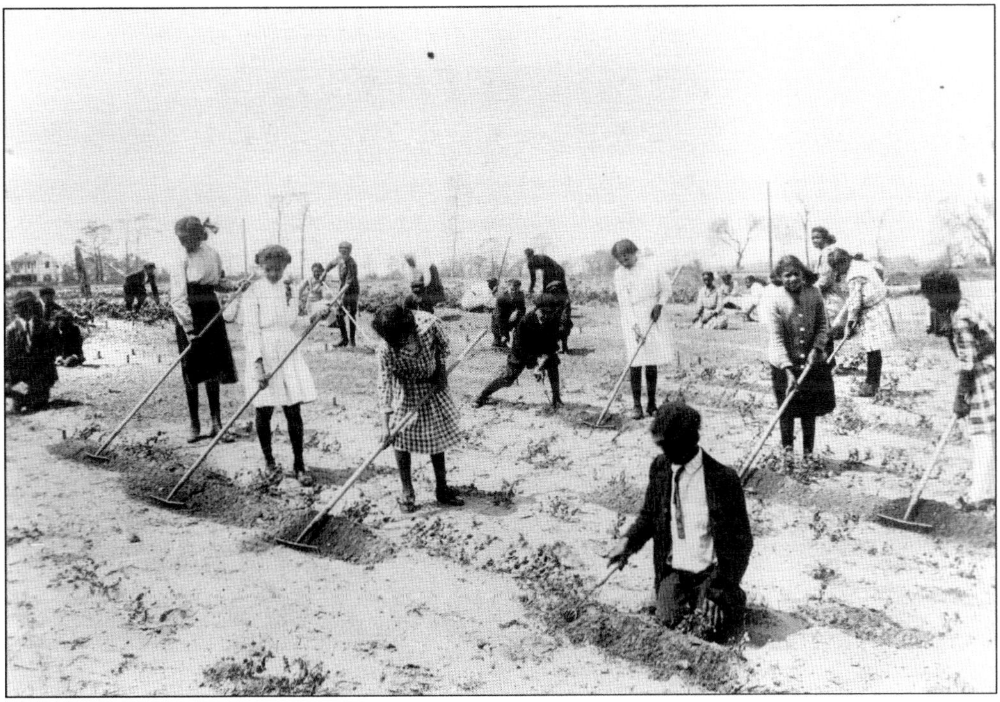

Around 1920, students who sought additional education beyond the fifth grade were sent to the Charleston Industrial School (Burke School) for an additional three years of vocational training as indicated in these two images. The image above portrays agriculture for boys and girls. Pictured below are young women preparing laundry. (Courtesy of the Avery Research Center.)

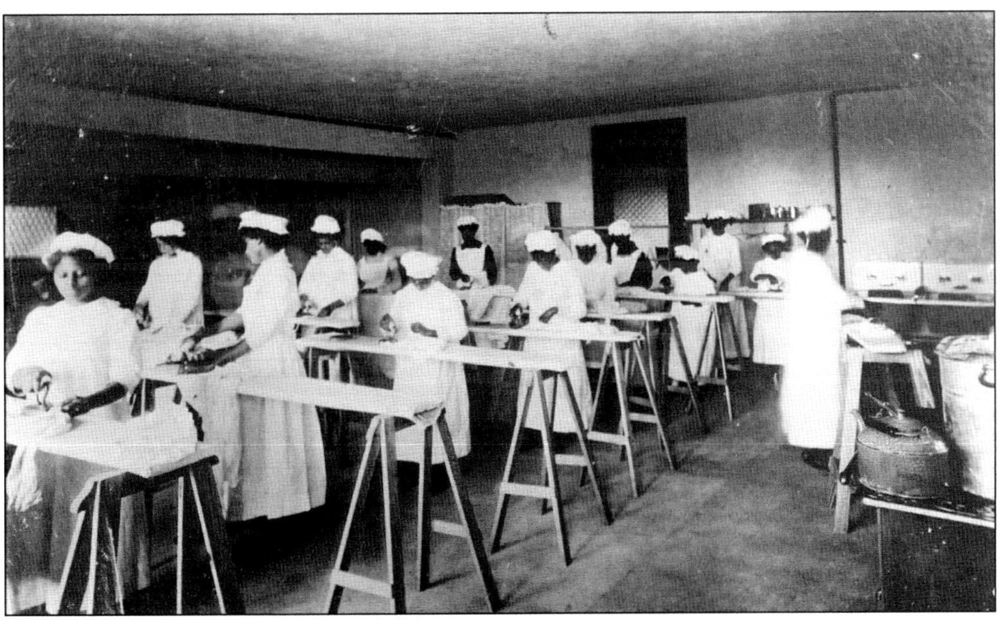

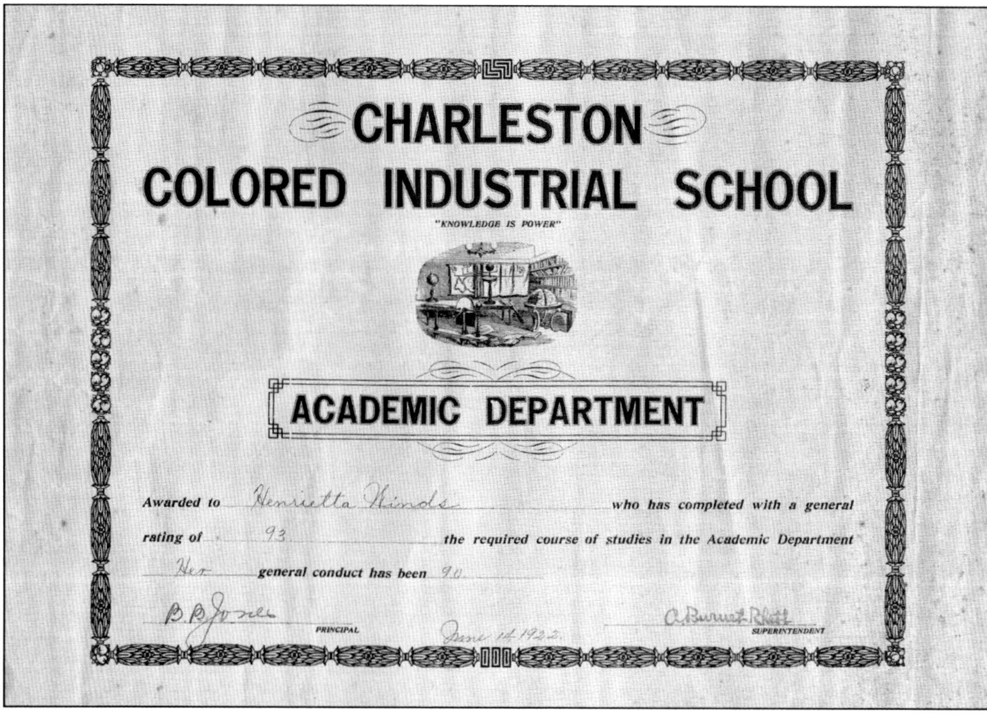

CHARLESTON
COLORED INDUSTRIAL SCHOOL
"KNOWLEDGE IS POWER"

ACADEMIC DEPARTMENT

Awarded to Henrietta Winds who has completed with a general rating of 93 the required course of studies in the Academic Department Her general conduct has been 90

B. B. Jones PRINCIPAL June 14 1922 A. Burnet Rhett SUPERINTENDENT

One of these documents reveals the type of subjects offered in 1922 in the industrial department and the names of the teachers. The other document indicates that there was an academic department; however, the certificate did not reveal what courses were offered. (Courtesy of the Avery Research Center.)

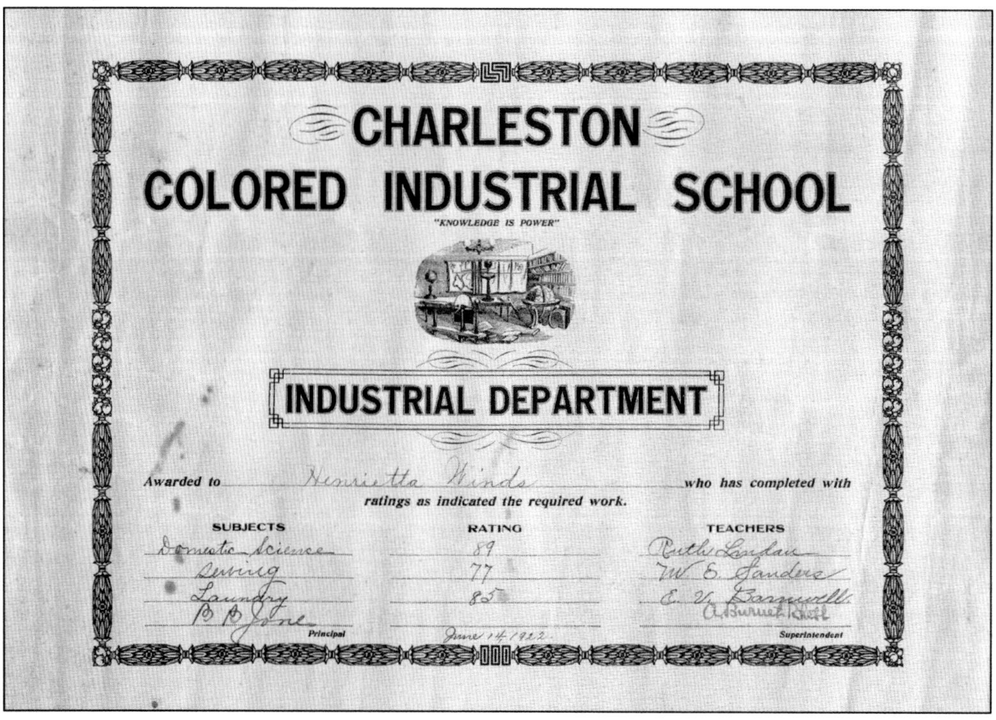

CHARLESTON
COLORED INDUSTRIAL SCHOOL
"KNOWLEDGE IS POWER"

INDUSTRIAL DEPARTMENT

Awarded to Henrietta Winds who has completed with ratings as indicated the required work.

SUBJECTS	RATING	TEACHERS
Domestic Science	89	Ruth Landau
Sewing	77	M. E. Sanders
Laundry	85	E. V. Barnwell

B. B. Jones Principal June 14 1922 A. Burnet Rhett Superintendent

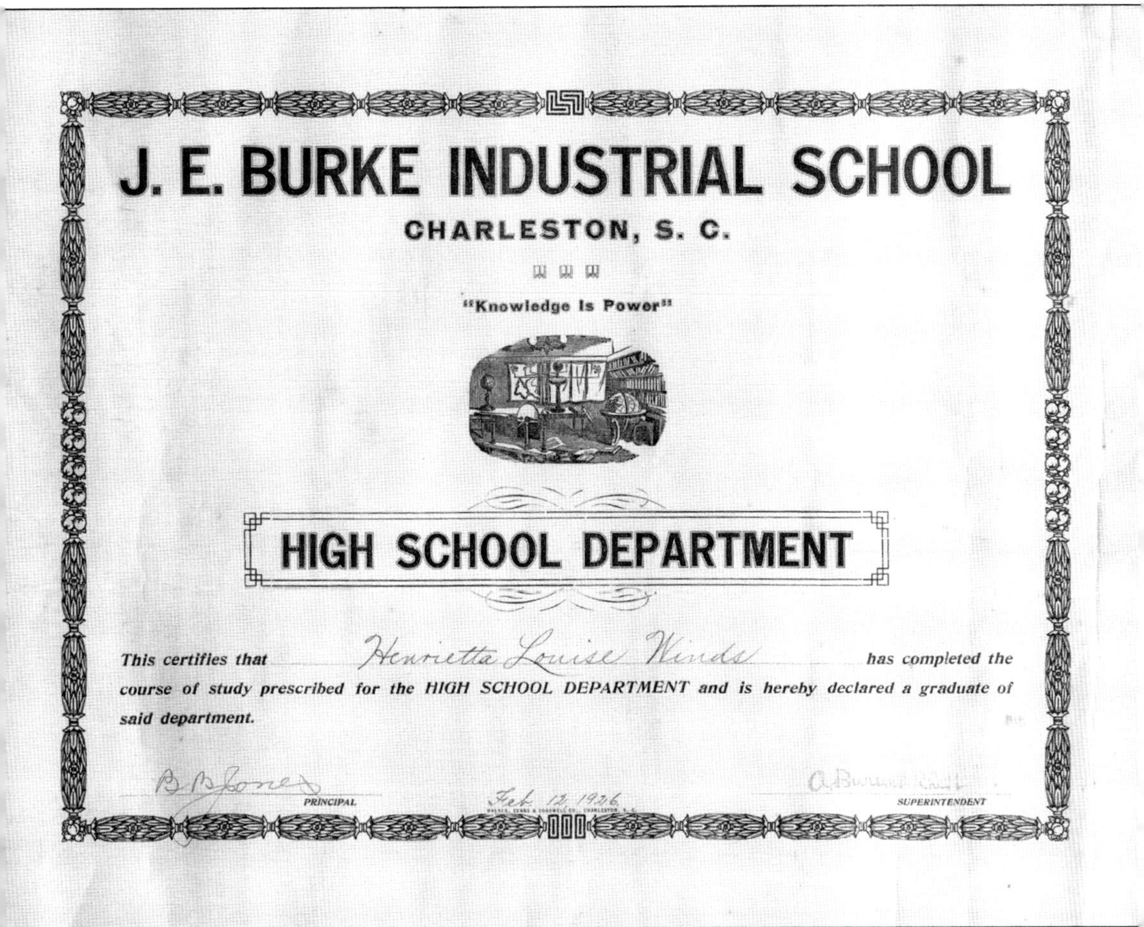

J. E. BURKE INDUSTRIAL SCHOOL

CHARLESTON, S. C.

"Knowledge Is Power"

HIGH SCHOOL DEPARTMENT

This certifies that Henrietta Louise Winds *has completed the course of study prescribed for the HIGH SCHOOL DEPARTMENT and is hereby declared a graduate of said department.*

B. B. Jones
PRINCIPAL

Feb. 12, 1926

[illegible]
SUPERINTENDENT

According to this certificate dated 1926, the official name of the school was J. E. Burke Industrial School, and the school included a high school department. The 11th grade was the highest grade that one could obtain in the department until 1948, when the 12th grade was added. (Courtesy of the Avery Research Center.)

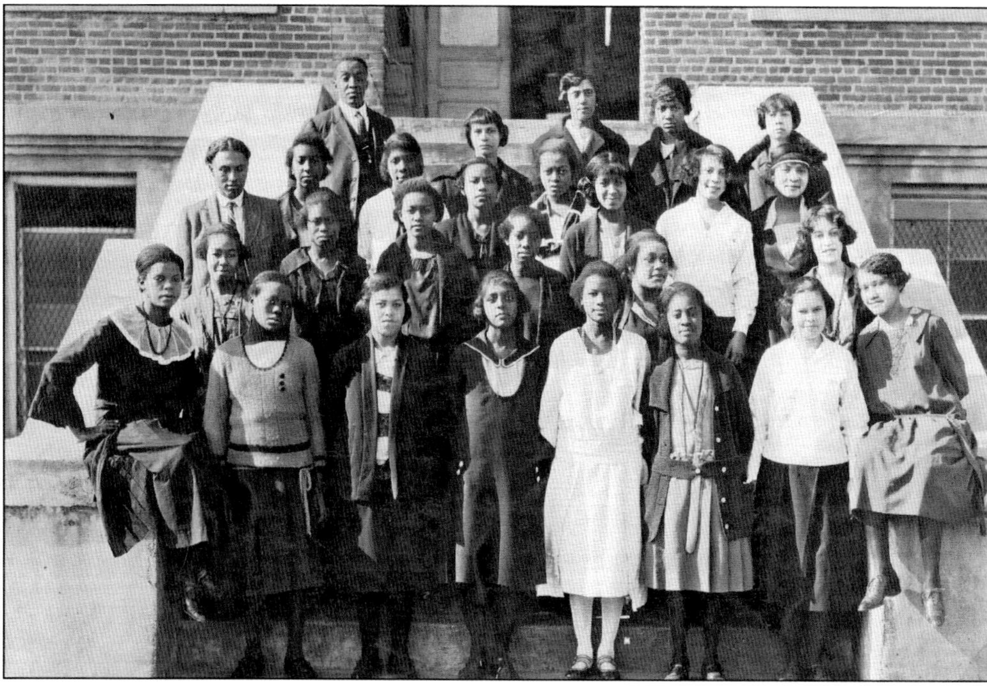

In 1924, this became the second senior class to complete the requirements for graduation. There was only one male student pictured in the class, as shown to the far left. (Courtesy of the Avery Research Center.)

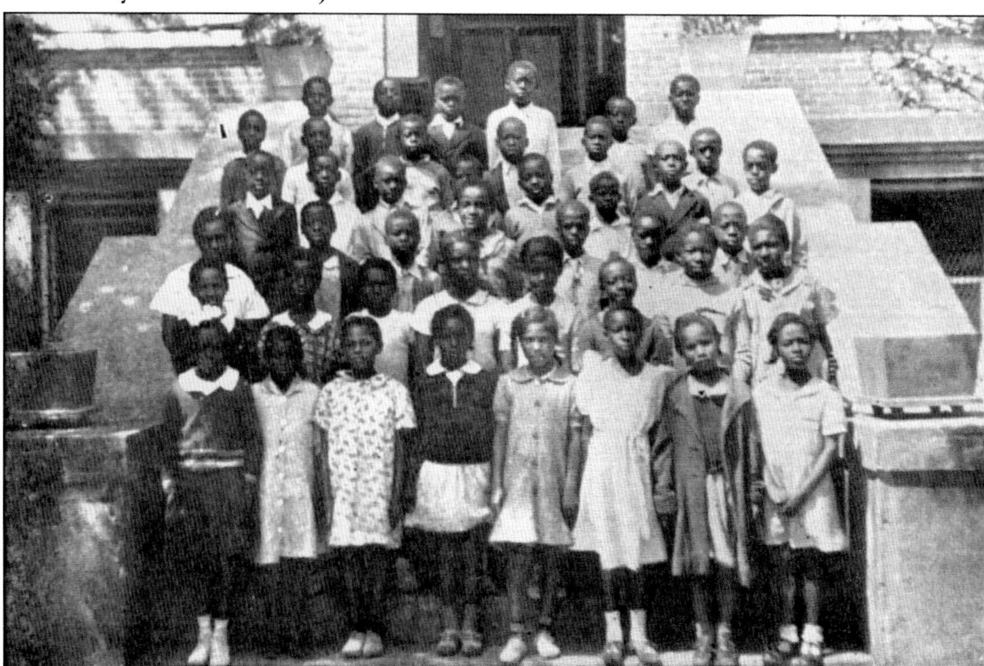

By 1925, the school had expanded to serve elementary and high school students. This 1937 image showed a typical third-grade class, housed with students from the high school department. (Courtesy of Burke High School.)

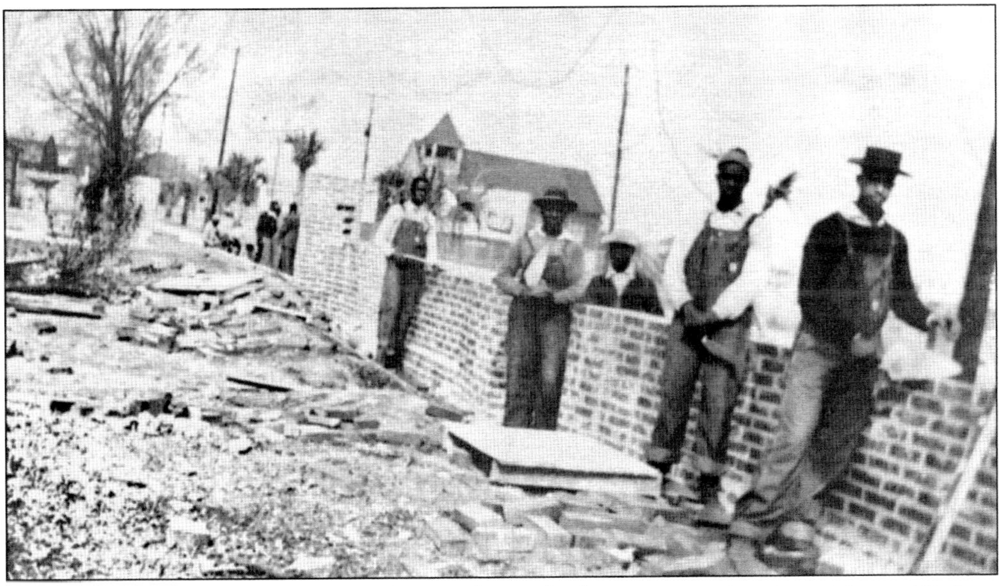

As early as 1936, students were perfecting the craft of masonry under the tutelage of Robert Fields. It was during this time that Fields and his students built a brick fence to enclose the campus. Also during the early 1940s, Fields, with the aid of his students, added a wing to what was then known as the annex building. (Courtesy of Burke High School.)

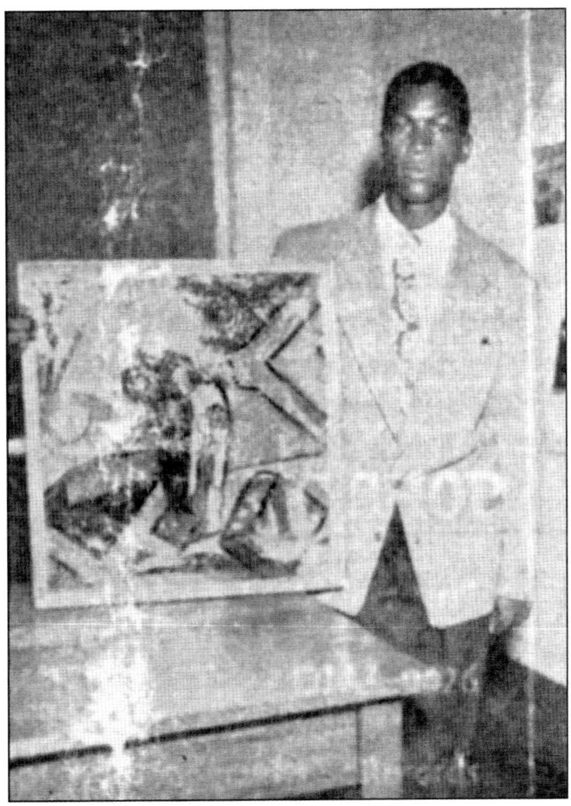

Merton Simpson was chosen outstanding artist of his senior class in 1948, and deservedly so. Simpson was known as one of Charleston's young and gifted artists. During his junior and senior years at Burke, he was awarded first prize for his oil paintings, which were exhibited at the Central Agriculture Fair in Virginia. While still a student at Burke, his works were exhibited at the Gibbes Art Gallery, a museum that catered to the white elite in Charleston. (Courtesy of the Avery Research Center.)

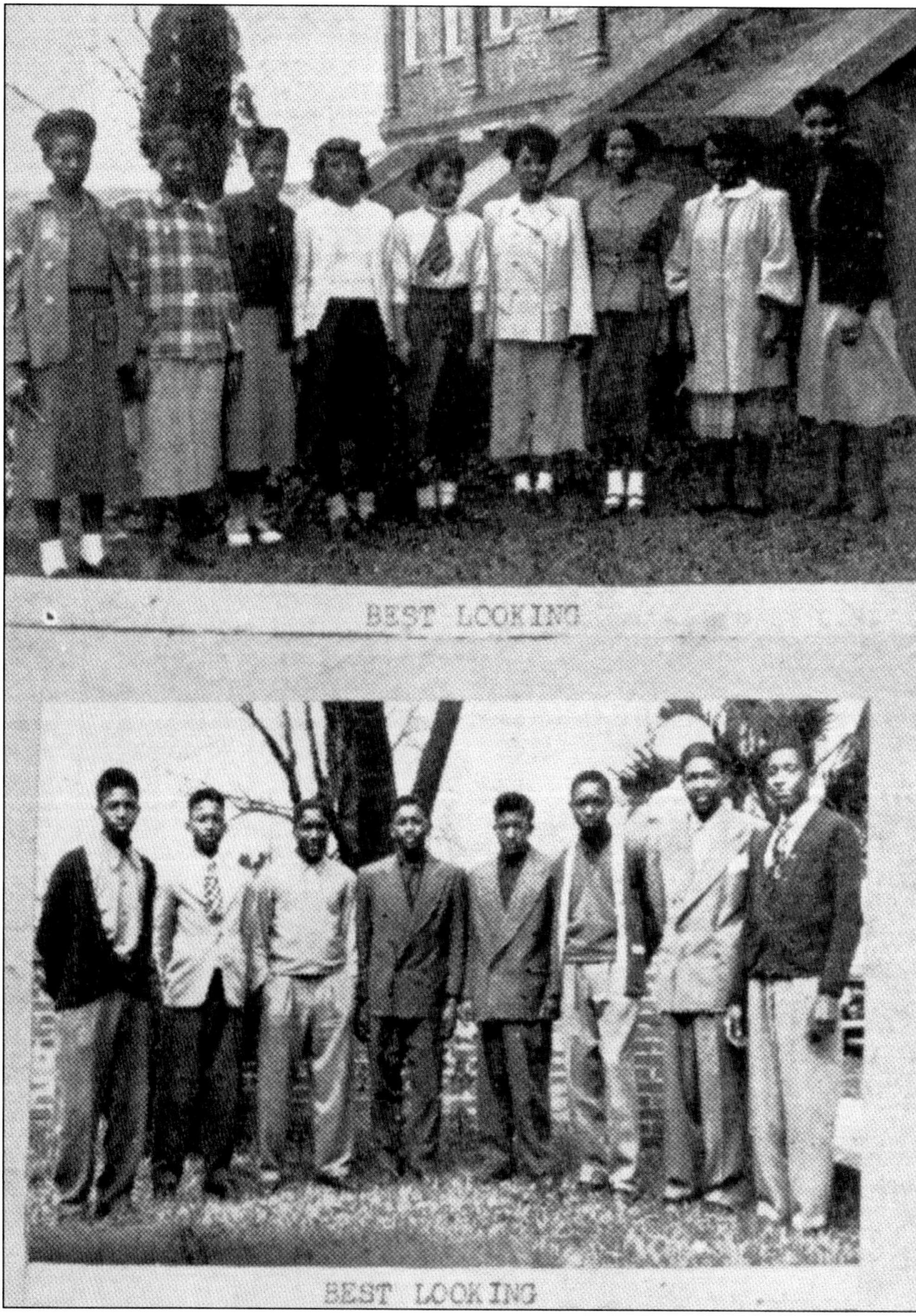

During the 1940s, it was customary for the senior class to choose several seniors in each of the superlative categories, as shown in this 1949 photograph. The image above featured those students chosen best looking. (Courtesy of the Avery Research Center.)

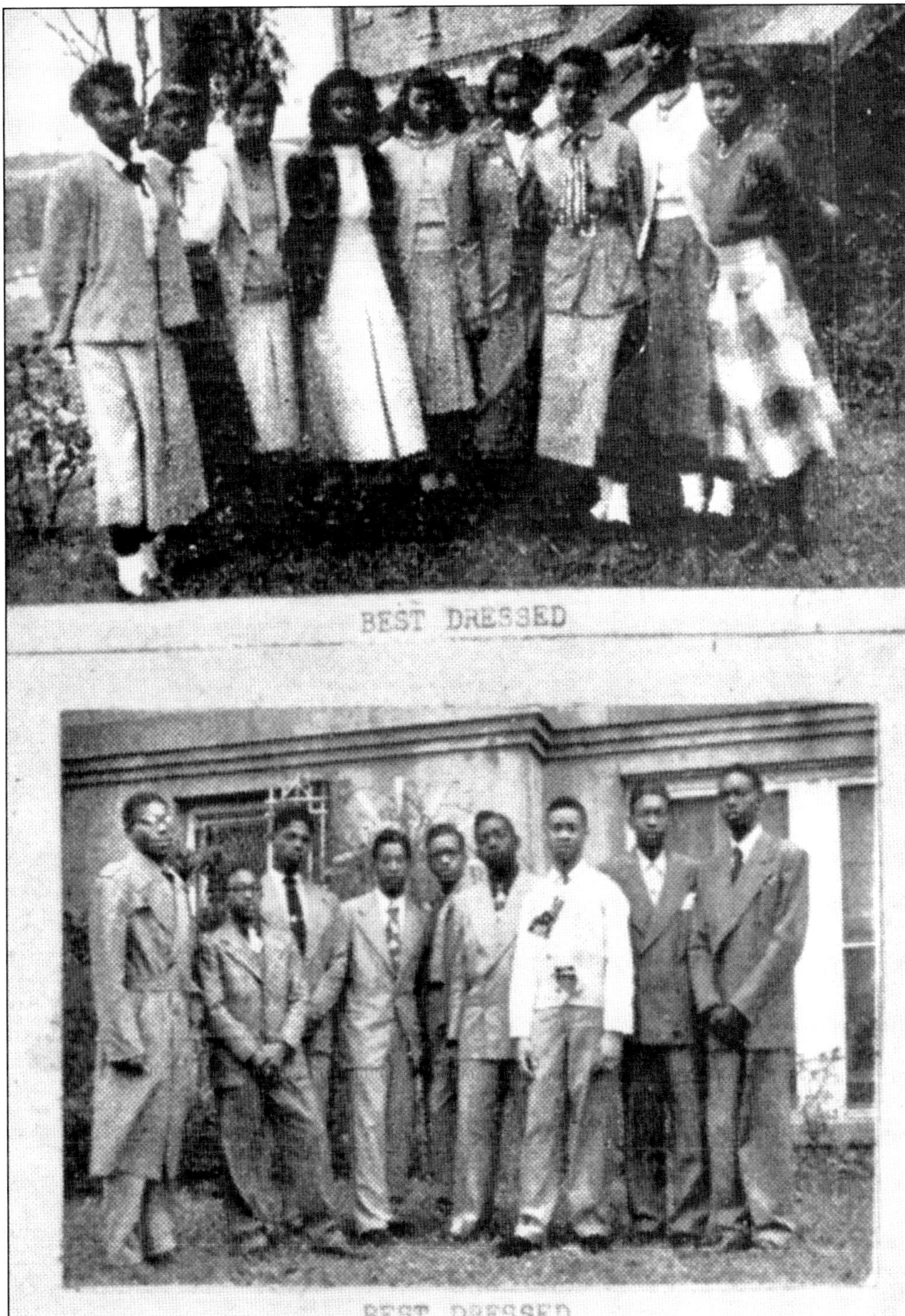

This 1949 photograph featured those seniors who were voted by their peers as best dressed. By the 1950s, only one student was voted for in these different categories. (Courtesy of the Avery Research Center.)

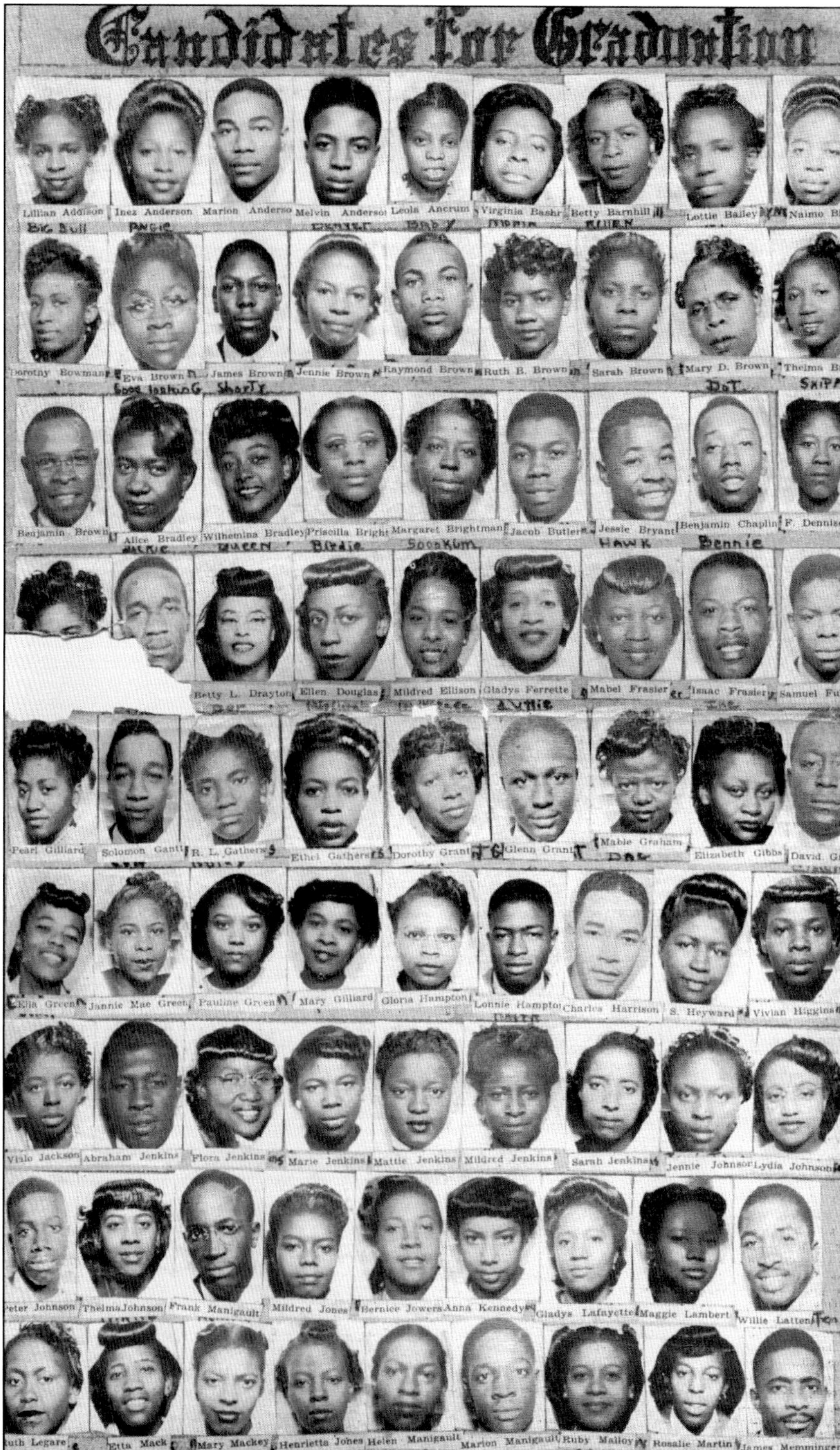

In 1948, Burke graduated its first 12th-grade class. This image shows the last senior class to complete the 11th grade in 1947. (Courtesy of the Avery Research Center.)

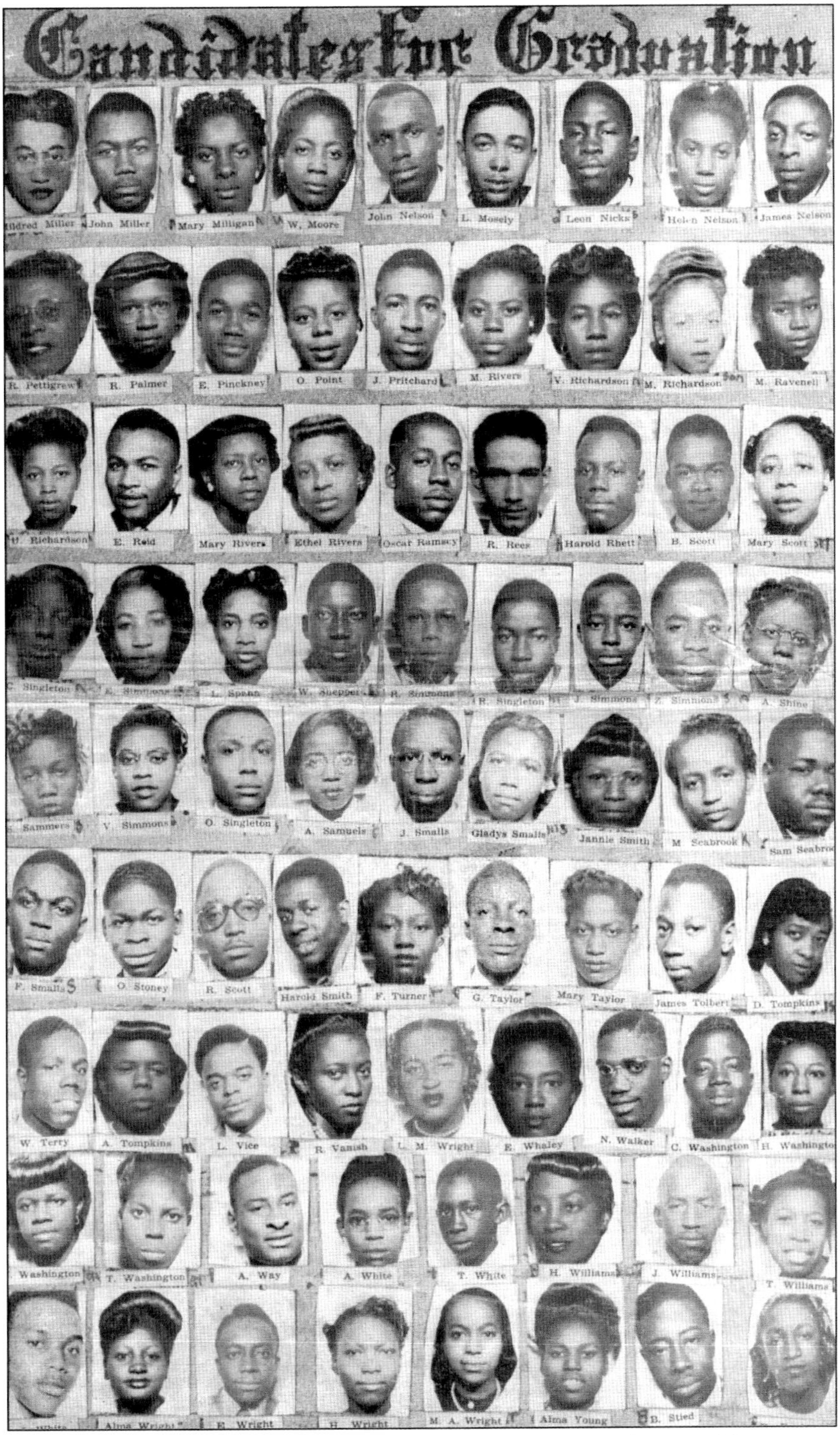

Prior to 1948, the 11th grade was the highest grade that a student could attain at Burke school. Several of these male graduates were returning veterans of World War II. (Courtesy of the Avery Research Center.)

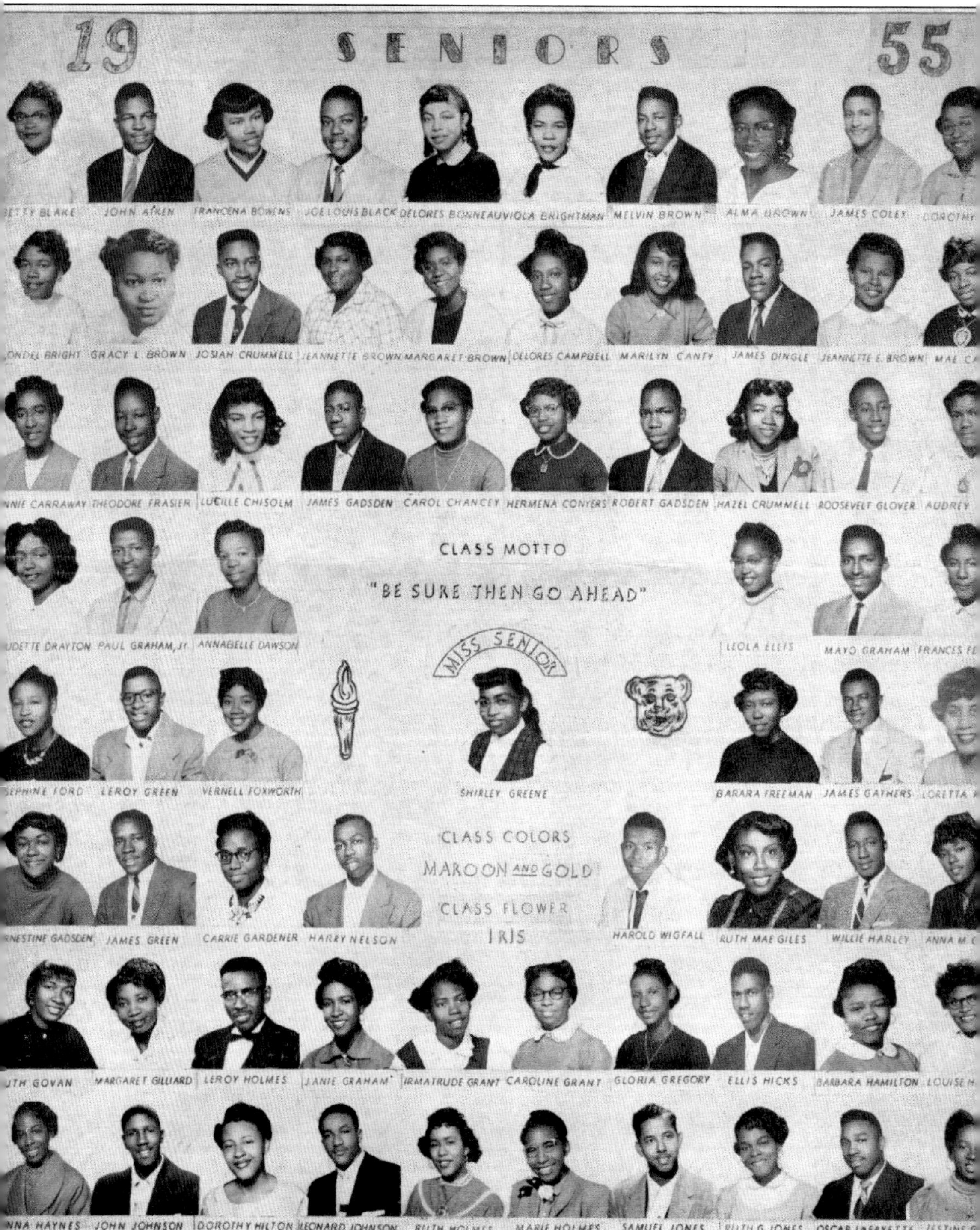

This senior class became the first graduating class of Burke that included students who had recently attended Avery High School. Avery's last graduation took place in 1954. (Courtesy

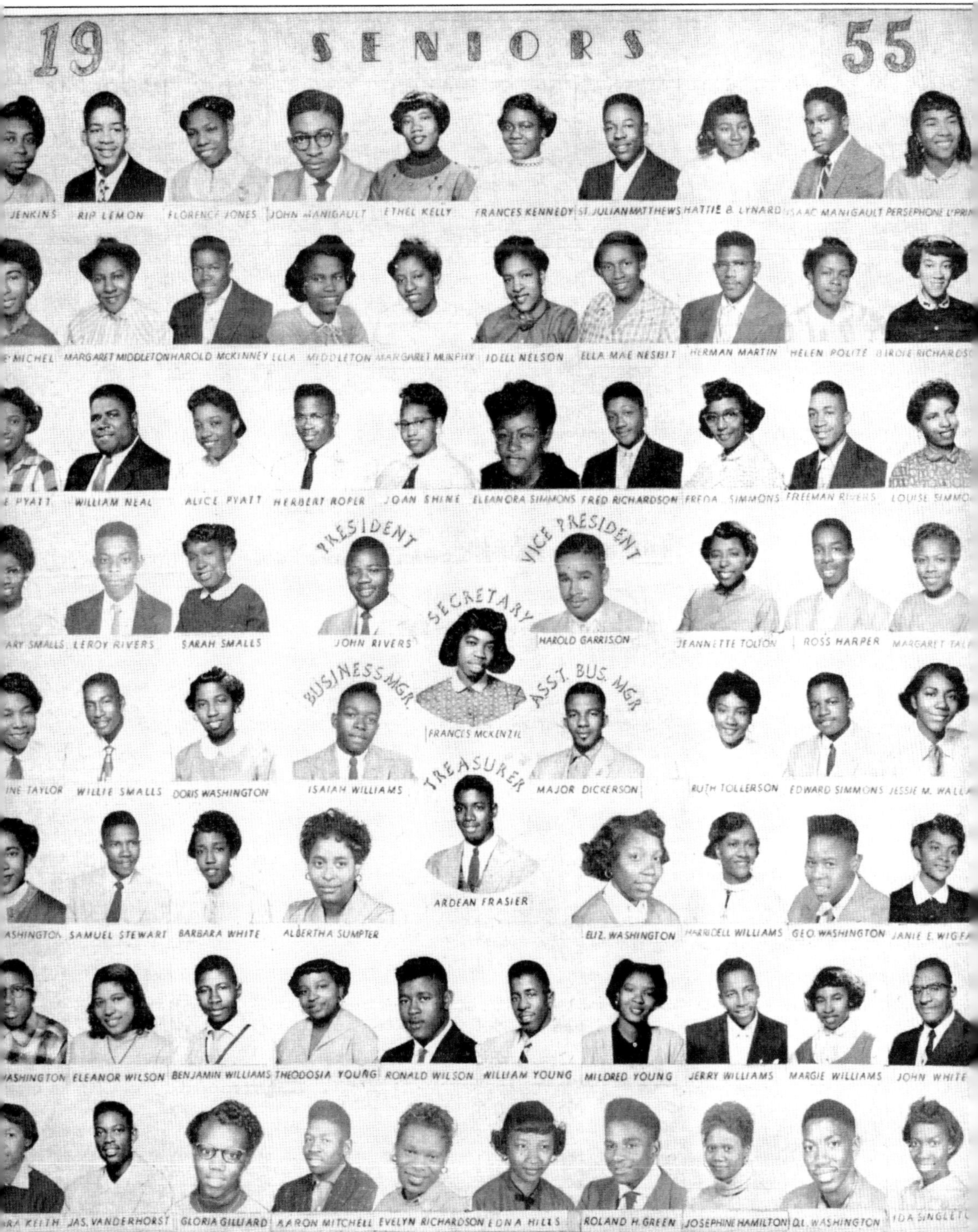

of the Avery Research Center.)

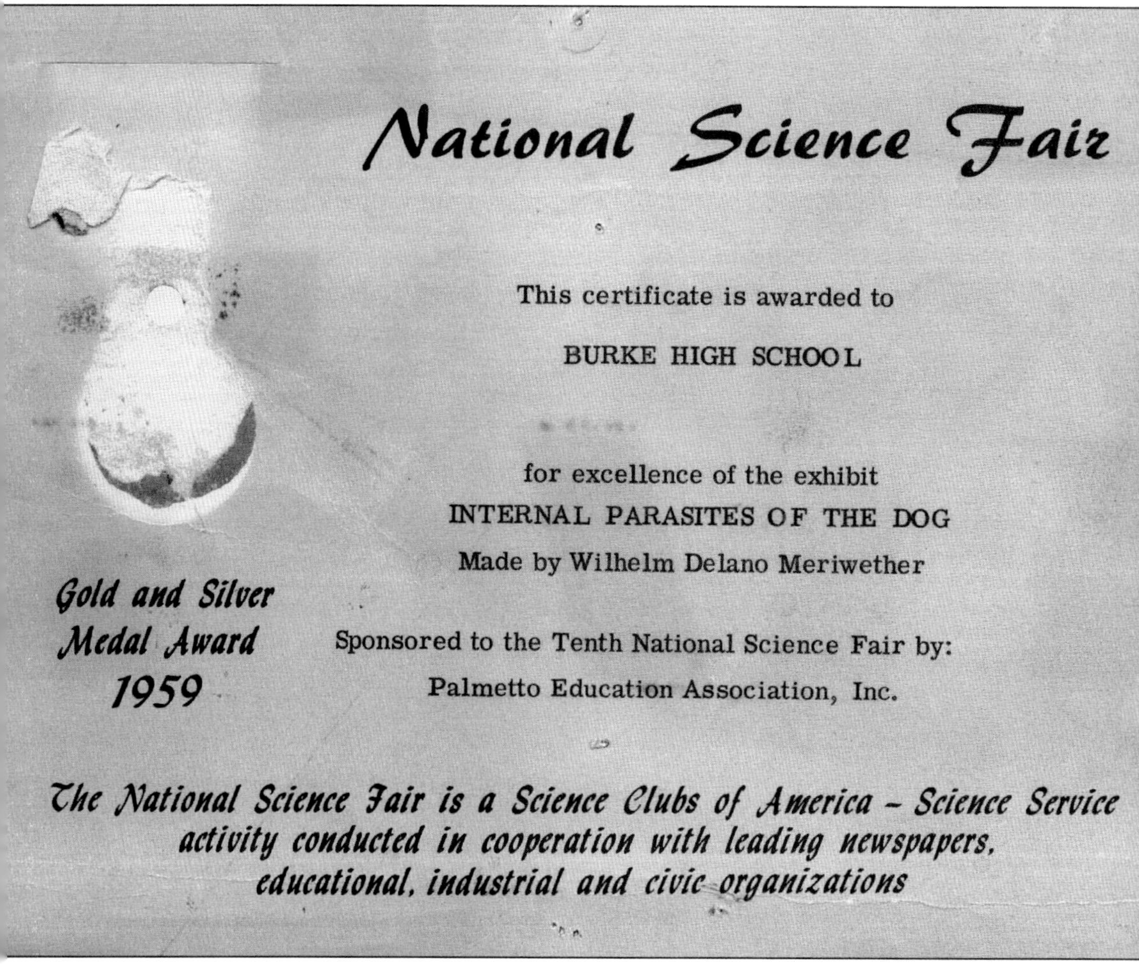
National Science Fair

This certificate is awarded to

BURKE HIGH SCHOOL

for excellence of the exhibit

INTERNAL PARASITES OF THE DOG

Made by Wilhelm Delano Meriwether

Gold and Silver Medal Award 1959

Sponsored to the Tenth National Science Fair by:

Palmetto Education Association, Inc.

The National Science Fair is a Science Clubs of America - Science Service activity conducted in cooperation with leading newspapers, educational, industrial and civic organizations

This certificate symbolized a major accomplishment for the school and especially for Delano Meriwether. In 1963, he became the first African American to integrate Duke's School of Medicine. (Courtesy of the Avery Research Center.)

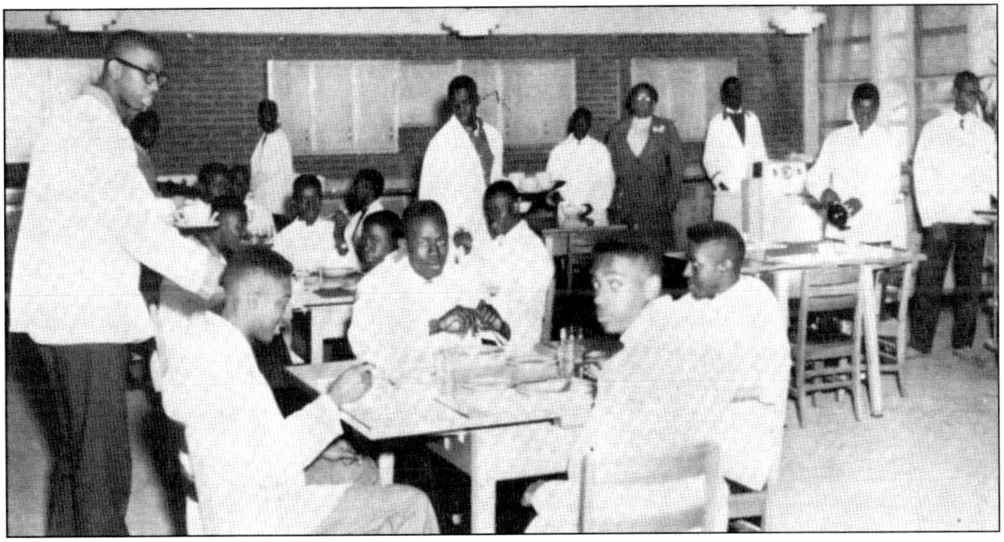

Pictured in this 1959 photograph are some of the 25 male students enrolled in a home economics class specifically for young men. Susie Simmons is the instructor. (Courtesy of the Avery Research Center.)

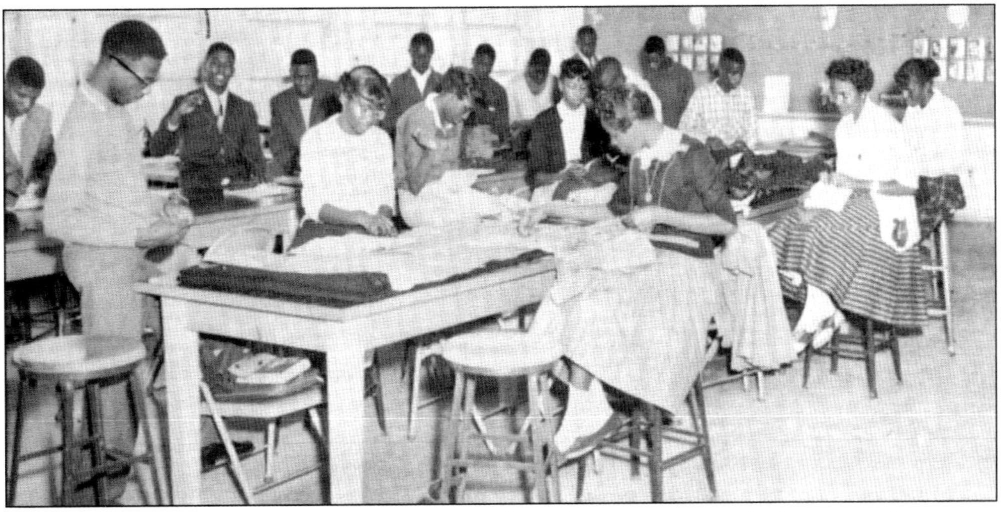

This 1959 image shows students hard at work in this advanced tailoring class. It was not unusual to find young men enrolled in these classes, because tailors were in high demand during the 1950s. (Courtesy of the Avery Research Center.)

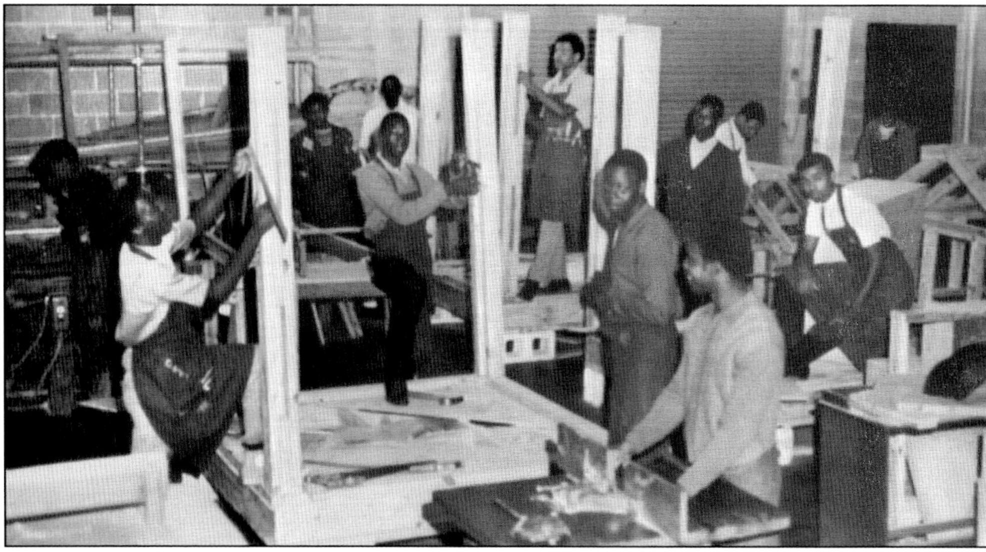

Carpentry was offered as early as 1920 under the direction of William G. Wright. Initially, it was mandatory that every physically fit male student enroll in the carpentry and woodworking course for at least one year. During the school year of 1944–1945, students enrolled in the carpentry class made a table for the cosmetology class, built a stage for the auditorium, remodeled the principal's home, and built gates. (Courtesy of the Avery Research Center.)

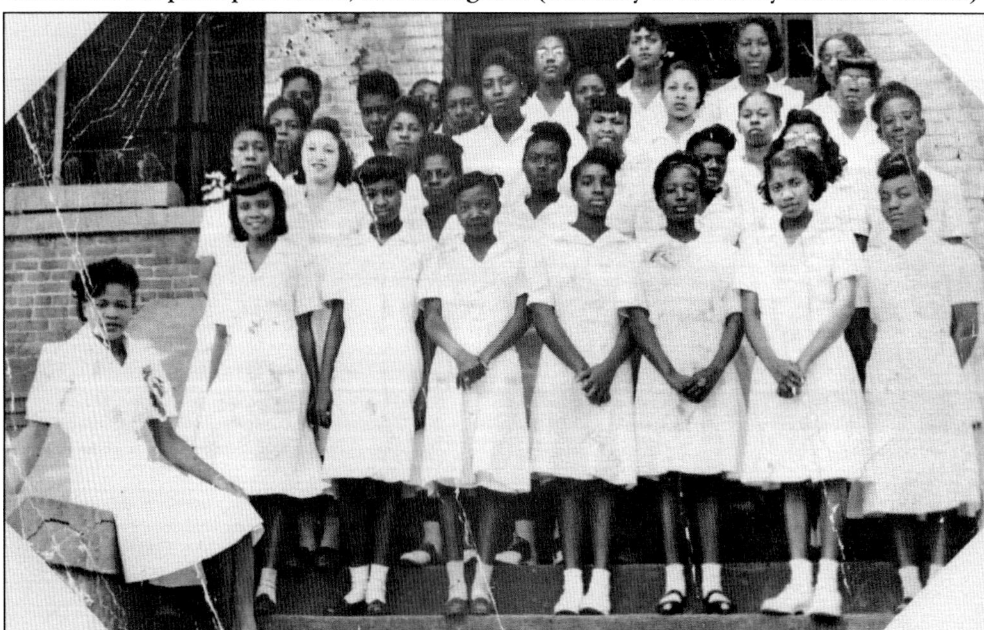

Classes for cosmetology began in 1944 under the supervision of Laura Mack Sims, pictured at left. The class had a total enrollment of 37 young ladies from the junior and senior classes. The students were required to pay an annual laboratory fee, furnish textbooks and uniforms, and spend 1,000 hours in training. It was reported that for 35 consecutive years, all of Sims's students passed the state board examination. She was recognized for her years of dedication by having her name placed on the vocational building at the school, dedicated in 1980. (Courtesy of Burke High School.)

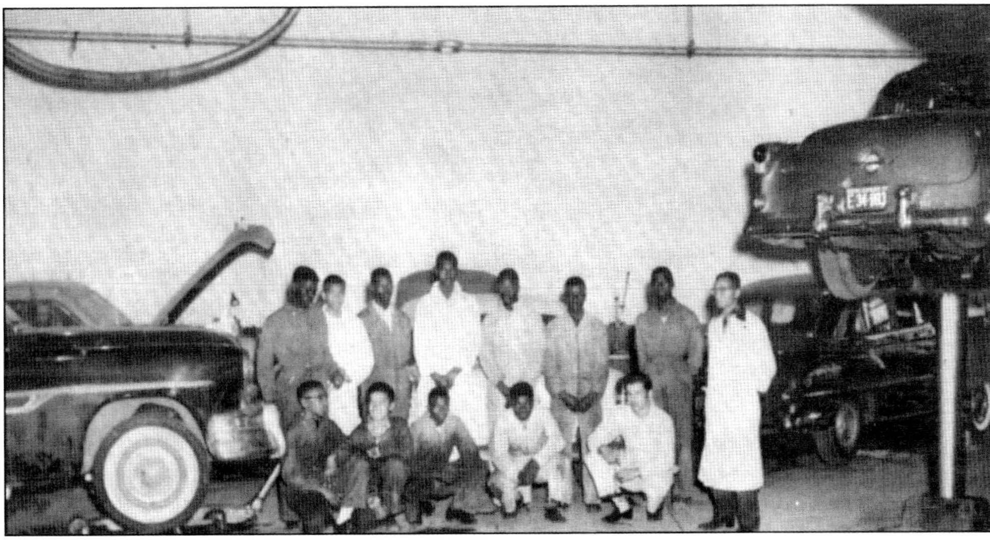

In 1954, students were introduced to auto mechanics, as shown in this image taken in 1959. By 1969, auto mechanics was offered as an adult trade class to those interested in advancing their careers in the area of auto mechanics. (Courtesy of the Avery Research Center.)

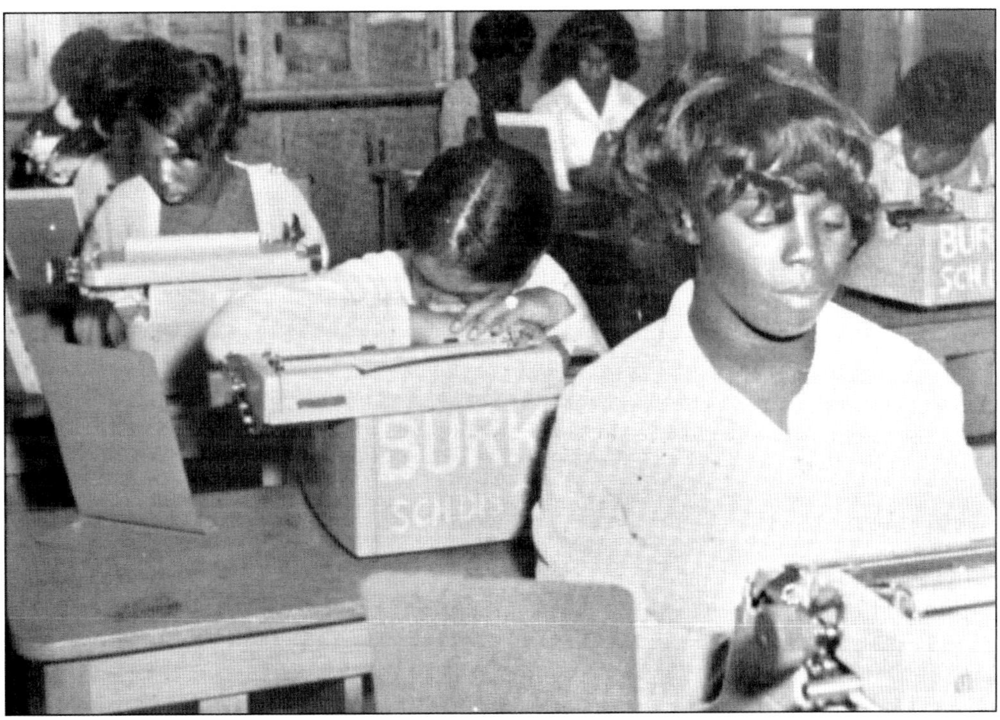

Typing was one of the most requested courses by female students who had an interest in secretarial or office work as a career, as shown in this 1971 photograph. (Courtesy of Burke High School.)

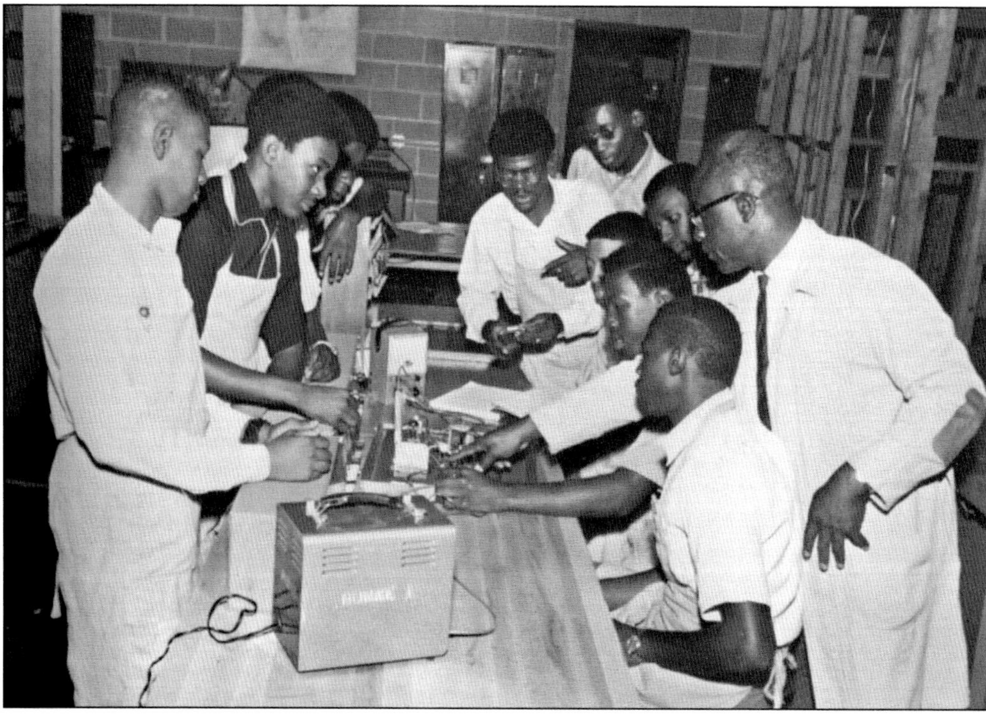

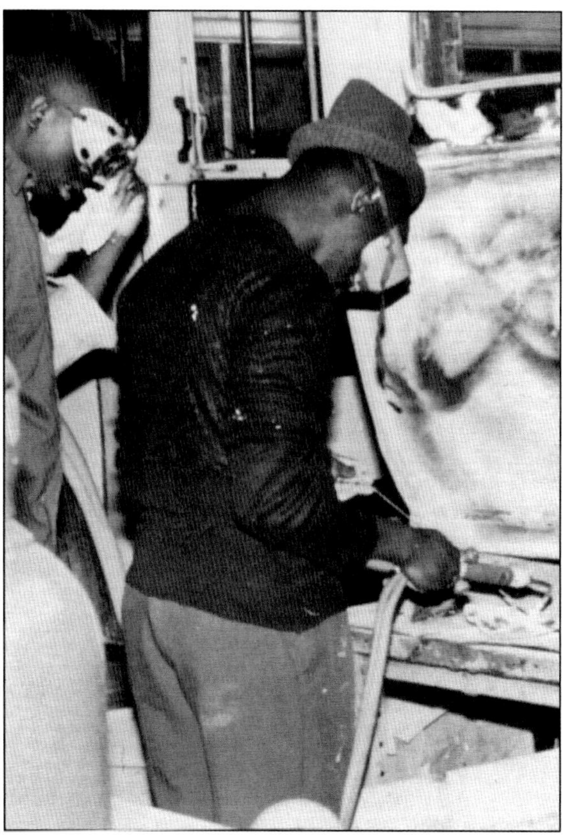

Electronics was first introduced to the students around 1954. This course was taught as a day and night subject, which allowed veterans returning from the 1950 Korean War to pursue a career in the field of electronics. (Courtesy of Burke High School.)

This 1984 image shows students enrolled in a welding class. Welding was first added as a new course around 1940. (Courtesy of Burkc High School.)

Seven

THE *PARVENUE*

In the final analysis, journalism is the engine of a free press, an institution that is protected under the first amendment to the Constitution.

—Rudolph A. Pyatt Jr. (Class of 1951)

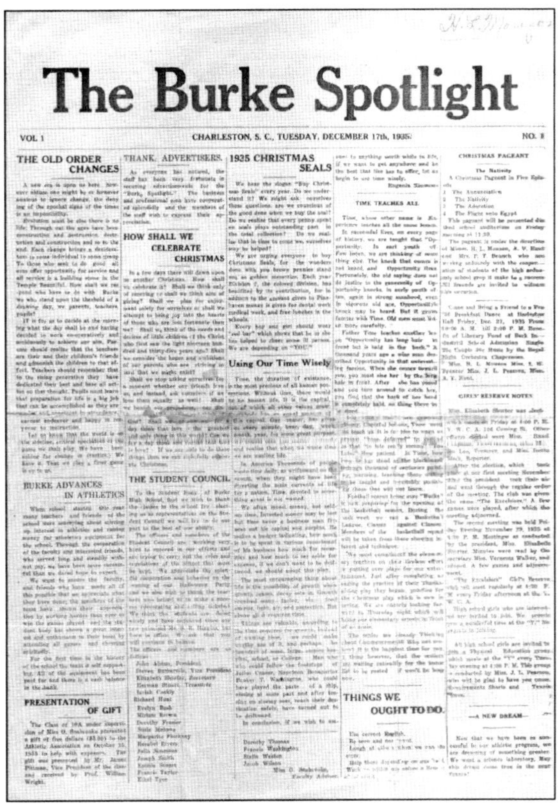

The Burke Spotlight

VOL. 1 CHARLESTON, S. C., TUESDAY, DECEMBER 17th, 1935.

THE OLD ORDER CHANGES

THANK ADVERTISERS

1935 CHRISTMAS SEALS

TIME TEACHES ALL

CHRISTMAS PAGEANT

HOW SHALL WE CELEBRATE CHRISTMAS

Using Our Time Wisely

GIRLS' RESERVE NOTES

THE STUDENT COUNCIL

BURKE ADVANCES IN ATHLETICS

PRESENTATION OF GIFT

THINGS WE OUGHT TO DO

A NEW DREAM

A precursor to the *Parvenue* was the *Spotlight*, which was published in 1935. This issue consisted of four pages front and back. There was an article on page one addressing the faculty, friends, and students regarding their efforts to raise funds to support athletics at the school. Also, on page two, it was revealed that the school's mascot was originally the panther and not the bulldog. (Courtesy of the Avery Research Center.)

The Parvenue

"A Guide To Ideas and Ideals"

VOL. X — Burke Industrial School, Charleston, S. C., November, 1948 — NO. 1

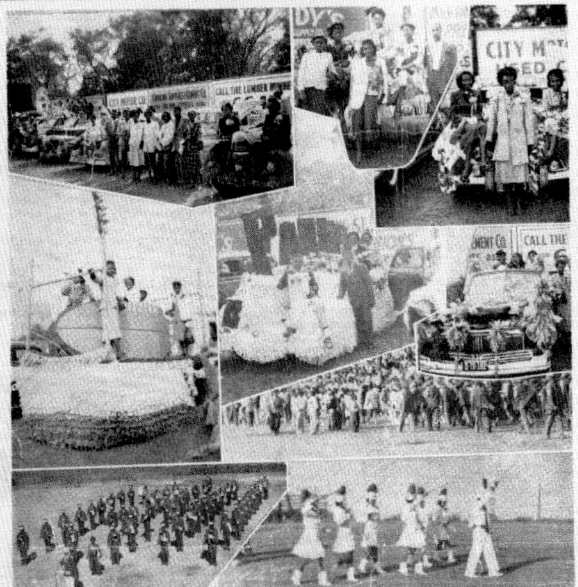

HOMECOMING SHOTS—Shown above are shots of Burke's Homecoming celebration. Top row from left to right are parade ... Parvenue"; "Miss Senior"; spectators. Bottom row—The Band and Majorettes.

Bulldogs - Tigers Clash in Annual Turkey Day Tilt

BOTH TEAMS PREDICT WIN

By ESTELLE ANCRUM

Here it comes again, the day of all good eatings; and the fighting Bulldogs and the brave Tigers are raring to go on their annual turkey day classic at Harmon Field November 25, 1948.

Avery Tigers have a ten game schedule. So far this season she has won four games, lost one and tied one.

She has a well balanced team this year. They run from both box and "T" formation as well.

Outstanding men are: H. Murphy, fullback; F. Wright, quarterback; E. Iracks, right halfback; Oscar Fordham, left halfback; W. Farrette, C. Duncan, C. Seabrooke, T. Haynes, T. Hart.

Coach Bligen has said "Last year's game was a tough one to lose. We had an accident on the first play of the game which really hurt us, but

(Continued on Page 5)

Homecoming Day Is Successful

By JUANITA WIGFALL

Charleston is reminiscing today about the Homecoming celebration of Burke Industrial School held Friday, October 29, which climaxed a week of preparation for an elaborate welcome for the alumni and friends.

The celebration got under way at 1:30 p. m. when thousands gazed at the variety of floats, which depicted the truth of what life at Burke means in: journalism, music, language, art, government, dramatics, trades, sports, gardening, scouting, debating and Christian living. There were thirty-two groups on parade.

The parade, which featured "Miss Burke" and representatives from all organizations in the school went down President to Line street; from Line to Ashley Avenue; Ashley Avenue to Morris, Morris to Coming, Coming to Line, Line to Rutledge, Rutledge to Cleveland, and Cleveland to College Park, where the Burke Bulldogs and the Howard High Tigers of Georgetown, S. C., met in a football match.

The Bulldogs came out victorious with a score of 19-0. At half time, the eighth graders formed the two school letters. The veterans also entertained the spectators by displaying the unique manner in drilling.

American Education Week Begins; Many Discussions Planned

By FRANCENA SANDERS

"Strengthening the Foundation of Freedom" is the theme of American Education Week observance which began November 7 and will end November 13. During this week schools and communities everywhere will join together to observe a common purpose.

The theme has been outlined into daily topics as follows: Monday, "Improving the Education Program"; Tuesday, "Securing Qualified Teachers"; Wednesday, 'Providing Adequate Finance"; Thursday, "Safeguarding Our America"; Friday, "Promoting Health and Safety"; Saturday, "Worthy Family Life"; Sunday, "Living to Live Together".

Information about these topics will be conveyed through plays, radio programs, bulletin boards displays, public program, and classroom discussion.

5th Annual Red Feather Campaign Underway

By VIOLA ROBINSON

Charleston County Community Chest started the fifth annual Red Feather campaign October 18, for advance gift section and November 1, for general solicitation. Burke's faculty's goal was $500. Up to the time Parvenue went to press approximately $453.50 was pledged.

Students Enter Letter Writing Contest

Sixty-one letters were sent by the English department, of Burke, to be

(Continued on Page 3)

Night Courses Again Offered at Burke

By LEONA MIDDLETON

Courses in masonry, tailoring, carpentry and domestic services began at Burke October 5, and courses in first aid, child care and home nursing began November 2.

The courses in trade are open to men and women who expect to work in specific trades. The instructors are Mr. Wright, carpentry; Mr. Fields, masonry; Mr. Graham, tailoring and Mrs. Edwards, sewing.

The other courses are opened to

(Continued on Page 3)

Many Activities Mark Book Week Observance

Book Week observance November 16 to 22 will be highlighted with two assembly programs, a book fair, open house, and bulletin board displays. All activities will be centered around its theme, "Books Tell the Story".

Noted Author Guest Speaker

Miss Catherine Drayton Mayrant Simons will be the guest speaker at assembly November 17. Miss Simons, whose home is near Charleston, has published stories and poems in book form. She has written articles for "Saturday Evening Post", "New York Times" and other periodicals.

Her latest book "Sword for Galway" has been selected by the book league. "The Pattern is her first publication.

Miss Simons has traveled extensively in the United States and Western Europe. During the past summer she traveled in Spain and Ireland.

She is interested in sports and is a lover of dogs and horses.

Club to Present Play

At assembly, November 19, the Library club will present a play. This will convey to the meaning of the theme "Books Tell the Story".

Book Fair and Open House Featured

A book fair and open house will be given at 8 p. m. November 19. This affair is opened to parents, friends, and students. It will be highlighted with speakers from noted authors and an elaborate display of books. This marks the third annual Book Fair sponsored by Burke's Library.

The Annual Turkey Day Football Classic between Burke and Avery High School was played on Harmon Field. There were times when the game was played at College Park, but the game was always played on Thanksgiving Day. (Courtesy of the Avery Research Center.)

MERRY CHRISTMAS

The Parvenue

"A Guide To Ideas and Ideals"

VOL. XI — Burke Industrial School, Charleston, S. C., December 20, 1949 — NO. 2

YULETIDE SPIRIT PREVAILS AT BURKE

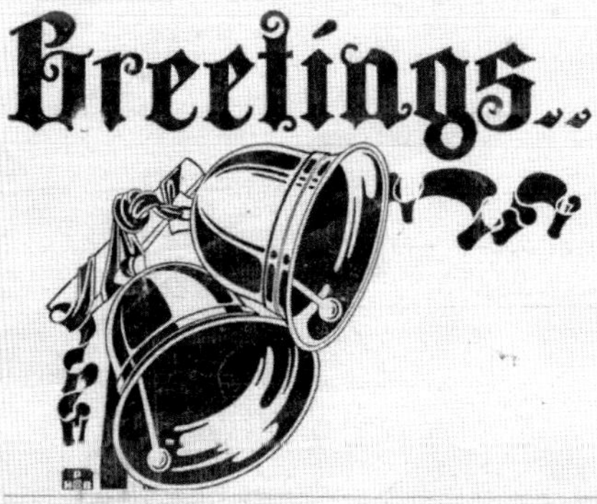

White Christmas Commences at Burke

By BEULAH JENKINS

In order to spread Christmas joy, and to help the students get the spiritual impression of Christmas, the Student Council, Dramatic Club, choral group, and the band will sponsor its annual Christmas Observance, December 20, 1949 during the school day in the Frasier Field Auditorium.

STUDENTS TO GIVE GIFTS TO NEEDY

Activities will be marked with the annual observance of White Christmas which is the collecting of useful gifts such as baskets for the less fortunate ones. Each homeroom class will prepare a box decorated as colorful as they have been in previous years. These boxes will be arranged artistically beneath the traditional Christmas tree. Other decorations will include holly, wreathes, candals, and bells.

DRAMATIC CLUB TO PRESENT, [illegible]

The main feature on the program will consist of a play presented by the Dramatic Club, entitled "The Carol of The World", by Roger M. Bushfield, Jr. This is a one-act play in two scenes. The characters are Josef Mohr played by Allen Breach, a village priest; Mistress Mott played by Lauretta Smith, his housekeeper; Herr Linck, played by Ernest King, a member of his Parrish, and Franz Grubers, played by LeRoy Nesbit, the village schoolmaster and organist.

The entire action takes place in a Church in Austria on Christmas Eve, 1818. Scene one is later evening and scene two is some hours later.

"The Carol of the World" is the story of the writing of "Silent Night". On Christmas Eve in 1818 a village priest is asked to bless a baby to be born that evening. Despite, the protestations of his housekeeper, he goes. Later the village schoolmaster organist read over the poem the priest was inspired to write. Because of the breakdown of the Church organ, composes a tune for the world's first Christmas carol.

(Continued on Page 4)

Burke Becomes an "A" Rated Institution

Mr. Nichols has announced that Burke has been named an "A" rated institution by the Southern Association of Colleges and Schools accrediting committee.

The announcement came from Houston, Texas, where the association was holding its annual meeting. Mr. Nichols was notified in Daytona Beach, Florida, where he was attending the Southern Association of Colleges and Secondary Schools annual meeting.

Having an "A" rating means much to the students and they seem to be very happy about it.

Christmas Seal Sale Conducted at Burke

During the month of December Burke, like other schools and communities all over the country is aiding the National Association in raising funds to help people in the prevention and cure of tuberculosis by selling and buying tuberculosis Christmas seals.

Promotional activities at Burke include special projects like attractive Bulletin boards in classroom and auditorium; all school participation in school press proejct and Student Council post office.

Approximately 53,000 Christmas Seals have been distributed at Burke: 40,000 to students and 13,000 to teachers. Up to date $100

(Continued on Page 3)

Christmas Vacation Will Be Enjoyed By Burke Students

By JOSEPHINE LEGARE

Throughout Burke reports indicate a fairly happy and joyous Christmas vacation. For when school closes for the holidays today students will begin to carry out their plans as follows: some are going away from home; some will relax at home some will engage in light fun like skating, bicycling and visiting friends and relatives. Of course there will be gift giving and gift receiving; and eating too.

Here are a few places some are planning to visit:

Jaunita Wigfall of class 3-2 is spending her vacation with her mother in San Francisco, California.

(Continued on Page 3)

BURKE - AVERY IN COMBINED XMAS CONCERT

By BEULAH JENKINS

Over one-hundred voices from Burke and Avery blended together in a Christmas concert at Morris Street Baptist Church on December 16, 1949, at 8:30 P. M.

This was the first time Burke and Avery have had a joint Christmas concert. Avery and Burke sang together "Lo How-A Rose E'er Blooming". This concert was under the direction of Mr. H. H. Fleming. Mr. J. Hall and Mr. J. M. Graves were accompanists.

BURKE'S CHOIR WORE NEW ROBES

Burke's choral group wore their new robes for the first time. They are made of blue satin, bell sleeves with white satin lining, square yoke and shirred in the front and back, the [illegible] work was done by Mesdames Bonaparte, Edwards, and Miss V. C. Green, and some of the students of the sewing department.

PROGRAM CONSISTED OF MANY SELECTIONS

The choral society and choir offered the following selections: Processional and recessional, "Hark! The Herald Angels Sing" (Mendelssohn), Burke's choir and Avery's choral society; prologue, "Lo, How a Rose E'er Blooming" (Praetorius), by both groups; "Break Forth O Beauteous Heavenly Light" (Bach), "The Carol of the Angels" (Niles), "Willie Take Your Drum" (Burgundian carol), "The Sleep of the Infant Jesus" (Gaveart), "I Wonder as I Wander" (Niles), "Carol of the Bells" (Leonovitch-Wilhousky), by Avery's choral society; "The First Christmas" (Gerrit Smith), "Sing We the Virgin Mary" (arr. Niles-Horton), "As It Fell Upon a Night" (arr. K. Davis), "Follow the Star" (arr. Fleming), "Go Tell It on the Mountain" (traditional), "Wasn't That a Mighty Day" (John Work), by Burke's choir; also "In the Stable" (arr. John Cozen), "Silent Night" (Gruber), "We Wish You a Merry Christmas" English folk song), by the society and the choir.

100% PARVENUE SUBSCRIBERS

By ESSIE LEE FORD

"High distinction" rating goes to the same class for the second consecutive year, Class 1-4 is the only 100% class subscribing to the Parvenue. When they were classified as eighth grade with Miss Smith as homeroom teacher and Leonard Ashby as reporter, they held the same rating. They are now ninth graders with Mrs. Caffey as their homeroom teacher and L. Gethers as the reporter.

Other classes that rate in per cent of subscription are: Mrs. Howard, 81.8% Lillie Mae Ferguson reporter; Miss Heyward 79.4%, Lorraine Ball reporter.

STAFF PLANS PARTY

At the staff meeting Wednesday, December 7, 1949, the staff planned to give Mrs. Caffey's class a party in January for being 100% for two consecutive years. They received a pennant with 100% engraved on it, the first year.

NINTH GRADE LEVEL RATES HIGHEST IN SUBSCRIPTIONS

The ninth grade level rates highest with 107 subscriptions. Eighth grade level 75; tenth grade level 70; eleventh grade level 55; and seniors 25 and veterans 17.

PERCENTAGE HIGHER IN STREET SALES

Street subscriptions rate as high as 344. Essie Lee Ford 86, Estelle Ancrum 54, Leomia Brown 48, Martha Sanders 41; Beulah Jenkins 34, Carolyn Smith 28; Ruth Grimes 25, Lillie Mae Ferguson 17, Sadie Jacobs 16, Pecola Moore 14, and Patsy Simson 11.

At the time of this writing approximately $278.46 has been collected for subscriptions whereas only a total of $151.86 was collected last year up to this time. This total does not include single copies. Total subscriptions are 693.

Parvenue Is Granted Certificate Award

By LEON GIBBS

Burke's student publication, The Parvenue, has received a national award certificate "for distinctive achievements in celebrating National Newspaper Week". The certificate was granted by the Quill & Scroll, an international honorary society for high school journalists.

The award was granted to the Parvenue Bulletin, which carried details of the part Parvenue played in the celebration of National Newspaper Week.

In 1949, it was announced that Burke was named an "A"-rated institution by the Southern Association of Colleges and Schools; however, the school was not fully accredited by that same body until 1954. (Courtesy of the Avery Research Center.)

Staff Submits Instructions for Annual Subscription Campaign

Plans were submitted to the homeroom classes last week for the Parvenue staff's annual subscription campaign which officially began October 1.

100% Goal

The goal, this year, is to make every Burke student a Parvenue subscriber through a special 100% class plan which was submitted to each homeroom September 27.

A class pledges 100%; each member must make the necessary down payment of 10c by October 5; the balance is to be paid in 60 days.

100% Classes

Up to date eleven classes have signed up to use this plan: Mrs. Howard, Miss Pyatt, Mrs. F. Grant, Mr. J. D. English, Miss I. H. Spencer, Mr. I. M. Hutchinson, Mrs. D. S. Holmes, Mrs. Simpson, Mrs. Seabrook, Mrs. P. T. Holmes, Miss B. Sheares, Mrs. V. Maconic, Miss H. Clark.

All 100% classes will receive a certificate.

"Miss Parvenue" Contest

The annual "Miss Parvenue" contest was also launched last week. Twenty-four classes sent candidates: they were from the homeroom classes of Mrs. Grant, Mrs. Howard, Mrs. Seabrook, Mrs. P. T. Holmes, Mrs. Bonaparte, Mrs. Oglesby, Mrs. G. O. Hutchinson, Mr. I. M. Hutchinson, Miss Simpkins, Mr. H. P. Hutchinson, Miss Pyatt, Miss Willams, Mr. Long, Miss McGriff, Mr. Hill, Mrs. Martin;

Also Mr. Moore, Miss Clark, Mr. Cook, Mrs. Moses, Mrs. Rhodes, Mrs. Carr, Mrs. Campbell, Miss Sheares, Mrs. D. S. Holmes and Mrs. H. G. Simpson.

The student selling the largest amount of subscriptions in the community will be crowned "Miss Parvenue". The contest began October 5 and will close October 12.

Forty-five reporters and forty-four candidates for "Miss Parvenue" met and received instructions on techniques of selling yearly subscriptions.

Reporters

The homeroom reporters are as follows: seniors, Norma Mack, Ruth Rivers, Ruby Morris, Donella Reid, Joseph Bacote, Leola Hankerson, Curtis McCormick, Effius Matthews;

Juniors—Delores Frazier, Ella Mae Middleton, Josephine Ford, Frances Nelson, Beatrice Gibbs, Carrie Gardener, Allen Smalls, Barbara Keith, Eulalie Jenkins;

Sophomores—Alma Bowles, Frank Smith, Helen Mack, Mary Lee Ballard, Vermelle Johnson, Edna Garrett, Marthena Mills, Juliette Devine, Martha Whaley, Bertha Mae Jones, Shirley Alston;

Freshmen — Cynthia Felder, Lillie M. Gladden, Margaret Prior, Mable Small, Delores Thompson, Geneva Payne, Sheran Duncan, Alfred Brown;

Eighth Graders—Mildred Graham, Evelyn Taylor, Francena Devine, Georgette Horry, Miriam Ramsey, Marietta Hayes, Elijah Walker, Rosalind Benton, Barbara Kinlock, Harold Jackson and Wendell Lawrence.

Candidates

The following are candidates for "Miss Parvenue":

Seniors —Norma Mack, Gloria Gibbs, Donella Reid, Theresa Mack.

Juniors — Loraine Robinson, Irene Washington, Vermelle Forworth, Dorothy Fell, Myrtle Grant, Clara Batie.

Tenth grade—Sylvia Dawson, Joan Broughton, Alma Bowles, Shirley Smalls.

Ninth—Martha Simmons, Cynthia Felder, Joel Duncan, Lillian Jenkins, Lillie Mae Lucas, Lillie Mae Kinlock, Helen Smalls, Thema Hutchinson, Ruth Conyers, Deleres Thompson, Ruth Gentry.

Eighth —Delores Williams, Barbara Kinlock, Marie Johnson, Doris Brown, Carrie Govan, Dolores Sanders, Anne Lawrence, Lillie Mae Ricks, Clara White, Irene Grant, Vermelle Holmes, Emily Newton, Marietta Hayes, Rosalind Benton.

Also — Alfreda Williams, Miriam Ramsey, Albertha Brooks, Martha Simmons, Georgetta Horry, Beatrice Smalls, Eleanor Felder, and Margret McBeth.

A Dedication to Freedom and the Free Press

October 1 to 8 marks the observance of National Newspaper Week throughout America. It is dedicated to the cause of freedom and the free press.

Freedom of the press, given to us by our forefathers through the constitution, has long since helped the true light of freedom.

In surpressed countries where freedom is just a word, people cannot express their ideas and ideals. They cannot print the facts or what they may think on the ways of the government.

We, Americans, should be ever thankful for the newspaper which is truly a light to freedom. For the newspaper prints the unbiased truth; it is unpredudiced. We can express our opinions through the newspaper without fear of imprisonment or even death.

We are blessed to be living in a country that is free and allows us to enjoy the privileges of a free press.

Barbara Johnson.

The Parvenue

"A Guide To Ideas and Ideals"

Vol. XV No. 1 — Burke High School, Charleston, S. C. — October 9, 1953

Home Ec. and Science Buildings to Be Ready by Jan.

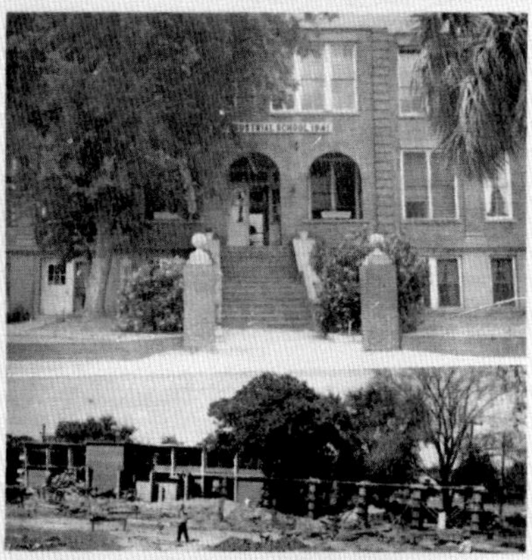

Top picture: Burke's main Building before it was demolished; bottom pictures: New buildings under construction.

School Board Considering Lot Behind Harmon Field For Burke's Gymnasium

One of the four buildings which is a part of Burke's extensive building program is now nearing completion. This building which will house the home economic department is scheduled for completion around the first of the year. Burke will then have the best home economic building in the state. A second building which is to house the science department is also scheduled to be completed at that time.

The Gymnasium

At a meeting September 18 the School Board abandoned plans for Harmon Field as a possible site for the proposed gymnasium. They are now considering a city owned lot behind Harmon Field.

This building program began May, 1953. Since then the old main building has been completely demolished. The foundation is now being laid for the buildings which will be occupied by the library and administration departments. These buildings are scheduled to be completed by September, 1954.

Across the street on the site of the old U. S. O. building an auditorium will be built. This construction has not been started.

A Special Assembly Climaxes Activities Of News Week

With a special assembly keyed to make students conscious of the importance of reading the school's publication and all newspapers, the Parvenue staff climaxed its National Newspaper Week activities October 7.

News week activities officially began October 1 when President Willis Goodwin issued a proclamation to each homeroom class. Other activities ncluded special units on the newspaper worked out in the English classes; also bulletin board and poster displays.

The assembly program was divided into two parts: the first part featured speeches by the editor and the president of the Student Council.

Editor Anderson explained the policies of the school paper; and President Goodwin reviewed last year's headline happenings.

The second part was a T. V. quiz program. Questions were taken from the speeches. Subscriptions to the Parvenue were given as prizes. The grand prize was a trip.

The music department under the supervision of Mr. Fleming furnished the music. Juliette Devine was chairman; Barbara Johnson quiz director and Joe Louis Williams gave the invocation.

Enrollment Shows 130 Less Students

1,599 students are now enrolled at Burke: 648 boys, 906 girls, and 45 veterans, according to a report of September 21. This is a 130 less students than last year.

The eighth grade has the largest number of students: 417. There are 193 seniors, 259 juniors, 331 Sophomores and 354 freshmen.

The greatest drop was in the ninth grade; there were 447 ninth graders last year; the seniors also dropped from 215. The other classes have remained practically the same.

Editor Anderson Explains Policies Of the School Publication for Term

Editor-in-chief Alvin Anderson said in assembly this week that there is a need for more emphasis on the third freedom.

The editor in a speech to the students of Burke at a special assembly in observance of Newspaper Week set forth the following policies:

"It will serve as a guide to ideas and ideals by reserving the right to censor any material that is detrimental to an individual or group.

"But at the same time be ever conscious of needed improvements and present these situations in a tactful manner.

"No debatable issues will be publicized without presenting the views of both sides.

"The authenticity of all news will be carefully checked.

"It will publicize life at Burke—the achievements of individuals and groups.

Personal Expressions Part Of English Orientation

What's your line? What's on your mind? as a part of a unit on personal expressions were thoroughly enjoyed by English students at Burke.

This was a part of an intensive five-day orientation program initiated by the English department September 14 to 18.

Other phases of this program included such topics as know your school, administration, teachers and fellow students; greetings and conversations.

This issue revealed that the school was involved in a major construction project. Furthermore, there was a discussion about the possibility of a new gymnasium being built on the campus. The proposed gymnasium did not materialize until 14 years later. (Courtesy of the Avery Research Center.)

Charleston's Dream of A New Burke Soon To Become A Reality

That beautiful dream of so many Burke-ites and ex-Burkeites is about to become a reality. Work will begin on the construction of the new Burke in 90 days and is expected to be completed in a year.

A statement to this effect was obtained from Mr. George C. Rogers, Charleston's superintendent of public schools on March 23. Mr. Rogers sat behind his desk in his second floor St. Philip street office, looking statesman-like, wearing reading spectacles.

When questioned as to the exact time the construction of the new Burke will begin, the superintendent thought for a few seconds, then replied in a confident tone of voice, "Well, in 90 days anyhow". Indications were that it was possible that the construction would begin even sooner.

Mr. Rogers revealed that the construction program would include plans for six buildings: four academic, a gymnasium and an auditorium. These plans were made public for the first time in November; but at that time no date had been set for the beginning of the construction.

The site of the gymnasium is still uncertain. When queried about it, Mr. Rogers answered "I am still in favor of having it built on Harmon Field." He made it clear that there is no possibility of expanding the Burke school campus. "We'll have to make an agreement with the city to use a portion of Harmon Field", he added. (Harmon Field is owned by the city).

It has been disclosed that the auditorum will be built on the present site of the old U. S. O. building. The four academic buildings will be built in the foreground of the school at angles to the present buildings. The superintendent explained that the present main building "will be torn down to make room."

When asked to comment on the long lived rumor that Charleston's Avery high school will be dissolved when the new Burke is completed, Mr. Rogers replied, "That's not definite, it all depends on whether or not we'll be able to take care of all of the students up there" (at Burke).

This building program, coupled with the building of larger school in the surrounding areas, will make available to the young people of Charleston county much better facilities; and also greatly improve the over-crowded conditions at Burke.

Many new classrooms will be ready for use sometime in early 1954.

The building of the new Burke is part of a multi-million dollar school construction program, launched for the purpose of providing better educational facilities for South Carolina students; and was made possible by the three per cent sales tax enacted in 1951.

According to the superintendent, these new buildings will be equipped with the most modern facilities. The gymnasium will seat 1,080 and will house locker and shower facilities for boys and girls at the opposite ends of the building.

The auditorium will be dome-shaped. It will seat 800 and will contain practice rooms for choral groups and the band.

Editor's Note: Construction has

The Parvenue

"A Guide To Ideas and Ideals"

Don't Miss The Opera

Vol. XIV | Burke High School, Charleston, S. C., April, 1953 | No. 4

Burke Choral Society To Present 'The Bartered Bride' Comic Opera

Burke high school's choir will present a comic opera "The Bartered Bride" (Bedrick Smetana) at 8:15 Monday, May 4 at the Henry P. Archer school's auditorium.

This three act opera is centered around a Feast-day celebration in a Bohemian village . . . where two families are arranging the marriage between the daughter of a peasant Krushina and the son of a wealthy landowner. The entire action of the play takes place from noon immediately after church, until twilight, about 1850.

Vernell Foxworth, soprano, will sing the lead role of Marie, the daughter of the peasant Krushina; and Robert Brown, tenor, will play the leading male role of Jenk, Micha's son by a former marriage, who is posing as a youth in the village.

Other featured soloists will include James Foxworth, bass, as the village marriage broker; Mathew Brown, baritone, a peasant; Mary Bligen, soprano, his wife; Daniel Brown, bass, a landowner; Lillian Wrighten, messo-soprano, his wife.

Alvin Anderson will act the role of Vashek, the simple son of Micha, the wealthy landowner. Ethel Weston will play Esmeralda, a member of the troupe.

More than fifty voices will be in the supporting chorus.

Directors are Miss Naomi Williams, dramatic chariman; and Mr. Harleston Fleming, chairman of the music department. Mr. John Hall is the accompanist.

Tickets are now on sale. Mr. Holland W. Daniels is publicity chairman.

Dramatists Present Two One-Act Plays

Two one-act dramas "The Valiant" by Holworthy Hall and Robert Middlemas; and "The Last Trip Out" by Walter Hackett, was presented by the Dramatic club on April 29 in the annex auditorium.

Ernestine Gadsden played the leading role in "The Last Trip Out" and Theodore Grant lead in "The Valiant".

"The Valiant" is a story of a young man who refuses to reveal his identity and goes to the electric chair for a murder in which he feels quite justified in committing. This play was directed by Mr. E. A. Roper. Supporting roles were played by John Rivers, Nathaniel Green, Isiah Williams, Archie Heyward and Persephone La Prince.

"The Last Trip Out" is the story of a mother and a young woman's experience in the hardship of losing loved ones at sea. The cast was directed by Mrs. R. E. Brown; and included five girls and two boys.

This is the Dramatic club's only production this year.

Staff Members Hold Top Post In P.S.P.A. Receive Awards

Secretary, P. S. P. A. editor, assistant director posts went respectively to Barbara Johnson, Alvin Anderson, and Mrs. M. H. Howard of the Parvenue at the association ninth annual spring meeting, Saturday, April 18, Lincoln High school Sumter.

Parvenue won three awards in the newspaper publication contest: 2nd place poem, Major Dickerson, 3rd place poem, Ernest Thompson, 3rd place news article to Gwendolyn Robinson. The Avery Tiger won best all around and most of the top awards.

Mr. John H. McCray, editor of the Lighthouse and Informer was featured speaker. He did not arrive on schedule so he spoke at the beginning of the business session. His speech was practical and journalistic.

Journalistic workshop were held in the following areas: Make up and type, advertising, photography and yearbook. Barbara Johnson assisted with photography.

Burke Student Leaders End Yearly Projects; Look Toward Graduation

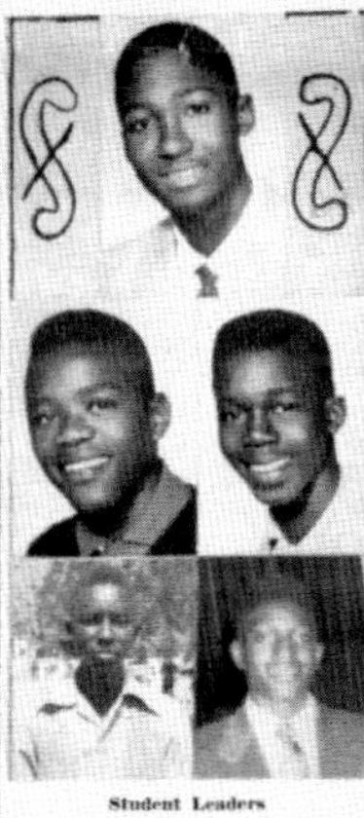

Student Leaders

Presidents (starting from top—reading left to right) William Wright, senior; John Rivers, sophomore; Isaac Brown, eighth grade; Nathaniel Green, junior; Herman Singleton, freshman.

Burke's grade level leaders have completed a full year of activities; and now they are turning their attention to the traditional graduation activities.

William C. Wright, president of the senior class, probably has been the busiest of all leaders and he still has a heavy program ahead of hm: class day, baccalaureate and graduation.

William has assumed his responsibilities very well; and has also taken an active part in other activities like the Dramatic club, Future Teachers, Science club; also president of the Booster club.

Among his greatest accomplishments is writing a play about Father's Day which was presented at the Delta Sigma Theta Sorority's Jabberwock at County Hall February 16.

William plans to study at Hampton Institute Virginia.

Nathaniel Green, president of the junior council, has been very busy also. His major project was the junior-senior prom.

He plans to study law at Fisk university, Nashville, Tennessee. He is president of the Dramatic club. His hobbies are stamp collecting and music.

The sophomores' successful program may be attributed to John Rivers, who is president. He is a very able leader.

He likes chemistry. He is president of the Honor society, president of the Hi-Y, a member of the Dramatic club and Science club.

Much credit should go to Herman Singleton, president of the freshman council for the well conducted "Freshman Day" celebration. He would like to further his study in dramatics. He is a member of the Junior Dramatic club, the Student council and the student patrol. He likes singing.

Isaac Brown holds the title as mayor of the eighth grade. He is over a well planned set up. He would like to be a pharmacist. He is a member of the student patrol. He likes all sports and photography.

Trade Students Receive Awards Willis Goodwin Heads Association

Trade students of Burke won six awards in the Palmetto state tournament which was held at Carver high school, Spartanburg, Thursday, April 23. At that same time Willis Goodwin was elected president of the State Industrial Club.

For first place in tailoring Claretta Gethers received a gold cup. Other Burke winners are 2nd place painting, John Brown; 3rd place carpentry, Louis Stretch; 4th place masonry, James Taylor; 5th place cosmetology, Martha Campbell; 5th place in auto mechanic (Diversified Occupation) Samuel Anderson.

Edward Hamilton was named the photographer for the day.

Bulletin: Doris Brown will be crowned "May Queen" May 8. Her class raised $202.51 in the recent contest.

COMING EVENTS

Physical Educational Exhibition and Coronation of "Miss Burke" .... May 15
May Day Festival, Harmon Field .... May 8th
Baccalaureate .... May 24
Class Night .... May 29
Graduation .... June 4

According to the headlines, plans were finalized for the construction of a new Burke school. George Rogers, Charleston's superintendent of public schools, would not confirm a rumor that upon completion of the school, Avery High School would close and those students would become a part of Burke's student body. (Courtesy of the Avery Research Center.)

Burke's Enrollment Approaches the 2,000 Mark

Increase Shown In 8th Grades

Burke's enrollment nears the 2,000 mark—1,975, not including the 108 veterans who are taught in an afternoon session. This is an increase over the 1,599 students enrolled at Burke Sept. 21, 1953, which included 45 veterans.

The upward surge in enrollment is caused by the abandonment of Avery and the merging of all of the city's Negro high school students at Burke.

The enrollment picture per grade level, as recorded Oct. 20 shows 257 seniors, 367 juniors, 458 freshmen, and 536 eighth graders. This compared with last year's enrollment shows an increase in all grades with the greatest increase in the eighth. Last year there were 417 in the eighth grades, 354 freshmen, 331 sophomores, 258 juniors, and 193 seniors.

This is the largest enrollment in the history of Burke. Only one other time did the enrollment near this mark: in 1950-'51 the enrollment was recorded as 1,922 and that included 166 veterans.

Burke is the largest school in Charleston. According to the Sept. 21 enrollment figures, there is a combined total of 1,635 students in the city's three other high schools.

Burke's Staff Has Four New Teachers

New appointments to the faculty and staff of Burke include only four new teachers.

Miss Mildred D. Jones, a graduate of Burke, is teaching English speech and theory in cosmetology. She received her bachelor of science degree in speech and drama from New York University. Her hobbies are doll making, dancing, sports and many other things.

Frank Miller is teaching art. He is a graduate of Booker Washington High School, of Columbia, S. C., and Claflin college, Orangeburg. This is his first year of teaching. He declared sports to be his hobby, with basketball as his favorite.

Elijah Johnson is teacher of auto mechanics. He received his high school training in Orangeburg. He has worked with the diversified occupatons program for a number of years. He stated that his hobby is working with automobiles.

Mrs. Thelma J. Rice is the newest appointment to the faculty. Her high school training was received at Avery. She received a bachelor of science degree in home economics from Hampton Institute, Va. Her experience includes two years at Jamestown Junior High School. She is teaching civics in the eighth grade. Her hobbies include sewing and reading.

With New Teachers Faculty Numbers 82

Burke's faculty consists of 82 members, not including the principal, vice principal, three secretaries, custodian staff and cafeteria management.

With the exception of D. Jack Moses, who is supervisor of music in the elementary schools, and John F. Potts, who resigned to accept the presidency of Voorhees School and Junior College, Burke's personnel includes the complete faculty and staff of Avery.

The entire faculty was introduced to the student body at an orientation assembly, Wednesday, September 15. At this time Samuel Jones, president of the student council, welcomed the students and other student heads explained the purposes of the various activities.

DRAMA GUILD IN CONTEST

The Drama Guild will present "The Twelve Pound Look" by James N. Barrie, in the annual drama contest which will be held Thursday and Friday Nov. 11-12 at Buist auditorium.

November 11 Is Important Date for Burke Parents

P.T.A. Meeting, American Education Week

Mr. Hoursey Compares Old Burke With New Burke High School

"Mr. Collins may not know it but where his office is now there was a burial ground. I'm not talking about 1952, 1951, 1950, 1949 or 1948; but I'm talking about 1916, the year I was graduated from what was Burke then. In fact when the first building was built, workmen dug up skeletons."

A. W. Hoursey, teacher of journalism, declared this to a Parvenue reporter last week when he was approached concerning a comparison of the new and old Burke.

According to Mr. Hoursey, there is not much left to compare, because the framed shop building is the only one left of the original structures. He stated that at that time there were white teachers and Burke's highest grade was an advanced eighth.

He spoke with frankness and sincerity. He emphasized that it is important that students today should recognize and appreciate the present teachers and cooperate with them in establishing a school of high standards.

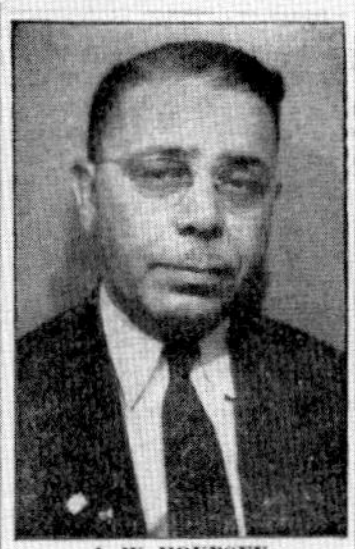

A. W. HOURSEY

Mr. Hoursey, for 21 years, was adviser to the Avery High School publication, and a teacher at Avery for 28 years. Besides journalism, he has worked for years with the Hi-Y club.

Library Personnel Plans Book Fair

November 11 is an important date for Burke parents; for besides being the regular PTA meeting night, it is the time that the school will be in the midst of the observance of American Education Week, which will begin the week of Nov. 7.

During that time, the library personnel plans a Book Fair in observance of Book Week.

"Good Schools Are Your Responsibility" is the theme of Education Week; and activities will feature special assemblies, homeroom discussions. Parents will have a chance to view the physical plant of Burke.

Daily topics will be Sunday, Ideals to Live by"; Monday, "Teachers for Tomorrow"; Tuesday, "Investing in Good Schools", Wednesday, "Working Together for Good Schools"; Thursday, "Effective Citizenship"; Friday, "Teaching the Fundamentals Today"; and Saturday, "How Good Are Your Schools?"

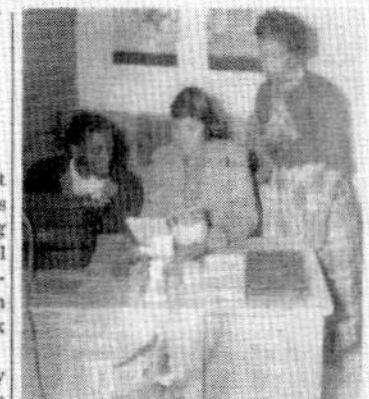

PLANNING BOOK WEEK—Walter Dilligard, left, looks over Book Week plans with librarians Mrs. H. E. Jenkins, center, and Miss T. Brown standing, in one of the offices of the library.

Principal W. G. Nichols states that committees are now being formed; and specific plans are not complete for American Education Week as of this date.

Library Club Plans

During Book Week, the Library club plans to have an assembly program; also a Book Week tea. The club's enrollment consists of seven boys and eleven girls. The purpose is to stimulate reading and to encourage the use of the library.

The officers of the club are Dorothy Stanyard, president; Barbara Fetterson, vice president; Barbara Leach, secretary; Andrea Brown, treasurer; Walter Dilligard, reporter and Gwendolyn Simmons, program chairman.

The Parvenue

A Guide to Ideas and Ideals

Vol. XVI No. 1 — Burke High School, Charleston, S. C., October-November, 1954

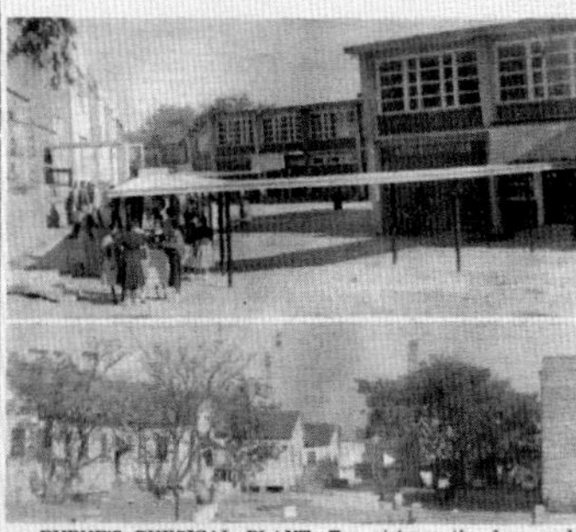

BURKE'S PHYSICAL PLANT—Top picture: the four modern buildings: administration, library, science and home making; also to the left the 35-room section; the covered way connecting the buildings. The administrative offices and the doctor and nurse's offces take up the entire first floor of the administration building; the library extends the entire length of the first floor of the second building.

Bottom picture: the framed trade buildings; the curved roofed building in the foreground houses the cafeteria and the auto mechanic shop. A part of the rear of the 35-room building is shown here also.

Physical Plant Comprises 71 Teaching Units Including 4 Modern Buildings

Burke's physical plant consists of 71 teaching units. Twenty teaching units are in the four modern new structures: adminstration building, four; library, three; science, six; the homemaking building seven.

The old addition, which has 35 rooms, stems from a four room annex to later, eight rooms; then still later a 23-room addition connecting a four room building. The four room building was erected as a science building in 1944. Most of the ninth grade classes are in this section now.

Ten teachers share rooms with other teachers; thus they move to a different classroom each period of the six-period day, which begins for eighth graders and students who take trade at 8 a. m. The eighth grade students' school day ends at 1:15 p. m. The remainder of the student body go home at 3:20 p. m., with the exception of the diversified occupations students who leave for on the job training at 1 p. m.

Mr. Nichols Praises Pupils' Adjustment

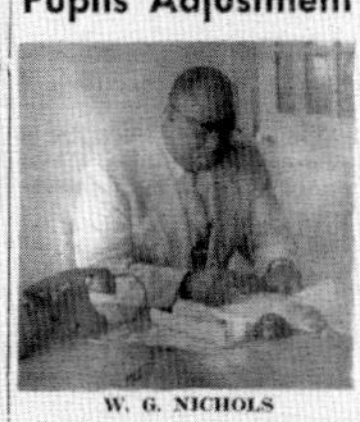

W. G. NICHOLS

Old and new students are making nice adjustments in the opinion of Principal W. G. Nichols, when asked his impression of the students. He expressed hopes that it continues that way.

He pointed out that there is a lot of room for improvement, especially in changing classes. "We need to pass to recess more quickly and quietly," he declared, "for other classes are still in session."

Mr. Nichols, whose office has been located for the past year in the 35-room annex building, was in the midst of moving to his new streamlined office in the modern attractive administration building. He says he'll miss the bustle of the heavy traffic of the old building.

Mr. Nichols has been principal of Burke for the past eight years. His sunny personality and understanding has made him a favorite among students.

He emphasized that "As high school students, everybody has a job."

He sincerely believes in the students and expressed confidence that each student is trying to fulfill his obligations.

Seven New Courses Added to Curricula

Auto mechanics is among the seven new courses added to Burke's curriculum this year. Other courses include art, Spanish, speech and journalism which is now offered for full unit credit. Also trade mathematics, senior survey mathematics and senior advanced mathematics.

For years, auto mechanics was promised as a course. The building was built since 1944 and used for welding during war time; later as a gym and auditorium, then as a masonry shop; last year as a library; and even now a study hall is in one corner of it; also a book room along with the auto mechanic class.

Teaching auto mechanics is Elijah Johnson; art, Frank Miller; journalsm, A. W. Hoursey; speech, Mrs. M. D. Seabrook, Mrs. F. E. Hicklin and Miss Mildred Jones. Mrs. Hicklin also teaches Spanish. I. M. Hutchirson teaches trade mathematics, J. Michael Graves, senior survey and Mrs. G. P. Singleton, senior advanced mathematics.

Radio, Television Among Courses Offered at Night

Night school courses include radio and television; also auto mechanics this year. This is the first time adults have had the opportunity to take this course at Burke.

The first classes were held Monday, Oct. 11, and classes will continue to be held two nights a week, Monday and Wednesday, for six months.

Randolph Perry of Simonton is the instructor in radio and television.

Other courses offered include masonry, painting, typing, bookkeeping, tailoring.

By 1954, the school population had reached 2,000. Also, the faculty consisted of 82 members, including the majority of Avery's faculty and staff. In addition, details were given about the new courses that were added to the curriculum in 1954. (Courtesy of the Avery Research Center.)

The Parvenue

"A Guide to Ideas and Ideals"

Vol. 26:3 Burke High School, Charleston, S. C. March, 1966

Bulldogs Await New Home

It seems that Burke will finally get a long overdue and much needed gym. The preliminary plans for the gym which will seat approximately 1,200 for basketball games and 2,000 for assembly programs have been drawn. In addition to gym and auditorium facilities the building is proposed to house facilties for the band and choir.

The tentative plans for the band compound provide for a general practice area to accommodate its 120 members, individual sound proof practice rooms, office area, storage rooms, and a musical library. Also, included in these plans are air-conditioning and intercommunications systems.

The plan for the chorale area is similar to that of the band area including a general practice area, individual practice rooms, office, dressing rooms and musical library.

The actual gymnasium area will have provisions for classrooms for instructions in theory, office area, storage rooms, first-aid room, and separate dressing rooms for stage area and gym classes. The gym's playing area will have the dimensions of a regulation basketball court with the plaing areas for other games such as shuffleboard, badminton, and tennis marked out on the floor.

If these plans materialize we will have a gym that we can point to with pride. No longer will we have to be ashamed to entertain visitors in our gym because this new gym promises to be representative of Burke High School.

By Harriett E. Jenkins

New Teachers Join Faculty

We are proud to welcome to the staff this semester, four additional teachers. They are: Mrs. C. M. Washington, a native of Charleston, is a graduate of Bonds-Wilson High School. She attended Claflin College in Orangeburg, South Carolina where she received her Bachelor of Arts Degree in English. She formerly taught at Bonds - Wilson. Mrs. Washington plans to attend summer school this summer to work on an Advanced Degree.

Mrs. T. B. Henry, a native of Newberry, South Carolina, is a graduate of Gallman High School. She attended Allen University in Columbia, South Carolina where she majored in English and minored in Social Studies.

Mrs. M. F. Bennett is a native of Bamberg, South Carolina and a graduate of Richard Carroll High School. She majored in Biology, minored in General Science, and received her Bachelor of Science Degree at Morris College in Sumter, South Carolina. She attended Union College in Schenectady, New York where she received her Masters of Science Degree. She has done additional work at the Univefsity of South Carolina and is a former teacher of Rhett Elementary School.

Mr. M. Dennis, a native of Charleston, is a graduate of Burke High School and of South Carolina State College. He majored in Social Studies and minored in Sociology and Biology.

To our new faculty members, we welcome you and hope your experiences here at Burke will be enjoyable ones.

By Elaine Washington

Music Society Gets Charter

Burke High school has received a charter to establish a chapter of modern music master on its campus. Membership in this honor society is the highest recognition that can be given to a music student in senior high school. The sponsor of this international music honor society will be Mr. R. A. Faord. The chapter promises to bring new, youthful and many musical adventures to students at Burke. Students chosen are reminded by the sponsor that they are to keep their high ideals and set a fine example to the rest of the student body. The requirements are based on excellence in performance or performance practices and good Character, Service, Leadership, Scholarship, Musicianship, and Cooperation. Mr. Foard reminds us that it is important for all of us to encourage these fine young people in their efforts, not only by enjoying their tribute to music, but by letting them know how much their music means to us.

By Elaine Washington

Betty Crocker Winner Named

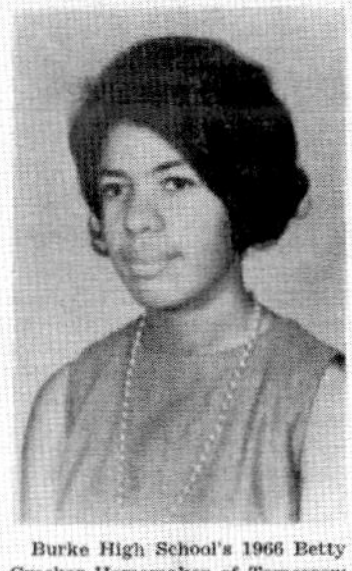

Burke High School's 1966 Betty Crocker Homemaker of Tomorrow is Harriett E. Jenkins, a member of Mrs. C. E. Michel's homeroom. She scored highest in a written knowledge and attitude examination taken by senior girls December 7, 1965, and is now eligible for national scholarship awards. Harriett has already earned a special award pin from the program's sponsor, General Mills. She is also one of the ten State Finalists for the state of South Carolina.

Test papers of all school winners in the state are being judged, and a State Homemaker of Tomorrow and runner-up will be selected soon. The State Homemaker of Tomorrow will receive a $1,500 college scholarship, and her school will be awarded a complete set of the Encyclopedia Britannica by Encyclopaedia Britannica, Inc. The second-ranking girl in the state will receive a $500 educational grant.

Next spring, the State Betty Crocker Homemaker of Tomorrow from every state and the District of Columbia, each accompanied by a school advisor, will join in an expense-paid educational tour of Colonial Williamsburg, Virginia, and Washington, D. C. Then, the 1966 All-American Homemaker of Tomorrow will be announced at a dinner in Washington. Chosen from state winners on the basis of original test score and personal observation and interviews during the tour, she will have her scholarship increased to $5,000. Second-, third-, and fourth-ranking Homemaker of Tomorrow in the nation will be awarded $4,000, $3,000 and $2,000 grants respectively.

The Betty Crocker Search for the American Homemaker of Tomorrow was instituted by General Mills in 1954-55 to emphasize the importance of homemaking as a career. The program has enrolled 4,627,943 senior girls, with total scholarship grants exceeding $1,261,000. The 570,824 girls and 14,714 schools participating in the 1965-66 Search establish a new record enrollment.

Junior Honor Society Selects New Members

The Margaret Poinsette Chapter of the National Junior Honor Society of Burke High School was established to recognize the outstanding qualities of students in the eighth, ninth and tenth grades. It has prospered and met a great need in this school from the beginning of its operation.

Members are selected on the basis of Citizenship, Scholarship, Service, Leadership, and Character. To be eligible for candidacy for membership, all candidates must have a scholarship rank in the upper third of the class and a scholarstic average of no less than "B".

A wide variety of business has been transacted in the meetings of the National Junior Honor Society. Plans have been made for the Initiation and Induction Ceremonies which will take place during the latter part of the month, for the election and installation of officers of the Society and for the assembly program to be held in April.

Now that we are diligently working toward the "grand finale" of the second semester, I take great pride in announcing that fifty Burke scholars in grades eight through ten maintained a scholastic average of 85 or better which entitles them to full pledged membership. They are as follows: Deronda Baxter, Christine Caffey, Alfred Jones, and Delores Shepard, 10-Z; Gristella Bennett, Izetta Chapman, Rosalee Fleming, Rita Hector, Irving Smalls, and Albert Thompson, 10-Y; Sandra Burch, Patricia Coley, Margaret DeCosta, Alethia Johnson, Clarence Mays, 9-Z; Isaac Bass, Janice Heyward, Jacqueline Ritter, William Wineglass, and Gwendolyn Wrighten, 9-Y; Arnold Benson, Alonza Bolton, Scuvillia Graham, Ed James, Larry Washington, and Cynthia Wright, 9-W; Myra Bennett and James Johnson, 9-O; Bernard Brown, 9-H; Anna Cook, Bernandette DeVoe, Louis Gadsden, Deanne Gantt, Jennifer Harbour, Marjorie Miller, Cheryl Powell, Earl Richards, Cheryle Roper, and Zoe Seabrook, 8-W; Stanley Jones 8-V; Rosalie Lewis, 8-U; Elmore Black, and Henry Smalls, 8-T; Archibald Stoney, and Deborah Walker, 8-S; and Joyce McPhail 8-R.

As advisor to this organization, I sincerely thank the homeroom teachers of these students for their co-operation in encouraging good scholarship and stimulating the students to observe and practice those acts of others that develop strength of character.

Miss G. E. Coleman, Advisor

Ex-Party Member Speaks To Upperclassmen

The controversial Mrs. Julia C. Brown was presented at the assembly program February 1, 1966. Mrs. Brown was once a member of the Communist Party after which she became a spy for the F.B.I. Mrs. Brown devoted her speech to a discussion of Communist activities, and her introduction into the Communist Party in Cleveland, Ohio. Mrs. Brown asserted that there is great danger of infiltration of communism into every level of American society. She spoke of communism as an "Ideology which so many of us have been so eager to follow out of ignorance." She gave herself as an example of one who entered the party out of ignorance. She also made a statement concerning the intense need of a new Americanism. Her statement indicated that there must be in America a new and greater respect for law and order. This remains one of similar statements by various persons, and other groups. She made many accusations, but did not readily specify those accusations by figures or numbers. All in all, Mrs. Brown made it seem like a crime to question the American way of life. The experiences she related of herself were quite interesting.

Mrs. Brown was brought to Charleston for an address at Memminger Auditorium by the Freedom Forum.

By Martha McCord

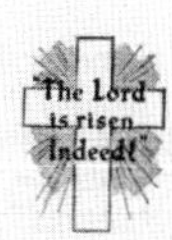

Juniors To Take Cooperative Test

For the past five years, the cooperative English Tests have been given in the spring of the year to all eleventh grade English students at Burke. The purpose of the test is to group eleventh graders for instruction in English IV in their senior year. Results of the tests are studied and used to strengthen the students in those areas in which they show weakness.

There are two parts to the test. Part one deals with reading which covers vocabulary, level of reading comprehension and speech of reading comprehension. Part two deals with English Expression which covers effectiveness and mechanics. Effectiveness refers to the choice of the written expression which precisely conveys the meaning intended. About two-thirds of the items in this part require the student to complete a sentence by choosing the best single word from among four presented. The remaining items require completion of sentences with the most effective phrases or clauses. Mechanics refers to usage, spelling, punctuation, and capitalization.

The Cooperative English Tests will be given on Thursday, March 24, 1966 in the Burke gym.

By Zoe Seabrook

Graham Earns Purple Heart

Spec. Earl C. Graham was awarded the Purple Heart posthumously. Col. Charles S. Campbell, Commander of the Charleston Army Depot presented the award to Mrs. Barbara Ann Graham, widow of Spec. Graham, at a televised presentation.

Spec. Graham was among the 1st Cavalry Division which left for Viet Nam from Charleston in August of 1965. He was assigned to one of the troops stationed along the Cambodia border. It was while fighting there that he is reported to have been killed when he stepped on a land mine.

By Arthur Gilliard

Department Plans Career Month

The guidance department is now in the process of getting ready for career month which will extend through the month of March.

March ninth will be set aside as Career Day. Consultants from various occupations will be invited to Burke to speak to students on his occupation.

A career fair will be held on the tenth and eleventh of March in the library. The theme for this year's fair is, "Occupation Space Age." Individual students will be asked to do exhibits centered around occupations dealing with the space age. Prizes will be awarded to the best exhibits.

Sometime during Career Month a rerpesentative from the Gulf Oil Company will come to speak at the eighth and ninth grades' assembly program. Also, at our next P. T. A. meeting a panel discussion will be held for the parents on jobs in the Charleston area along with a film.

During the month of March take advantage of the opportunities to learn more about careers, particularly the one you're most interested in.

By Christine Caffey

Plans for the long-awaited gymnasium were finally approved in 1966. Construction was completed in 1967. The structure is no longer in existence; however, a new gymnasium was built in 2005 near the same location. (Courtesy of the Avery Research Center.)

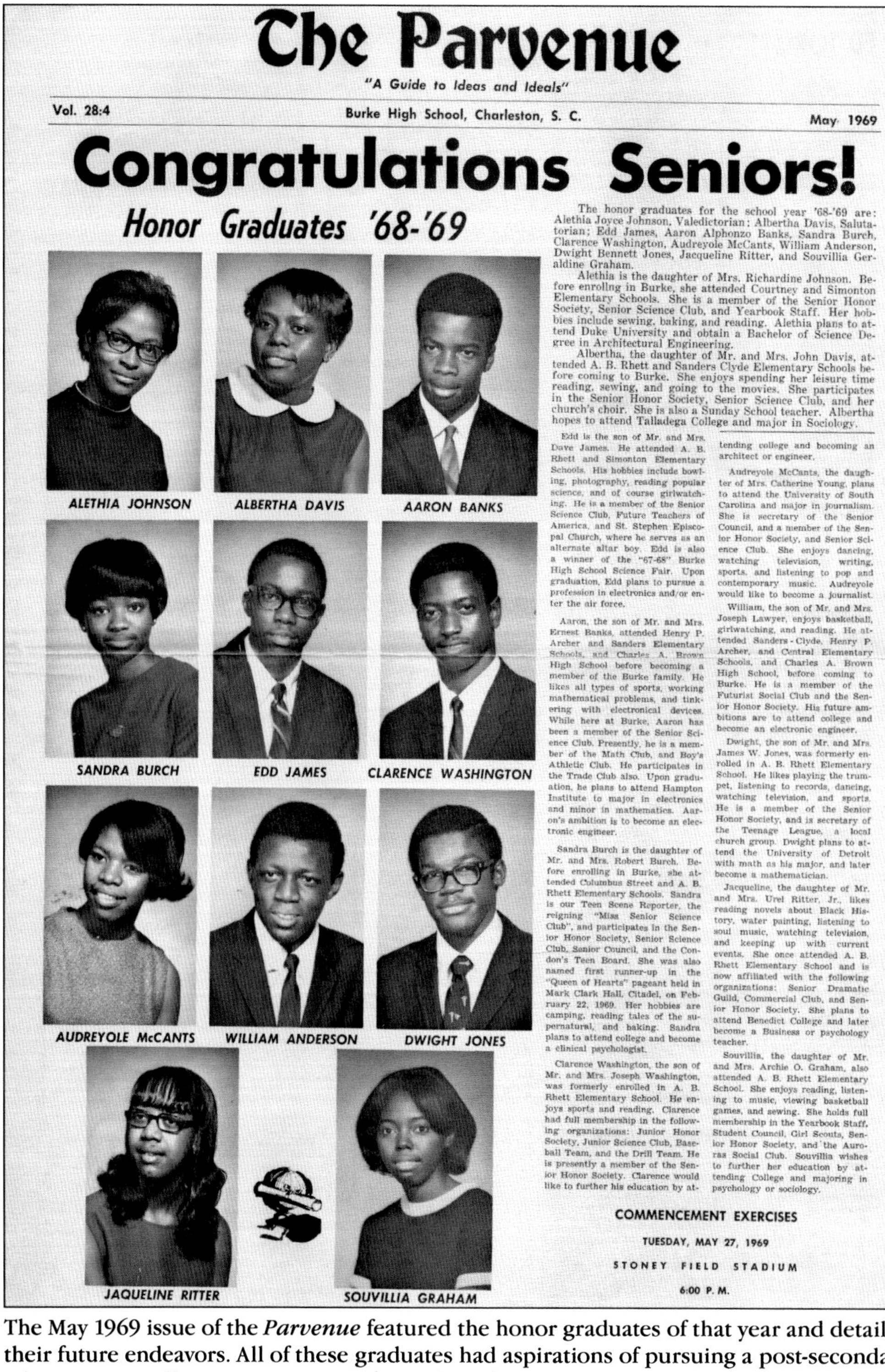

The Parvenue

"A Guide to Ideas and Ideals"

Vol. 28:4 — Burke High School, Charleston, S. C. — May 1969

Congratulations Seniors!

Honor Graduates '68-'69

ALETHIA JOHNSON — ALBERTHA DAVIS — AARON BANKS

SANDRA BURCH — EDD JAMES — CLARENCE WASHINGTON

AUDREYOLE McCANTS — WILLIAM ANDERSON — DWIGHT JONES

JAQUELINE RITTER — SOUVILLIA GRAHAM

The honor graduates for the school year '68-'69 are: Alethia Joyce Johnson, Valedictorian; Albertha Davis, Salutatorian; Edd James, Aaron Alphonzo Banks, Sandra Burch, Clarence Washington, Audreyole McCants, William Anderson, Dwight Bennett Jones, Jacqueline Ritter, and Souvillia Geraldine Graham.

Alethia is the daughter of Mrs. Richardine Johnson. Before enrollng in Burke, she attended Courtney and Simonton Elementary Schools. She is a member of the Senior Honor Society, Senior Science Club, and Yearbook Staff. Her hobbies include sewing, baking, and reading. Alethia plans to attend Duke University and obtain a Bachelor of Science Degree in Architectural Engineering.

Albertha, the daughter of Mr. and Mrs. John Davis, attended A. B. Rhett and Sanders Clyde Elementary Schools before coming to Burke. She enjoys spending her leisure time reading, sewing, and going to the movies. She participates in the Senior Honor Society, Senior Science Club, and her church's choir. She is also a Sunday School teacher. Albertha hopes to attend Talladega College and major in Sociology.

Edd is the son of Mr. and Mrs. Dave James. He attended A. B. Rhett and Simonton Elementary Schools. His hobbies include bowling, photography, reading popular science, and of course girlwatching. He is a member of the Senior Science Club, Future Teachers of America, and St. Stephen Episcopal Church, where he serves as an alternate altar boy. Edd is also a winner of the "67-68" Burke High School Science Fair. Upon graduation, Edd plans to pursue a profession in electronics and/or enter the air force.

Aaron, the son of Mr. and Mrs. Ernest Banks, attended Henry P. Archer and Sanders Elementary Schools, and Charles A. Brown High School before becoming a member of the Burke family. He likes all types of sports, working mathematical problems, and tinkering with electronical devices. While here at Burke, Aaron has been a member of the Senior Science Club. Presently, he is a member of the Math Club, and Boy's Athletic Club. He participates in the Trade Club also. Upon graduation, he plans to attend Hampton Institute to major in electronics and minor in mathematics. Aaron's ambition is to become an electronic engineer.

Sandra Burch is the daughter of Mr. and Mrs. Robert Burch. Before enrolling in Burke, she attended Columbus Street and A. B. Rhett Elementary Schools. Sandra is our Teen Scene Reporter, the reigning "Miss Senior Science Club", and participates in the Senior Honor Society, Senior Science Club, Senior Council, and the Condon's Teen Board. She was also named first runner-up in the "Queen of Hearts" pageant held in Mark Clark Hall, Citadel, on February 22, 1969. Her hobbies are camping, reading tales of the supernatural, and baking. Sandra plans to attend college and become a clinical psychologist.

Clarence Washington, the son of Mr. and Mrs. Joseph Washington, was formerly enrolled in A. B. Rhett Elementary School. He enjoys sports and reading. Clarence had full membership in the following organizations: Junior Honor Society, Junior Science Club, Baseball Team, and the Drill Team. He is presently a member of the Senior Honor Society. Clarence would like to further his education by attending college and becoming an architect or engineer.

Audreyole McCants, the daughter of Mrs. Catherine Young, plans to attend the University of South Carolina and major in journalism. She is secretary of the Senior Council, and a member of the Senior Honor Society, and Senior Science Club. She enjoys dancing, watching television, writing, sports, and listening to pop and contemporary music. Audreyole would like to become a journalist.

William, the son of Mr. and Mrs. Joseph Lawyer, enjoys basketball, girlwatching, and reading. He attended Sanders - Clyde, Henry P. Archer, and Central Elementary Schools, and Charles A. Brown High School, before coming to Burke. He is a member of the Futurist Social Club and the Senior Honor Society. His future ambitions are to attend college and become an electronic engineer.

Dwight, the son of Mr. and Mrs. James W. Jones, was formerly enrolled in A. B. Rhett Elementary School. He likes playing the trumpet, listening to records, dancing, watching television, and sports. He is a member of the Senior Honor Society, and is secretary of the Teenage League, a local church group. Dwight plans to attend the University of Detroit with math as his major, and later become a mathematician.

Jacqueline, the daughter of Mr. and Mrs. Urel Ritter, Jr., likes reading novels about Black History, water painting, listening to soul music, watching television, and keeping up with current events. She once attended A. B. Rhett Elementary School and is now affiliated with the following organizations: Senior Dramatic Guild, Commercial Club, and Senior Honor Society. She plans to attend Benedict College and later become a Business or psychology teacher.

Souvillia, the daughter of Mr. and Mrs. Archie O. Graham, also attended A. B. Rhett Elementary School. She enjoys reading, listening to music, viewing basketball games, and sewing. She holds full membership in the Yearbook Staff, Student Council, Girl Scouts, Senior Honor Society, and the Auroras Social Club. Souvillia wishes to further her education by attending College and majoring in psychology or sociology.

COMMENCEMENT EXERCISES

TUESDAY, MAY 27, 1969

STONEY FIELD STADIUM

6:00 P. M.

The May 1969 issue of the *Parvenue* featured the honor graduates of that year and detailed their future endeavors. All of these graduates had aspirations of pursuing a post-secondary education. Equally impressive was the number of male honor students as compared to the numbers of females. (Courtesy of Burke High School.)

The Parvenue

"A Guide to Ideas and Ideals"

Vol. 29:6 Burke High School, Charleston, S. C. May 1970

Congratulations Seniors!

Honor Graduates '69-70

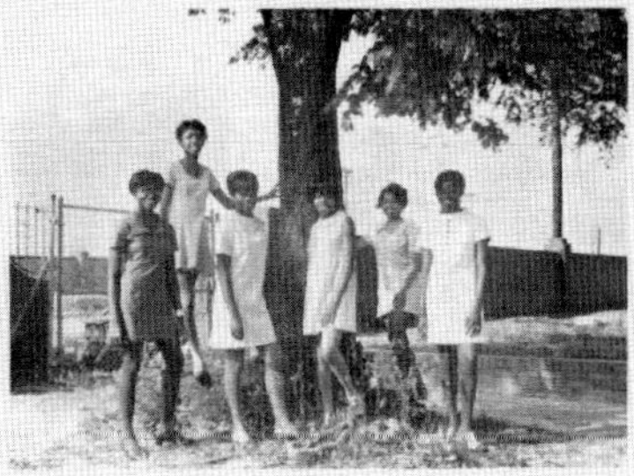

(From l. to r.): Judy Manigault, Deanna Gantt, Emma Broughton, Vernell Sanford, Valedictorian; Marjorie Miller, and Vermelle Washington, Salutatorian.

The honor graduates for the school year '69-'70 are: Vermell Sanford, valedictorian; Vermell Washington, salutatorian; Marjorie Miller, Judy Manigault, Emma Broughton, and Deanna Gantt.

Vermell Sanford is the daughter of Mrs. Janie Aflada. She attended Columbus Street Elementary School. At Burke she is business manager of the Senior Honor Society, a member of the Senior Dramatic Guild, the Yearbook Staff, reporter and business manager of the Y-Teens, and she presently reigns as "Miss Y-Teens".

Also, Vermell has been selected Star Student and is recognized by Who's Who in America, Outstanding American Society for High School Students, Eastern Star, and has received the Broader Education Finer Womanhood Award. Her hobbies are listening to records, dancing, and sewing. Vermell plans to be a physical therapist.

Vermelle Washington, the daughter of Mr. and Mrs. Elijah Washington, attended Rhett, Simonton, and Mitchell elementary schools. She is secretary of the Senior Honor Society, business manager of the Senior Council, editor of the Yearbook Staff and a member of the Students for Black Culture. She is presently regning as "Miss Senior Honor Society".

Her ambition is to attend Winthrop College and become a dietitian. Vermell has been selected by the Outstanding American Society for High School Students and Who's Who in America. Her hobbies are sewing, cooking, reading and dancing. She comments, "When I found out I was salutatorian I was surprised because I knew I had a lot of competition. It is an honor to have such a title."

Marjorie Miller is the daughter of Mr. and Mrs. Carl B. Miller. She attended Rhett Elementary School. At Burke she is a member of the Senior Science Club, exchange editor of the Parvenue Staff, vice-president of the Senior Choir, president of the Senior Honor Society, and business manager of the Modern Music Masters. Marjorie has been selected by Who's Who in America, and Outstanding American Society for High School Students. Her ambition is to attend U.S.C. and become a food technician.

Judy Manigault resides with Miss Mabel Young. She attended Courtenay Elementary School. At Burke she is affiliated with the Commercial Club. Her hobbies are sewing, writing poetry, reading and singing. Her ambition is to attend Knoxville College and major in social studies.

Emma Broughton is the daughter of Mrs. Bedell Broughton. She attended Simonton Elementary School. Emma is a member of the Commercial Club. Her hobbies include watching T.V. and listening to the radio. She plans to travel and then become an accountant. "It's been a terrible year," said Emma, "and I'm happy that it's over."

Deanna Gantt, the daughter of Mr. and Mrs. Christopher Gantt, Sr., attended Rhett Elementary School. She is a member of the Yearbook Staff, the Parvenue Staff, the Senior Honor Society and the Senior Dramatic Guild. Deanna presently reigns as "Miss Senior". She plans to attend U.S.C. and major in journalism. She is the recipient of the Betty Crocker Award.

Two Burke Juniors Receive Awards From Presbyterian College

Twenty Charleston high school juniors have been cited by Presbyterian College in Clinton, South Carolina, as PC Junior Fellows in recognition of unusual scholastic attainment, president Marc C. Weersing announced recently.

From Burke High School — Bernard Jerome Washington, son of Mr. and Mrs. Joseph Washington of 137 Spring Street; and Annette Sherelyn Spann, daughter of Mr. and Mrs. McKeever Spann of 98 Congress Street were selected.

The Presbyterian College Junior Academic Achievement Award is presented to the young man and young woman who — after the first semester of their junior year in high school — have the highest cumulative averages for the previous 2 1/2 years af academic work.

The award carries a special citation, a minimum scholarship grant and automatic consideration in PC's new Summer Honors program.

Commencement Program Planned

The sixtieth graduation exercise, which will be a combination of the commencement and baccalaureate exercises this year will be held Wednesday, May 27, at 6:00 p.m. at the Stoney Field Stadium.

The class motto for this year is: "Great revolutions are the work of principles rather than of bayonets." The honor speakers are: Vermell Marie Sanford, Vermell Washington, Marjorie Miller, Judy Manigault, Emma Broughton and Deanna Gantt.

The graduates will present a skit in wihch the problems of today will be featured: the theme, "The Black Revolution Speaks: for youth, to the establishment, for the law, for democracy, for education, for religion."

The speaker, Reverend J. B. Butler, is a native of Newberry, South Carolina. He received his education in the public schools of Newberry, S. C.; Allen University, and the University of Chicago.

He has served as the pastor of churches in Denton, Md., Columbia, S. C., and Georgetown, S. C. At present he is the pastor of Emanuel A.M.E. Church.

Music will be rendered by the band under the direction of Mr. Benjamin Brockington, and the choir under the direction of Mr. R. A. Ford.

Alumni Notes

First Lieut. Leroy Palmer

A former Burkeite, and a Hurlburt Field junior officer has been named one of the United States Air Force's Outstanding Supply Officers for 1969.

First Lieutenant Leroy R. Palmer, III, a native of Charleston, South Carolina, and a 1962 graduate of Burke High School, was recently notified of his selection for the coveted award. The lieutenant serves as supply officer with the 319th Special Operations Squadron (SOS). The 319th SOS is responsible for flying C-123 cargo transport missions.

In a citation signed by General John D. Ryon, USAF chief of staff, the supply officer was recognized as " . . . having demonstrated outstanding proficiency in fulfilling supply responsibilities." A 1968 graduate of North Carolina Agricultural and Technical State University, Lieutenant Palmer received a bachelor of science degree in economics.

Lieutenant Palmer was chosen on the basis of a comprehensive review of his performance record by the Headquarters USAF Selection Board.

Sgt. Kenneth Brown

Sgt. Kenneth Brown, son of Mr. and Mrs. Thomas James Brown of 222 President Street has been named as one of America's Outstanding Young Men for 1970.

Chosen for his many professional and civic endeavors, Brown was one of a select number of young men in our country to be awarded this distinguished honor.

Kenneth Brown was a graduate of Burke in 1961, and a graduate of Morgan State College in 1965, of Morgan State College in 1965. As an outstanding young man, Kenneth will be honored in the 1970 volume of outstanding young men of America.

Former Burkeites Receive Diplomas

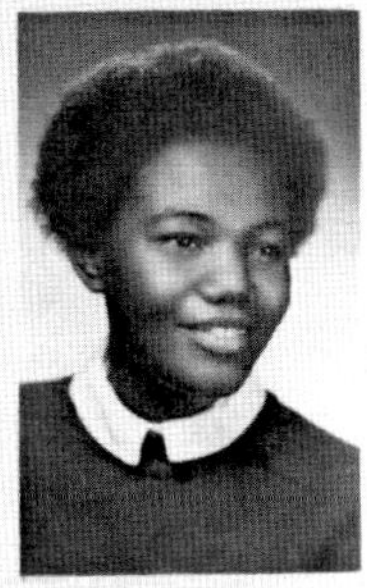

Joyce McPhail Receives Award

Joyce McPhail, a former member of Miss Lucille A. Williams' class, was selected in 1968 into the Student Transfer Education Program, a project of the Education Department of the National Urban League. The project is an "effort to provide a select group of able and highly motivated Southern Negro students two years (11th and 12th grades) of secondary education in strong college preparatory northern high schools which will strengthen and deepen 9th and 10th grade foundations."

Joyce is now a prospective graduating senior at Princeton High School in Princeton, New Jersey. She is a feature editor of the school paper, **The Tower,** a member of the yearbook staff and president of the Black Students Union. She was selected to appear in **Who's Who in American High Schools and Colleges,** and is a recipient of a scholarship awarded by the National Scholarship Service and Fund for Negro Students. Of the 200 seniors at Princeton High, Joyce was the only one to be accepted by four of the major colleges in the United States. They are Lincoln University, Mount Holyoke, Cornell University and Douglas College. Joyce has decided to attend Cornell University in Kittytown, New York, where she will major in political science. She has also been invited by the Director of Admissions at Cornell to attend a summer school program.

Joyce is the daughter of Mrs. Pearl McPhail of 343 Sumter St. and Mr. Allen McPhail of Mavin, Mississippi. In a recent letter she said that she misses the social activities at Burke and the pleasant company of "soul" people. But she added that her experience at Princeton has enriched her earlier training at Burke and has enabled her to compete and communicate with others of different races and social backgrounds.

Welcome Class of 1960

The members of the Class of 1960 presented a bench to the school at the Class Night Exercises.

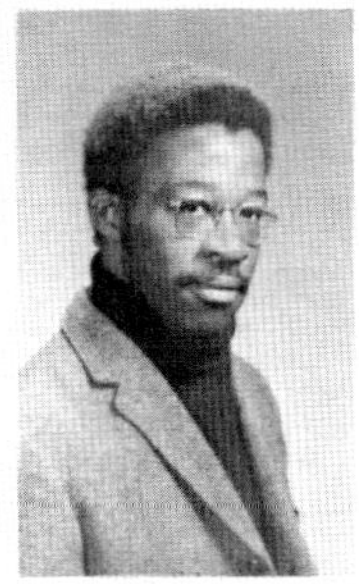

Harold Whack Receives Honors At Harvard

Harold Whack was born October 19, 1948, in Charleston, S. C., to Mr. and Mrs. Harold L. Whack, Sr. At the age of six, Hal began his formal education training at the elementary schools of Courtenay and A. B. Rhett respectively. Hal entered Simonton Junior High School and later transferred to Burke High School.

An organization then known as the American Friends Society noticed the academic achievements of this student. He was offered the opportunity to go to Wheatley High Schol in Roslyn Heights, New York. Hal took this opportunity and graduated with honors from the Wheatley High School June 27, 1966. With some of the largest universities in the United States, including Princeton University, Syracuse University, and Harvard University vying for his attendance, Hal chose Harvard University in Cambridge, Mass.

While attending Harvard on a government grant in 1968, Hal visited some foreign countries including Paris, France; Trinidad, Spain; Portugal, and London, England. He majored in political science. In June of 1970, Hal Whack will graduate with honors from Harvard. He plans to further his education in his chosen field upon graduation.

Hal attributes his greatest educational aspirations to the following teachers at Burke:

Mr. J. G. Thompson, Mrs. M. D. Seabrook, now retired, and Mrs. H. M. Stewart, now teaching at St. Andrew's High Schol.

INDEX:

Two former Burke students, Joyce McPhail and Harold Whack, were accepted into elite high schools in the north because of their academic potential and acumen, indicated in the 1970 issue of the *Parvenue*. (Courtesy of Burke High School.)

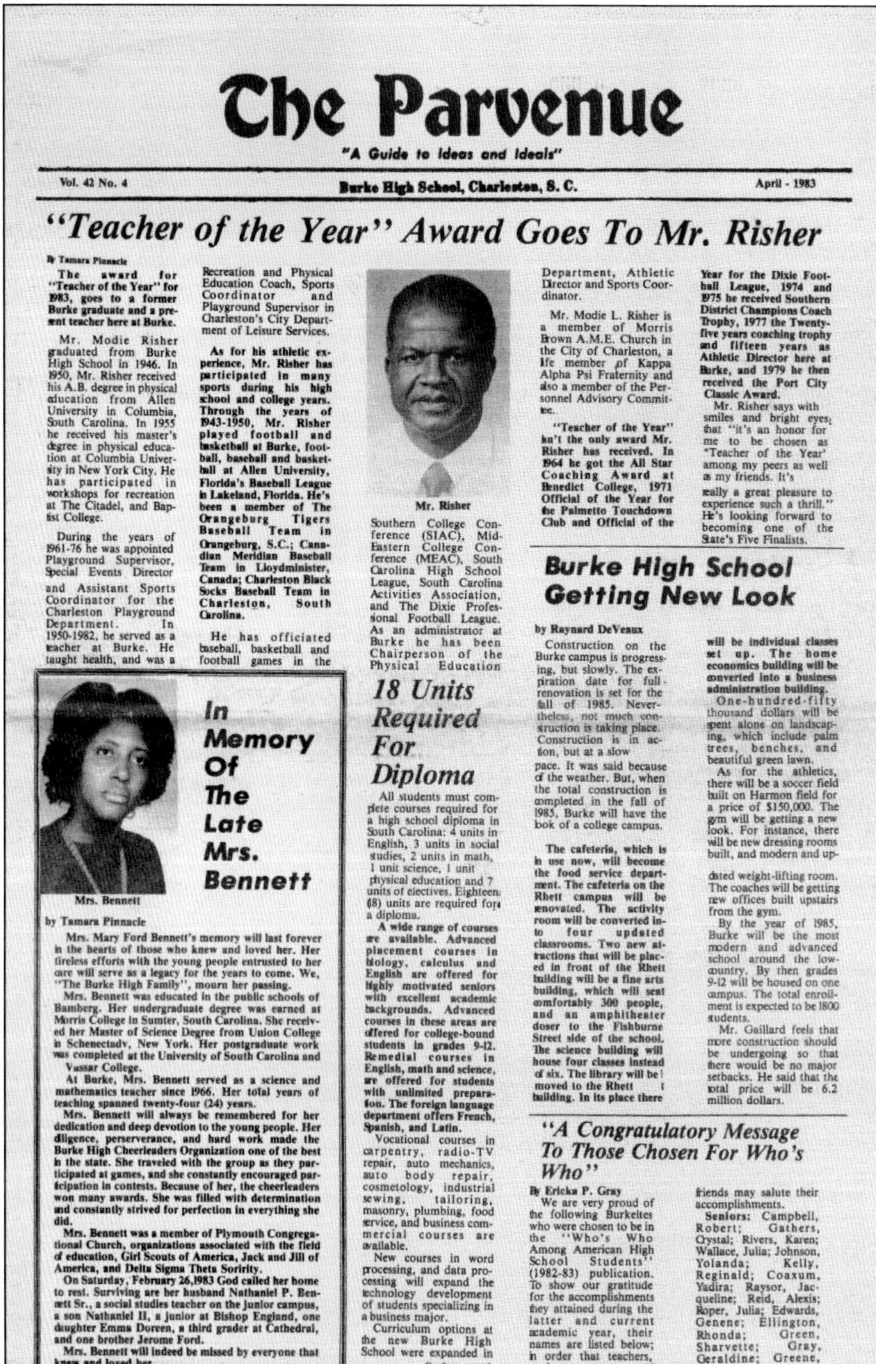

The Parvenue

"A Guide to Ideas and Ideals"

Vol. 42 No. 4 | Burke High School, Charleston, S. C. | April - 1983

"Teacher of the Year" Award Goes To Mr. Risher

By Tamara Pinnacle

The award for "Teacher of the Year" for 1983, goes to a former Burke graduate and a present teacher here at Burke.

Mr. Modie Risher graduated from Burke High School in 1946. In 1950, Mr. Risher received his A.B. degree in physical education from Allen University in Columbia, South Carolina. In 1955 he received his master's degree in physical education at Columbia University in New York City. He has participated in workshops for recreation at The Citadel, and Baptist College.

During the years of 1961-76 he was appointed Playground Supervisor, Special Events Director and Assistant Sports Coordinator for the Charleston Playground Department. In 1950-1982, he served as a teacher at Burke. He taught health, and was a Recreation and Physical Education Coach, Sports Coordinator and Playground Supervisor in Charleston's City Department of Leisure Services.

As for his athletic experience, Mr. Risher has participated in many sports during his high school and college years. Through the years of 1943-1950, Mr. Risher played football and basketball at Burke, football, baseball and basketball at Allen University, Florida's Baseball League in Lakeland, Florida. He's been a member of The Orangeburg Tigers Baseball Team in Orangeburg, S.C.; Canadian Meridian Baseball Team in Lloydminister, Canada; Charleston Black Socks Baseball Team in Charleston, South Carolina.

Mr. Risher

He has officiated baseball, basketball and football games in the Southern College Conference (SIAC), Mid-Eastern College Conference (MEAC), South Carolina High School League, South Carolina Activities Association, and The Dixie Professional Football League. As an administrator at Burke he has been Chairperson of the Physical Education Department, Athletic Director and Sports Coordinator.

Mr. Modie L. Risher is a member of Morris Brown A.M.E. Church in the City of Charleston, a life member of Kappa Alpha Psi Fraternity and also a member of the Personnel Advisory Committee.

"Teacher of the Year" isn't the only award Mr. Risher has received. In 1964 he got the All Star Coaching Award at Benedict College, 1971 Official of the Year for the Palmetto Touchdown Club and Official of the Year for the Dixie Football League, 1974 and 1975 he received Southern District Champions Coach Trophy, 1977 the Twenty-five years coaching trophy and fifteen years as Athletic Director here at Burke, and 1979 he then received the Port City Classic Award.

Mr. Risher says with smiles and bright eyes; that "it's an honor for me to be chosen as "Teacher of the Year' among my peers as well as my friends. It's really a great pleasure to experience such a thrill." He's looking forward to becoming one of the State's Five Finalists.

In Memory Of The Late Mrs. Bennett

Mrs. Bennett

by Tamara Pinnacle

Mrs. Mary Ford Bennett's memory will last forever in the hearts of those who knew and loved her. Her tireless efforts with the young people entrusted to her care will serve as a legacy for the years to come. We, "The Burke High Family", mourn her passing.

Mrs. Bennett was educated in the public schools of Bamberg. Her undergraduate degree was earned at Morris College in Sumter, South Carolina. She received her Master of Science Degree from Union College in Schenectadv, New York. Her postgraduate work was completed at the University of South Carolina and Vassar College.

At Burke, Mrs. Bennett served as a science and mathematics teacher since 1966. Her total years of teaching spanned twenty-four (24) years.

Mrs. Bennett will always be remembered for her dedication and deep devotion to the young people. Her diligence, perserverance, and hard work made the Burke High Cheerleaders Organization one of the best in the state. She traveled with the group as they participated at games, and she constantly encouraged participation in contests. Because of her, the cheerleaders won many awards. She was filled with determination and constantly strived for perfection in everything she did.

Mrs. Bennett was a member of Plymouth Congregational Church, organizations associated with the field of education, Girl Scouts of America, Jack and Jill of America, and Delta Sigma Theta Soririty.

On Saturday, February 26,1983 God called her home to rest. Surviving are her husband Nathaniel P. Bennett Sr., a social studies teacher on the junior campus, a son Nathaniel II, a junior at Bishop England, one daughter Emma Doreen, a third grader at Cathedral, and one brother Jerome Ford.

Mrs. Bennett will indeed be missed by everyone that knew and loved her.

18 Units Required For Diploma

All students must complete courses required for a high school diploma in South Carolina: 4 units in English, 3 units in social studies, 2 units in math, 1 unit science, 1 unit physical education and 7 units of electives. Eighteen (18) units are required for a diploma.

A wide range of courses are available. Advanced placement courses in biology, calculus and English are offered for highly motivated seniors with excellent academic backgrounds. Advanced courses in these areas are offered for college-bound students in grades 9-12. Remedial courses in English, math and science, are offered for students with unlimited preparation. The foreign language department offers French, Spanish, and Latin.

Vocational courses in carpentry, radio-TV repair, auto mechanics, auto body repair, cosmetology, industrial sewing, tailoring, masonry, plumbing, food service, and business commercial courses are available.

New courses in word processing, and data processing will expand the technology development of students specializing in a business major.

Curriculum options at the new Burke High School were expanded in

Con't on page 4

Burke High School Getting New Look

by Raynard DeVeaux

Construction on the Burke campus is progressing, but slowly. The expiration date for full-renovation is set for the fall of 1985. Nevertheless, not much construction is taking place. Construction is in action, but at a slow pace. It was said because of the weather. But, when the total construction is completed in the fall of 1985, Burke will have the look of a college campus.

The cafeteria, which is in use now, will become the food service department. The cafeteria on the Rhett campus will be renovated. The activity room will be converted into four updated classrooms. Two new attractions that will be placed in front of the Rhett building will be a fine arts building, which will seat comfortably 300 people, and an amphitheater closer to the Fishburne Street side of the school. The science building will house four classes instead of six. The library will be moved to the Rhett building. In its place there will be individual classes set up. The home economics building will be converted into a business administration building.

One-hundred-fifty thousand dollars will be spent alone on landscaping, which include palm trees, benches, and beautiful green lawn.

As for the athletics, there will be a soccer field built on Harmon field for a price of $150,000. The gym will be getting a new look. For instance, there will be new dressing rooms built, and modern and updated weight-lifting room. The coaches will be getting new offices built upstairs from the gym.

By the year of 1985, Burke will be the most modern and advanced school around the low-country. By then grades 9-12 will be housed on one campus. The total enrollment is expected to be 1800 students.

Mr. Gaillard feels that more construction should be undergoing so that there would be no major setbacks. He said that the total price will be 6.2 million dollars.

"A Congratulatory Message To Those Chosen For Who's Who"

By Ericka P. Gray

We are very proud of the following Burkeites who were chosen to be in the "Who's Who Among American High School Students" (1982-83) publication. To show our gratitude for the accomplishments they attained during the latter and current academic year, their names are listed below; in order that teachers, students, parents, and friends may salute their accomplishments.

Seniors: Campbell, Robert; Gathers, Crystal; Rivers, Karen; Wallace, Julia; Johnson, Yolanda; Kelly, Reginald; Coaxum, Yadira; Raysor, Jacqueline; Reid, Alexis; Roper, Julia; Edwards, Genene; Ellington, Rhonda; Green, Sharvette; Gray, Geraldine; Greene,

Con't on page 4

By 1983, according to the *Parvenue*, additional construction was taking place on the campus to accommodate the students that were being sent from Charles A. Brown and Charleston High Schools. Another article addressed a change in the curriculum that was mandated by the school board. Eighteen units were required to earn a diploma. (Courtesy of Burke High School.)

Eight

EDITORIALS AND QUOTES

It was the worst of times. It was the best of times.

—Virginia F. Howard (Class of 1961)

AN OPEN LETTER TO LOWER CLASSMEN

The results of April 23 showed that about 560 citizens of United Burke participated in the annual election of Burke's student government. I am most certain that these few votes were cast by upper-classmen. Only 50% of the school voted.

Do you as citizens of United Burke consider the importance of voting? Do you realize what an important part voting will play in your lives in future years? Have you ever given these questions a thought? As a citizen of United Burke, it seems that in the past four years the students haven't been taking full advantage of the democratic form of student voting.

Student voting will enable you in future years to understand and enlighten your minds to the value and great importance of voting. Belonging to a race that is striving to greater heights, you should take more interest in development of voting. A partial vote will not count as one. If your man is a candidate for office, will you let him down by casting a partial vote which will not be counted? No. YOU would never think of it. Then why not be a loyal Burke-ite and cast a whole vote and have 100% election next year at Burke. This is my advice to you.

Miriam Rivers.

Miriam Rivers addresses the lack of voter participation by the students for their annual student government elections in May 1945. (Courtesy of the Avery Research Center.)

AN OPEN LETTER TO MY SCHOOLMATES

"It has been brought to my attention on many occasions that the general behavior of the Negro children of our city schools is unsatisfactory. The way they carry themselves; rudeness to others, especially their attitude to adults who correct them; these things have made them unpleasantly conspicuous."

This is a direct quotation of a letter written by Mr. Grayson to all city school principals. What have we to say concerning this? Are we guilty of any of these things? If we are, there is room for disciplinary training.

We, as students of the city schools, especially Burke, should be alert, active, obedient, and efficient at all times if we expect to advance in life.

Quoting further: "I, myself, have noticed recently what appears to be a series of conflicts; monopoly of the sidewalks and at corners; uncouth talk and a disregard for property in and around the school."

Every Burke-ite knows and is conscious of the fact that school property is for our benefit. Let us show Mr. Grayson our finer traits. We should make him proud of us. Burke is the only high school in the city that Mr. Grayson is supervising.

Charles Walker.

In 1945, Charles Walker wrote about the general behavior of African American students in the city schools. He asked students at Burke to be respectful to others and to obey all of the school's rules and regulations. (Courtesy of the Avery Research Center.)

This Issue

No doubt you have noticed that this issue features activities that are going on around the school—termed as "Life at Burke". Equally as important are the heads that are portrayed on a page of a book; also there are the groups of clubs and organizations. Each phase has a special significance.

The spectacular events that are in progress around the school denotes "Life at Burke"; for here you simply see students in every day life acting in the fashion of most high school boys and girls: in class, recess, and social gatherings. There is also a place for the outstanding in specific fields. The "Superlatives", though chosen by popular votes, also tell you something. In all toll all of this tells you who is who and what is what.

Those two pages of books also have a meaning. The seniors are now on their last leaf and as the book is closed they leave in it a picture; a picture of dignity.

The clubs and organizations are all potent parts of life at Burke.

All of these factors are acting as guides to ideas and ideals.

To create any idea or to achieve any ideal requires long and hard work. That is what this issue meant to the PARVENUE staff. It has required great coordination from the editorial and business staff.

For the editor-in-chief it meant hours in the library, hours of concentration, loss of sleep; for the photograph editor it meant working after midnight, improper rest, neglect of studies; also the business manager had his specific worries. Besides running in to money difficulties he worked with photography. In fact all members worked with undying effort to keep up PARVENUE ideas and ideals.

Therefore the publication of a school paper cannot be readily accepted as a bed of roses, as the saying goes; in most cases the thorns are felt more. The only thing that will heal these thorn pricks is to know that you, the readers, have enjoyed reading this issue. Geneva McHoney.

Geneva McHoney gave words of support and encouragement to the newspaper staff and asked that the student body display a measure of compassion toward the staff as they worked toward publishing the newspaper in March 1949. (Courtesy of the Avery Research Center.)

Rudolph Pyatt wrote about the importance of preparing for the future in November 1950. He asked the student body if they were prepared to handle the responsibilities that came along with adulthood. Pyatt became the first African American reporter for the *News and Courier* in 1964. (Courtesy of the Avery Research Center.)

What Does the Future Hold for Us?

When we were much younger, and down in the elementary grades, a question most frequently asked us was "What do you intend being when you grow up?" Soon the question will be "Did you get to be what you wanted to?"

This should give all perspective graduates something to think about, although it may be of interest to lower classmen also.

Each man has his own vocation. Talent is his tool. And it is solely up to each individual to maneuver his tool efifciently.

We must realize that as time marches on, our actions, looks, associates, and many other things change.

Speaking of associates, now is the time to be careful about the people we associate with and how we handle our selves.

Life is peculiar; or should we say the people who live in it are peculiar. The reason for this statement is this: nowadays it is not altogether what we know; it is who we know in some cases.

Now don't take this too seriously; that is do not fall into parasitic habits. This is one of the worse things a human who has his health and strength can do. Learn to be independent. Independence signifies a strong character.

We may not achieve the fame that so many people have, but we certainly can make the most of our opportunities.

Of course some of us may become doctors, teachers, ministers, and others may not. This is no reason to feel that our school career is a waste of time. Even if financial standings are not the same some where, there is a place in the puzzle for you to fit in.

Very soon, within less than eight months to be a little more exact, many of us will be on our own. There will no longer be situations where we can depend upon our parents for certain things, for we are the men and women of tomorrow.

Are you making the most of your opportunities? We hope you are, because it would be sad to learn that some of you may end up being failures.

"What does your future hold for you?"

Rudolph A. Pyatt

A Brief Pause

While kneeling down to thank the Almighty Being for having kept you still among the living, pause briefly and think of a gallant American soldier crawling up some gory hill in the heart of Korea. He is fighting for a country in which he hopes to enjoy justice.

Even as he crawls over the gore tinged rocks, many are skeeming to deprive him and his people of that which is justly theirs; to make him feel inferior; to promote a "supremacy" which really doesn't exist.

For instance: let's suppose a sales tax has been enacted in his native state, supposingly to equalize all schools; a huge equalization program is underway; newspapers encourage the program. This is all excellent except for the fact that a mathematical mistake has been made. More money was voted for one group than the other; and it is the group that already had the better educational opportunities that received the larger appropriation.

We cannot comprehend the possibility of such a mathematical mistake. But does he let this weaken his love for his country? No! He fights on! He realizes that there is hope in Americanism. Ernest Thompson.

Ernest Thompson talked about the meaning of Easter and how important it was that year due to the Korean War and the turmoil that was happening throughout the world in March 1952. (Courtesy of the Avery Research Center.)

BE POPULAR BUT BE RESPECTED

Can you be popular and still command the respect of your friends?

Can you be popular without telling that joke about the time Rev. John these days but we aren't faced with a depression as yet. Dignity is too went to Sister Mary's house?

Can you be popular without doing a 'jig' on top of your desk?

Can you be popular without wearing your cap back in front; your dress shirt's tail out of your trousers; and your tie about your neck like a scarf?

Can you be popular without following the crowd after the football game?

If you must bury your decorum to gain popularity then you have become popular at the expense of your dignity. True good 'stuff' comes high high a price to pay for popularity. Don't be a victim of the moral blackmarket.

Our student leaders have not been victims of this moral blackmarket, they are popular enough to have been elected to lead us; and yet they command the respect of their fellow Burke-ites. We know of no other school where student leaders command so much respect as here at good ole Burke. So be popular and be respected.

Ernest Thompson

———O———

AIM FOR THE TARGET

Here we are beginning another school year. We should ask ourselves the question: What targets are we aiming? Are we going to school just to be going; or are we going because we have a target at which we are aiming?

Let us face some of the facts: some are going to school because our parents compel us to go; some are going because we are dodging work; but still some are going because we have a target—a goal. Let us start aiming now, and aim straight.

"Be strong. We are not here to play, to dream, nor to drift. We have hard work to do and loads to lift. Shun not the days as toil. Be strong."

Willis Goodwin

In 1952, Willis Goodwin wrote about the importance of setting goals, while Ernest Thompson wrote about the difficulties of trying to balance the notion of being popular, yet still being respected. (Courtesy of the Avery Research Center.)

Let's Build Up Our School's Reputation

Will the faculty, Student council and students of Burke help make our school a better one? Let us all cooperate to build a good reputation.

Students, if you can't get along with your friends, then why don't you make new friends; or be alone.

Let us not fight and argue along the streets going home. We should be as one; for no matter what school we came from, we are all Burke students now.

Won't you please help us to keep the policemen from having to come on the school ground to settle our controversies. Let's make our school a good school instead of a jail. For it makes the faculty and students who want to build the school up, feel very badly.

The name we give our school reflects upon us, whether it is good or bad. Remember, our school is what we make it. So let's give it a good reputation.

Mary Louise Wine, '57.

Mary Wine asked the students to be mindful of their actions on and off the campus because it was a reflection on the school. Joe Louis Black sought to remind the students of the importance of appreciating the freedom of the press and how it could impact their lives, November 1954. (Courtesy of the Avery Research Center.)

A Free Press—'Freedom's Forum'

National Newspaper Week was celebrated October 1, through October 8, to recognize the free press throughout the United States. The Parvenue staff joined in this national observance and presented a special assembly which emphasized the week's theme "Your Newspaper—Freedom's Forum."

It was pointed out that no institution is more necessary to our way of life than a free press. Freedom of the press, given to us by our forefathers through the Constitution, has long since helped the true light of freedom. In order to maintain that freedom, we must keep faith with our Constitution.

Our newspaper is the source from which all of us seek information. It must serve as an informer for us so that we may discharge well our responsibilities as students.

Freedom of the press also improves the responsibility of stimulating freedom throughout the world by bringing knowledge to the uneducated.

As long as there is freedom of the press, the students should exercise their rights and their intelligence, by reading the newspapers.

Joe Louis Black "55".

School as I See It—A Vital Part of Life

School is a vital part of any young person's life. Through our school, we gain knowledge and skill. We as students are not taking school as a very important part of our life; but merely as a daily routine.

Let's go to school and prepare ourselves for tomorrow. Tomorrow holds great things in store for us if we are prepared. How can we get prepared? That's the big question.

Our schools prepare us for the competition that beset us. We are in a world of constant movement; we will have to compete with different races. As Mabel Newcombe said, "It is more important to know where you are going than to get there quickly."

We as students make up the school; and we should be loyal; and take full advantage of all of its opportunities; and live up to the ideals of high school students.

Delores Hutchinson '55.

Delores Hutchinson discussed the importance of school and why students at Burke should be loyal and take advantage of the opportunities that one could to obtain a diploma. Juliet DeVine examined the significance of participating in the democratic process. She talked about the importance of all people exercising their right to vote in November 1954. (Courtesy of the Avery Research Center.)

Free America and The Common Man

As Americans, we cannot allow a misconception of social justice to retard our progress in a free world. The eyes of the communistic world are cast upon America; and each false move we make is maligned, misjudged and misconceived. We as Americans have but one course to pursue; and that is through social justice chart the career of free American people to a haven of peace and progress.

November 2 is election day over the entire United States. This is the American way to learn the wishes of the common men; for everybody in America who is twenty-one or above has this right—the right to participate in free elections and to use the secret ballot.

Even those of us who are under twenty-one may help in a free election. For just as we make our elders mindful of our materialistic wants, we can use the same tactics in making them mindful of using the ballot.

We must call their attention to the fact that in places where the common men make voting their business, progress is their enjoyment.

The common men have made America. They were the pioneers; they gave a blood, sweat and tears, that this nation might become strong and powerful.

Today's weapon is the ballot; and we must think things out. The spirit of us as new men is practical, realistic and demanding. We are conscious of our guaranteed rights under the Constitution.

As new men we want to coordinate and fully inter-relate our freedoms with what we know of the world. As new men we are nearer to freedom than other people of the world. We want to know what in the future will be done to make us universally forceful and protective.

If we accept less than this we will find ourselves retrogressing.

Juliette Theresa DeVine.

Significance of Negro History

Negro History Week is of unusual importance this year. A study of the background, progress and cultural deevlopment of the race may enlighten many.

For a search into Negro history will reveal that some of us are superior, some above average, some average, and some below average. But the same differences in intelligence among us, exist in all racial groups.

During the twentieth century, notable improvement has been made in health conditions among Negroes. Great numbers have entered the professional fields, especially teaching, preaching, medicine and journalism.

Many of us have been named among the outstanding; thus we can boast of personalities like the late George Washington Carver, scientist; the late Mary McLeod Bethune, educator; also Paul Lawrence Dunbar, James Weldon Johnson and many others.

The accomplishments of this century should soothe and heal the bruises caused by a recent article that criticized the health, moral standards and intellectual background of the race.

However, we must not ignore these criticisms. We should accept them as a challenge and do something about them.

In other words, the only way good things can be said about us is for us to do good things. We must realize that to do the same as the other man is not enough. We must do better than the other man.

Le Walter Dilligard, '56.

As early as 1956, LeWalter Dilligard debated the merits of Negro History Week. He challenged the students to strive for perfection and not to settle for mediocrity. Juliette Devine asked the students if they were truly Americans and what did people think about them in February 1956. (Courtesy of the Avery Research Center.)

Examine Yourself

Have we examined ourselves and our community? Are we living in such a way that others are branding us? Just what are we doing? Are we proud that we are Americans; that we are citizens of a wonderful country; that the Almighty God created us all?

The world is watching each move we make. The world is waiting for the sunrise, when all of us will be men of justice and a product of a goodwill society.

Let us all join in the fight for peace, freedom and happiness. Join the vast choir of Brotherhood and sing joyously, sincerely and proudly "Let Freedom ring; I am an American."

Juliette Devine, '56.

Resolve on Self-Discovery

The new year always gives us a chance to begin life anew. Each year we usually make some resolutions, but how many of them do we keep? Is it weakness that makes us break them? or is it that they were not realistic to begin with?

Weren't they resolutions based on the kind of person we would like to be, rather than on the kind of person we actually are? We cannot change ourselves, but we can, if we really knew ourselves, improve the way we are. If we can do this, we'll be able, not only to live with ourselves, but to be happy with the people that we love.

Never try to be what you are not but what you are is what counts. And to be happy and to remain happy, always look at things with an open mind. Do not judge all events by any one bad example. So in this New Year of 1956, let us find ourselves. Then let us simply resolve to be our best selves.

Martha Scott, '59.

By Irvin Reid

We, who have been here at Burke for one or more terms, welcome you, our new-comers, to the school. You are no longer visitors but a part of us. Therefore you are expected to join in with us. We will join hands in an effort to carry out a tradition that originated here many years ago. This is to make Burke better.

Probably you already know that there are many students here at Burke. Suppose it were possible that each student or several groups of students would do something to improve our school. Maybe it has already crossed your minds how much progress can be made. This would not only make us proud, but it would make the faculty proud.

Here at Burke we try our best to make our faculty happy. You could join in and help us in this effort. Listed below are five ways by which you can please our faculty, (1) being respectful (2) being courteous (3) being cooperative (4) being honest and (5) being studious.

There are many worthwhile groups and organizations here which you can join. We have the Dramatic Guild which has planned a wonderful performance for this school term. Other organizations are, The National Honor Society, The Criterion Club, Burke's Glee Club, and the Library Club.

With the tips given, and the goals that you've set, I feel that your coming years at Burke will be more than pleasurable ones. Good Luck!

Martha Scott challenged the students to set realistic resolutions for the New Year in 1956. Irvin Reid gave advice to the incoming sub-freshmen on how they could make their tenure at Burke a rewarding and enjoyable experience in November 1957. Dr. Reid is currently the president of Wayne State University in Detroit, Michigan. (Courtesy of the Avery Research Center.)

What Do You Think?

By LaVerne Brisbane

The topic of a possible 1958 yearbook takes precedence over all others around the school.

Recently several students, mostly seniors, were asked, "Do you think the senior class of "58" is capable of assuming the responsibility of publishing a yearbook?" These were their replies.

Gary Bowden, "I would say, yes. Our senior class is capable of assuming the responsibility of publishing a yearbook. Of course it is not the work of the senior class alone. The whole school would have to develop an interest in this project. As a senior, I would stop at no ends in working towards this goal."

Samuel Pointsett, "Yes, I feel that our senior class is fully capable of carrying on the project of the yearbook. It is a project that will require the cooperation of not only the senior class, but of the student body. We can thoroughly accomplish this goal if all of us will work and work diligently."

Clarence McNeil, "Yes, I think the senior class is very capable of producing a yearbook. Burke is in need of a yearbook, and I am sure even if it is not completed this year, the seniors will be paving the way for the present juniors."

Mathew Devore, "Yes, I think the class of "58" is very capable of publishing a yearbook. It is a project that should have been started long ago, and with the help of the entire student body the senior class of "58" will produce Burke's first yearbook."

Alphonso Gooden, "I would say yes. Our class is very capable of publishing a yearbook. With the fine and efficient staff we have in our council, the cooperation of the faculty, and with a lot of work, we are most certain to succeed."

Cecilia Gordon, "Yes, I feel the class of "58" is capable of publishing a yearbook. I feel with the help of the student body and faculty they will produce Burke's *"first"* yearbook. The seniors are intelligent enough and have the ability to accept a responsibility such as this."

Ruby McFadden, "I am certain that the class of "58" is capable of assuming this responsibility. The seniors possess the same qualities that the seniors in other schools posess and if they can produce yearbooks so can the class of "58".

Rosalee Stanly, "Yes, I feel our senior class is most capable of assuming the responsibility of the publication of a yearbook."

Several members of the senior class of 1958 were asked if their class was capable of publishing a yearbook. At right were some of the responses to that question in November 1957. (Courtesy of the Avery Research Center.)

The Editor's Den

By James Blake

In every country of the world there is a problem that demands everyone's attention. This problem is Juvenile Delinquency.

Today's attitude towards delinquency is different. Every effort is made to solve the problem before taking it to court. Does this help the problem any? The world is looking upon us (the teen-agers) for the answer. Let us look at some of the thoughts that come to the minds of the adults:

1. The environment from which the child comes.

2. The resentment the child has towards the advice of his parents.

3. The crowd or gang that he follows when away from home.

From the adults' point of view, the fault lies chiefly with the teen-agers themselves.

Now for the teen-agers point of view.

The teen-agers believe:

1. They lack the needed love from the rest of the family.
2. Parents put too much emphasis on work and pleasure rather than the family and the home.

No one really has the reason or cause for Juvenile Delinquency. But, we, the teen-agers must give this problem our deepest thought and recognize that it is a problem. We are the ones who must be leaders tomorrow.

In 1957, editor in chief James Blake addressed the issue of juvenile delinquency. Reverend Blake was a leading figure of the civil rights movement during the early 1960s in Charleston and played an instrumental role in the integration of the Charleston airport terminal and the Municipal Golf Course in Charleston. (Courtesy of the Avery Research Center.)

Are We In The Know?

Now, when it is most important that we be aware of domestic and foreign happenings it is most frightening when we realize how poorly informed or shall I say misinformed we are. Most of us pride ourselves on being "hep" or in with the "in crowd". We know all the latest fads and fashions; these seem to be the only important things. But are they really important?

Wouldn't you like to know why your relatives, friends and old school mates are fighting and dying in Viet Nam? Do you have any idea why we are over there? Have you ever given it any serious thought? I will wager that nine out of ten of us have not.

We cannot pick up a magazine or newspaper without seeing some mention of the Black Muslims or the Black Nationalist. Who are they? Do their ideas and theories hold a blessing in disguise or are they a potential threat to us in our fight for equality and justice?

Our lack of answers to these and other questions of this nature were brought out most pointedly when a Mrs. Julia Brown appeared as a guest speaker at one of our assembly programs. She was given a rather warm reception by the students. Yet, when the majority of these same students were questioned on their comprehension of what Mrs. Brown had said and why she was here their responses were nil. We found out that we knew little or nothing about extremist groups. The John Birch Society could have been a club for tree lovers for all we knew about it. No one seemed to have any knowledge about the group right in our midst who sponsored Mrs. Brown.

Come on and admit it, we really do not know all that we should know about these and many other organizations and movements. Ignorance of vital happenings that occur in this Great Society is not funny it is pathetic. If you have not begun, now is the time to begin to read the newspaper. Not just our local newspapers but national newspapers and news magazines. Now is the time for inductive and deductive reasoning. Come on let's really be in with the "in crowd", let's add a general knowledge of the real important matter to our long list of lesser ones.

By Harriett E. Jenkins

In 1966, Harriett Jenkins gave several compelling reasons why students should consider broadening their reading. She encouraged students to broaden their scope of knowledge both nationally and internationally. (Courtesy of the Avery Research Center.)

TO THE ADMINISTRATION, THE FACULTY, THE STUDENTS, AND THE OTHERS OF BURKE HIGH SCHOOL:

When I came here, I said to my colleagues that I came, because I love you. Now that I am leaving, I reiterate that I love you. Four years ago, I loved you because of what I am; now it is because of what you are.

With the exception of a few isolated incidents, you have made my years here only pleasant, and I will always be grateful for your general acceptance of me. This has been a rewarding experience for me and I carry with me many happy memories.

I regret leaving THE BEAUTIFUL PEOPLE of 11-5 and my beloved Beta Club members. Carry on, people, and become as complete as you can.

Don't give up on The System – better to get in there and become the system and thus shape it to your liking.

Hang in there and
Peace. . .
Patricia Adams.

Patricia Adams was one of a few white teachers at that time. She expressed her views about her overall impression of the school. Curtis Harbour detailed his maturation as a student from the time he entered as sub-freshman until his senior year in May 1972. (Courtesy of the Avery Research Center.)

May 1972

Reflections . . . On Leaving

During the past five years at Burke, I went through many changes. I will always remember the many experiences, both good and bad, that I have encountered.

My sub-freshman year was a period of getting adjusted to new surroundings and new people. Getting adjusted to new and older people presented a problem. I was afraid that being fresh out of grammar school and being quite young, the older students would not accept me as a part of the Burke family.

After a very long and disappointing sub-freshman year, I began to feel a little more at ease. In my freshman year, I joined my first organization, the Marching Band. Being in the band was and still is one of my most rewarding experiences.

My sophomore year came and the big Seniors did not seem so big. I began participating in more extra-curricular activities. This was my most memorable year because I really began to get involved. I also began to socialize more.

When I became a Junior, I realized that I was just a step away from embarking into my future; therefore, I started to really think more about the future and about school. I began to study harder and really think seriously about my subjects for I knew that the next step would be not only a step higher in school, but a start into life and also adulthood. At this moment, I could feel myself changing from a once playful youngster into a matured, well-rounded young man.

Well, finally it came! My Senior year! This was a most exciting and expensive year. I will always remember it as a year that I filled out applications, applications and more applications. More and more responsibilities pressed me.

Now that it is all over, I can say that it was a great challenge to me and I hope that in the future those five years will prove to be of great value in my endeavors.

Curtis Harbour

Huff and Puff and Blow Our School Down

Stacey Young

The deplorable condition of our school is not conducive to learning. Students are never settled in one classroom because of the inundated floors, leaky ceilings, and the pungent odor.

Whenever there is inclement weather, the rain leaks through the ceilings and the carpets become soaked. When classrooms are closed up, the odor arises and becomes unbearable. Walking down the hallway is comparable to walking through a swamp.

In 1983, Burke began the renovation of its campus, and here in 1988, it seems as if no work has been done. So what are we, the student body, supposed to do? Stay home whenever the meterologist predicts any percentage of rain? Then our limited, unexcused ten days would be up and no one would receive credit for any courses, even if passing.

It is now the end of the school year and no definite action has been taken to ensure us of a drip-free, swamp-free, odor-free educational environment.

We are hoping to meet brand-new learning environment in the next school year.

Stacey Young addressed one of the major concerns that have plagued Burke since its inception. She expressed hope that something would be done in the near future to resolve the deplorable physical conditions at the school in June 1988. (Courtesy of the Avery Research Center.)

TIMELINE

1894 Rev. John L. Dart establishes the Charleston Normal and Industrial Institute, first located at the corner of Bogard and Kracke Streets.

1910 Construction of the new school is completed.

1911 The Charleston Colored Industrial School opens January 3 with 375 students and 8 teachers. Philip P. Mazyck serves as principal until February. James R. Guy becomes principal.

1912 E. T. Healy succeeds Guy as principal.

1919 A legislative act allows for 16 African American teachers to replace the all-white faculty, and David Hill becomes the first African American principal of the school.

1921 After the death of J. E. Burke in January, the school's name is changed from Charleston Industrial School to Burke Industrial High School.

1923 Burke graduates its first 11th grade. A total of 21 students receive diplomas.

1925 Burke Industrial is expanded to serve elementary and high school students. During the school year of 1924–1925, David Hill is transferred to Buist Elementary School. Rev. B. B. Jones becomes principal.

1930 An athletic program is organized under the new principal, Joseph E. Berry. He also departmentalizes the high school from eighth grade up.

1932 The normal class, the senior class of the high school, and the senior class of the grammar school hold graduation exercises in the school auditorium.

1934 William Wright organizes the boys' football and basketball teams.

1935 The girls' basketball team is organized by J. L. Pearson and Ms. Hare. Samuel R. Higgins assumes the responsibilities as principal.

1936 A. D. Greene writes the school alma mater. The first annual Thanksgiving Day Classic football game is played between Burke and Avery Normal Institute at College Park.

1937 A school publication called the *Spotlight* is published. A. D. Greene directs the school's first opera.

1938 The football team wins the lower and state championship.

1939 W. H. Grayson becomes principal with M. A. Mouzon as vice principal.

1940 Diversified occupations are offered that give a student an opportunity to learn the trade of his choice under skilled artisans in the city.

1941 The band is organized under the direction of Holland W. Daniels. The group begins with an enrollment of 10 students. The string ensemble is formed under the direction of Ernest A. Roper. Marjorie H. Howard reorganizes the student newspaper. Once called the *Spotlight*, it is renamed the *Parvenue*. Elizabeth Frost Jenkins becomes the first professional librarian in Charleston County School District 20.

1943 Malissa T. Smith, a Burke High teacher, petitions the Charleston County School Board for equal pay.

1944 Cosmetology classes begin on the campus under the supervision of Laura Mack Sims.

1945 This is the first senior class since February 1942 to graduate in caps and gowns. William Grayson serves as principal. A biracial committee is formed to push for accreditation of Burke. Four buildings constitute the facilities on the campus.

1946 More than 70 veterans of World War II enroll at the school. Vice principal Wardell Nichols succeeds Grayson as principal.

1947 Burke plays its first night football game at College Park on October 30. The state board of education accredits Burke.

1948 The school graduates its first 12th-grade class. A cafeteria and 16 classrooms are added to help alleviate crowded conditions. Courses in tailoring, masonry, carpentry, and domestic services are implemented in October.

1949 The school receives an "A" rating by the Southern Association of Colleges and Schools Accrediting Committee.

1951 Baseball is started with Modie Risher appointed coach.

1953 The school enrolls 50 Korean War veterans.

1954 An open house is held for the public to view the newly constructed portions of the school. Seven new courses are added to the curriculum. The Southern Association of Colleges and Secondary Schools accredit the school.

1955 There are 25 boys enrolled in home economics with Susie U. Simmons as the instructor. Drivers' education classes begin with an enrollment of 13 students. F. J. Cook is the instructor. The football team wins the state high school championship. The girls' basketball team wins the city and state championship.

1960 A. W. Hoursey serves as acting principal. Work on the remodeled gymnasium is completed.

1961 H. H. Marshall is named principal.

1962 W. R. Meriwether is named principal.

1966 The school receives a charter to establish a chapter of modern music masters on the campus.

1968 The new gymnasium is completed.

1969 Adult trade classes begin with courses offered in auto mechanics, radio and television repair, carpentry, brick masonry, tailoring, commercial sewing, and blueprint reading. The wrestling team is organized.

1970 The school offers a three-track program: vocational, general, and college preparation.

1972 Students stage a walkout because of poor physical conditions at the school.

1976 The basketball team wins the state 4A boys championship. John Wilford is named South Carolina High School Coach of the Year.

1977 The sub-freshman class is abolished at Burke.

1979 The gymnastics team is organized under the direction of John Wilford. Leckyler Gaillard is named principal.

1980 The Fields-Sims-Wright Vocational Center is dedicated. The renovation and new construction began in 1977 and was completed a year later.

1982 Charleston County School Board member Everett Presson proposes that the name Burke be changed to the High School of Charleston.

1983 Renovations are completed on Burke and Rhett Schools, merging both campuses into one high school. The library is moved to the Rhett building. The Junior ROTC program begins at the school. Students from Charles A. Brown and Charleston High Schools are now a part of Burke's student body.

1984 The boys win the South Carolina High School Basketball 4A State Championship.

1988 The Charleston County Magnet School is located at Burke's campus.

1993 Burke becomes the first school in South Carolina to have a campus-based health clinic.

1994 The school ends its vocational studies program.

1995 Jeannetta Scott is named principal, becoming the first female to hold that position.

1996 The school becomes the first in South Carolina and the 53rd school in the country to benefit from the Class Link Program. The Academic Magnet High School moves from Burke's campus to the Charleston Naval Base.

1998 The first phase of renovations begins on the cafeteria, media center, and classrooms.

1999 Interim principal Andrea Heyer is moved to another school.

2000 Freshmen are moved to Courtney Middle School campus. Michael Tolley is named interim principal. Burke revises the curriculum into three career clusters. They are multimedia communications, community and consumer service, and health and science technology.

2001 Burke shares in a $2.5-million grant with North Carolina schools aimed at cutting the dropout rate.

2002 Groundbreaking ceremonies begin for the new Burke High School.

2003 Construction for the new school is on schedule.

2005 The new gymnasium is named in honor of former coach and athletic director Modie Risher. A dedication program is held in December for the grand opening of the new school.

2006 Principal Curtis Amos resigns after one year in the position. Charles Benton is named principal of Burke.

BIBLIOGRAPHY

Anderson, James D. *The Education of Blacks in the South, 1860–1935*. Chapel Hill: UNC Press, 1988.

Avery photograph file, 1890–1990. Avery Research Center. Charleston, SC: College of Charleston.

Babcock, Carl. "Burke High School Gets its Name Back." *Evening Post*, August 10, 1982, 1A.

Barone, Florence. "Alumni Oppose Making Burke Vocational." *Evening Post*, July 20, 1981, 1B.

———. "Burke, Brown Students Lose Name-Change Plea." *Evening Post*, June 15, 1982.

Bolden, Ethel. *Susan Dart Butler—Pioneer Librarian*. Master's thesis, Atlanta University, 1959.

Bullock, Henry Allen. *A History of Negro Education in the South from 1619 to the Present*. Cambridge: Harvard University Press, 1967.

Burke High School Yearbook, 1958–2006. Charleston, SC: Burke High School.

"Burke Night Classes to Begin." *Charleston News and Courier*, September 23, 1956, 14A.

"Burke Students Walkout: Building is Depressing." *Evening Post*, March 7, 1972.

"Burke to Dedicate Vocational Center." *Charleston News and Courier*, March 24, 1980, 5B.

Caldwell, A. B., ed. *History of the American Negro, South Carolina Edition*. Atlanta: A. B. Caldwell, 1919.

"Case for Accrediting Burke High School." *Charleston News and Courier*, September 30, 1945, 7: 4–8.

Charleston County School Board. *District 20 School Board Minutes*, 1956–1987. Charleston, SC: Charleston County School Board.

Courrege, Diette. "Leaders Rally to Support Burke." *Post and Courier*, July 18, 2006.

———. "Threat of School Take Over Rattles Burke." *Post and Courier*, July 14, 2006, 1A.

Drago, Edmund L. *Initiative, Paternalism, and Race Relations: Charleston's Avery Normal Institute*. Athens: University of Georgia Press, 1990.

Eugene Hunt Papers, 1940–1990. Avery Research Center. Charleston, SC: College of Charleston.

"Half Million Dollars Addition is Announced." *Charleston News and Courier*, December 24, 1952, 13: 1–3.

Hine, William. "Black Politicians in Reconstruction Charleston, South Carolina." *Journal of Southern History* 49 (November 1983): 555–584.

Hoit-Thetford, Elizabeth. *An Educational History of the Gullahs of Coastal South Carolina from 1700–1900.* Ann Arbor: University Microfilms International, 1986.

Holland, Davis R. *A History of the Negro Public Schools of Charleston, South Carolina, 1867–1942.* Master's thesis, School of Education, University of South Carolina, 1942.

Jackson, Luther. "The Educational Efforts of the Freedmen's Bureau and Freedmen's Aid Societies in South Carolina, 1862–1872." *Journal of Negro History* 8 (January 1923): 1–40.

Knight, Edgar W. "Reconstruction and Education in South Carolina." *South Atlantic Quarterly* 18 (October 1919): 350–364.

"Korean Vets Make Important Contribution While Learning Skills at Burke School." *Charleston News and Courier*, October, 4, 1953, 14A.

Manigault, Peter. "Negroes in City Schools Once had White Teachers." *Charleston News and Courier*, April 28, 1945, 10A.

McCarthy, David. "4-Building Addition Makes Burke City's Most Modern High School." *Evening Post*, September 29, 1954.

Murphy, Edward. "Proposed High School Would Cost $3.5 Million." *Evening Post*, October 16, 1981.

"Name Approved for Reorganized High School." *Evening Post*, June 8, 1982.

O'Neill, Stephen. "The Struggle for Black Equality Comes to Charleston: The Hospital Strike of 1969." *Proceedings of the South Carolina Historical Association, 1986*. Columbia: South Carolina Historical Association, 1986.

Parvenue newspaper collection, 1945–1988. Avery Research Center. Charleston, SC: College of Charleston.

Pyatt, Sherman E. *A Selective Index to the* Post and Courier *Newspaper About African Americans in Charleston, 1981–2005*. Charleston, SC: Avery Research Center, 2005.

Simms, Lois. *A Chalk and Chalkboard Career in Carolina*. New York: Vantage Press, 1995.

Tindall, George B. "The Question of Race in the South Carolina Constitutional Convention of 1895." *Journal of Negro History* 37 (July 1952): 277–303.

William Saxton Wilson collection, 1940–1990. Avery Research Center: College of Charleston.

Year Book of Charleston, S.C. 1910–1940. Charleston, SC: News and Courier Book Press, 1980.

AFTERWORD

The quotes on this page say more than any words that I can express about the deep feelings that students and faculty felt about Burke when they were there. The collage on the following page captures the essence of Burke High School throughout the years.

Academic success at Burke High School was, in the true sense, a team effort—parents, teachers, administrators, and students worked together to promote the school's mission.

—Edelle P. Gaillard
English Teacher (1970-1981)

The school was a major contributor to my foundation, i.e. character, integrity, and spirituality.

—Phalarma L. (Washington) Freeman
Class of 1972
Chief Child Support Specialist

The faculty was very professional—well dressed, talented, committed and dedicated to teaching. They were proud of the student's accomplishments.

—Alice A. Pyatt
Class of 1955
Retired Administrator (Education)

When I attended Burke, it was the original magnet school. Students who wanted an education came from Adams Run, Hollywood and other places to receive the best offered.

—Virginia F. Howard
Class of 1961
Retired Teacher

I considered myself fortunate to have entered and graduated from Burke.

—Richard Brewer Jr.
Class of 1949
Retired U.S. Army

Burke High School in the early nineties was still a place of discovery that was filled with many years of proud traditions.

—Rodney E. Jenkins
Class of 1993
Vice President (Wachovia Bank)

I say that students do a great deal for teachers in that they bring out the hidden qualities in the teacher that lead to her/his capacity to love.

—Lois A. Simms
Teacher (1945–1973)

All of the teachers really cared about you and encouraged you to always do your best. They continuously instilled a "can do spirit" in me.

—Dr. Gwendolyn Brown
Class of 1974
Dentist

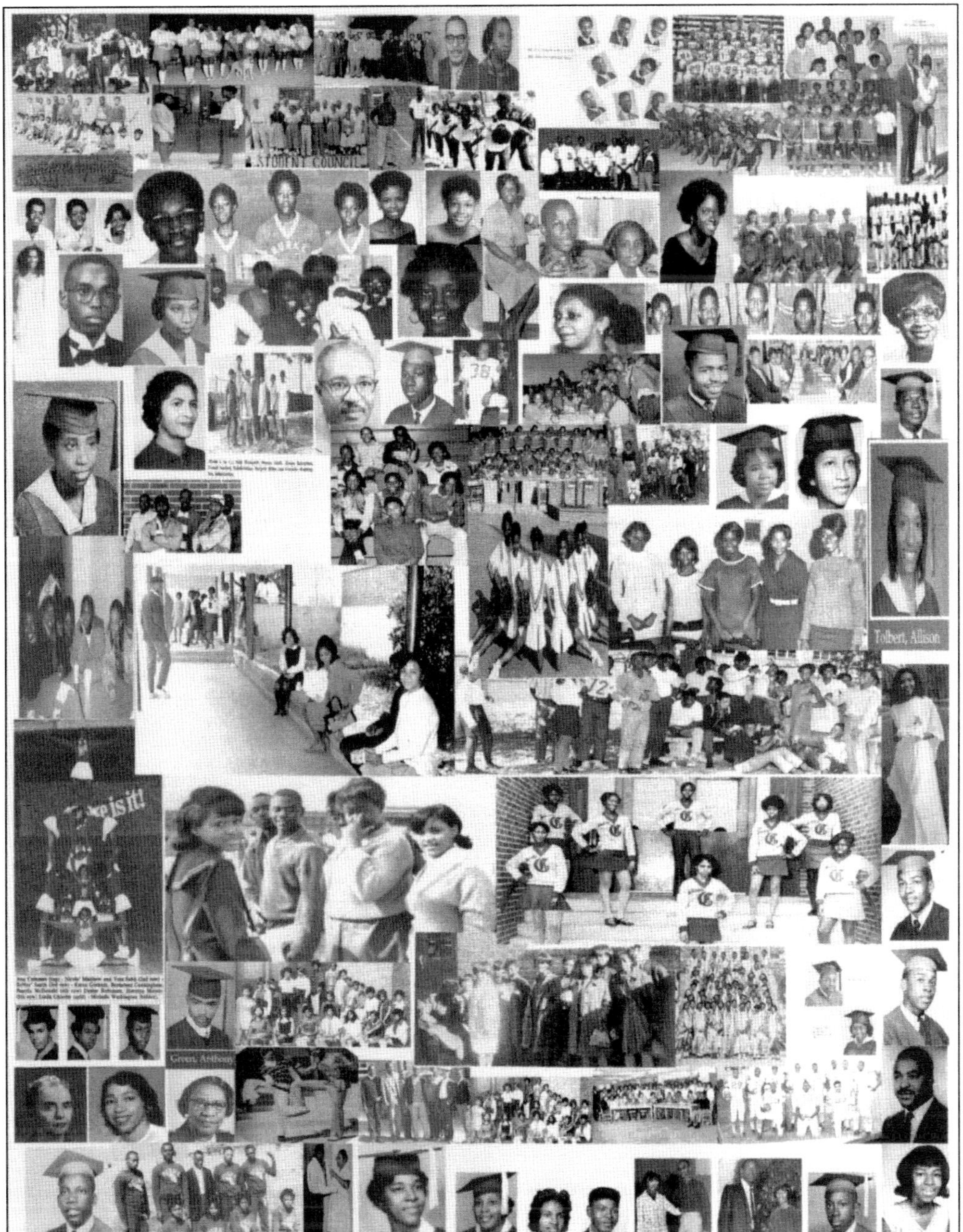

This collage represents some of the faces of students and faculty covering several decades. Also, one can glimpse some of the activities that took place throughout the years. (Courtesy of Sean Pyatt.)